"The Habitat International story is not only about the struggles and successes of people, but also about the challenges and growth of a small business in an increasingly competitive environment. The author blends these two compelling histories to tell the real-life tale of how a company is doing well by doing good."

GEORGE W. KESSINGER,
President and CEO of Goodwill Industries International

ABLE!

ABLE!

*How One Company's Disabled Workforce
Became the Key to*
EXTRAORDINARY SUCCESS

Nancy Henderson Wurst

BENBELLA BOOKS
Dallas, Texas

BenBella Books
6440 N. Central Expressway, Suite 617
Dallas, TX 75206
Send feedback to feedback@benbellabooks.com

PUBLISHER: Glenn Yeffeth
SENIOR EDITOR: Shanna Caughey
ASSOCIATE EDITOR: Leah Wilson
DIRECTOR OF MARKETING/PR: Laura Watkins

Printed in the United States of America

10 9 8 7 6 5 4 3 2 1

Library of Congress Cataloging-in-Publication Data

Wurst, Nancy Henderson.
    How one company's disabled workforce became the key to extraordinary success /
by Nancy Henderson Wurst.
        p. cm.
    Includes bibliographical references and index.
    ISBN 1-932100-44-X
    1. People with disabilities—Employment. 2. Habitat International, Inc.
3. Vocational rehabilitation. I. Title.
    HD7255.W87 2005
    658.3'0087—dc22

                                                                2004024650

Backcover photos Copyright © Mark S. Wurst Photography
Cover design by Todd Bushman
Text design and composition by John Reinhardt Book Design

Distributed by Independent Publishers Group.
To order call (800) 888-4741
www.ipgbook.com

For special sales contact Laura Watkins at laura@benbellabooks.com

For two fathers:

*To my dad, Mason Carpenter, who taught me that all human beings
are precious and valuable, no matter how different they are,*

and

*To David Morris's father, Saul, who built both a life and a successful,
compassionate business on this same belief.*

Thank you for showing the rest of us how it should be done.

Contents

Acknowledgments

I would like to thank the following people for their important contributions to this book:

To my agent, Bob DiForio, and my publisher, Glenn Yeffeth, for believing in this project and its potential impact on how we think about people with disabilities.

To my talented transcriptionist, Tammy Pinkston, for taking hours of tedious work off my hands.

To David Morris for supporting me in this project, for giving so much of his time to make it happen, and for making his staff so available for interviews. David, I salute you.

To the rest of the Habitat managers and administrative personnel: Jim Thomison, Connie Presnell, Sandra Ball, Jerry Treadwell, Damita Favors, and Patty Keith, for patiently answering all my interview and fact-checking questions, even when they were swamped with their own work.

To the wonderful Habitat employees and their parents and spouses, for their candor and willingness to tell such inspiring stories: Martin Arney and his mom, Lisa Blair; Lonnie Jacobs and his mom, Phyllis Schwarz; Terry Davis and his mother, Betty, father, James, brother, Tony, and sister-in-law, Yvette; Daniel Johnson and his parents, Sherry and Dick Taylor; Sharon Adams and her parents, Helen and Harvey; Carl Wallace and his wife, Juanita; Thomas Teg and his sisters, Y and Cheng, sister-in-law, Kiv, and wife, Rose; and Lincoln Sottong and his father, Phil. Thanks also to Jason Cook's parents, Dan and Freda, who granted permission to recount Jason's experience at Habitat.

To all the business leaders, customers, and community members who so openly shared their experiences and helped put the story into perspective: Carl Bouckaert, Ben Hahn, Hans Bakker, Kim Brown, and David Bagby, all from Beaulieu of America; Chuck Gearhart, Gearhart & Sutton; Dan Cellura and Mike Renahan, Izzo Golf Inc.; James Gibson and Fred Schnair, Jefferson Industries Inc.; Rick Parris, Millennium Packaging Solutions; Doug Marrelli, Lowe's Companies Inc.; Jim Moon, Lookout Mountain Community Services; Tom Henderson, Georgia Department of Labor; Melinda Wallins Lemmon, Bartow County (Georgia) Department of Economic Development; Alan Smith, First Citizens Bank; Darlene Jenkins, Siskin Hospital for Physical Rehabilitation; Tim Dempsey, Chattanooga Endeavors; Greg Sundell, Arkay Personnel Inc.; Judy Peasley, former buyer for Sears; Glenn and Kaye Vaughn, longtime civic leaders in Catoosa County, Georgia; and Joey DeVivo and Minnie Witcher, both from Orange Grove Center.

To the special-education teachers and other instructors who mean so much to Habitat: Robin Leventhal, Walker County School System; Wadene Livingston Bartoo, Ridgeland High School; Mike Carter, Catoosa Crossroads Academy; Cathy Griffith, Lakeview-Fort Oglethorpe High School; and Deanna Baker, Boynton Elementary School.

To David Morris's mother, Joyce, and his close friends, Hubert and Phyllis Shuptrine, who helped me trace the roots of this journey.

And last but not least, to my husband, Mark, who urged me to take a break from my more secure writing assignments to work on this important book, and who stood by me even when I had no time or energy for anything, or anyone, but this project.

Preface

"How far you go in life depends on you being tender with the young, compassionate with the aged, sympathetic with the striving and tolerant of the weak and the strong. Because someday in life you will have been all of these."
—GEORGE WASHINGTON CARVER

In November 1999, at the annual *Business for Social Responsibility* conference in Boston, a virtually unknown Georgia businessman stood before executives from the Gap, American Express, and other major corporations and explained why his company has been so successful.

"Simple," he said. "I hire the people no one else wants to hire."

As co-founder and CEO of Habitat International, Inc., an international supplier of golf putting greens, accent rugs, and indoor-outdoor mats for Lowe's, the Home Depot, and other major retailers, David Morris knows better than most how to work with special-needs employees. In 1986, five years after he and his father, Saul, launched their small rug company in Chattanooga, Tennessee, they agreed to host an enclave of eight social-services clients with mental retardation. Today, most of the workers at Habitat—more than 70 during peak production—have either a physical or mental disability, or both. People with autism, Down syndrome, and hearing impairments cut carpet next to those with cerebral palsy, mental illnesses, and brain trauma from car accidents and strokes. All earn real wages, not the usual $1 to $2 an hour state programs generally pay, and many make far more than the industry standard.

David, who balked at the idea when a friend approached him about hosting the first enclave two decades ago, is convinced his company has flourished not *in spite of*, but *because of*, his employees with disabilities. There is practically no absenteeism, very little turnover, and seldom

1

an attitude problem. Each worker is cross-trained on every task in the plant, from running the press to loading trucks to gluing foam pads to the backs of golf driving mats, so there is rarely a need to bring in extra help to cover for someone who's out. Quality control takes place naturally, and without prompting, as conscientious workers with developmental and other disabilities routinely point out faulty boxes, poor color matches, and shortages. Because of their willingness to focus on the task, and do it well, they frequently outperform their non-disabled co-workers and give Habitat an edge over its competitors. The employees with disabilities are, in a word, grateful for their jobs, and their appreciation shows in more ways than one.

Habitat has expanded a dozen times since it opened for business in 1981, and annual rug production has climbed from 85,000 to 1.5 million. Thanks in large part to the acquisition of a new home center account, revenues tripled between 2001 and 2004, at a time when other factories were bearing the brunt of an economic downturn, laying off staff members, and scurrying to carve more expenses. The company is so efficient that back orders are virtually non-existent; so is the return rate on defective goods. The practice of hiring unconventional workers has also strengthened Habitat's rapport with big-name retailers, mail-order firms, and sporting goods companies. "We've had major customers who were prejudiced about this," David says. "Once they come out here, they say, 'We want to buy everything from you from now on.'"

The irony is that the people who benefit most may be the ones without visible physical and mental challenges. "Our employees show us love, caring, and simplicity," David points out. "They haven't been spoiled by society, and they never will. They are the wise ones because they look at things with such a pure heart, and their love is contagious. They give us more than we could ever give back."

If you're tempted to think, "This issue doesn't affect *me*," think again. According to the National Organization on Disability (NOD), 54 million Americans—a full 20 percent of the population—are disabled. Most of us will be touched by a disability in some way—a parent's aging process, a friend's devastating accident, a child with a birth defect—at some point in our lives. Consider these far-reaching statistics:

- According to the American Society on Aging, 70 percent of people with disabilities are not born with them.
- One in 10 American families is directly impacted by mental retardation. The 140,000-member Arc of the United States (formerly known as the National Association of Retarded Children), esti-

mates that 6.2 to 7.5 million people in this country have this developmental disability.

- According to the Brain Injury Association of America, 1.5 million people sustain a traumatic brain injury each year—that's one every 21 seconds—and it is the leading cause of disabilities in children and young adults. The Centers for Disease Control estimates that at least 5.3 million Americans, or just over 2 percent of the U.S. population, currently live with disabilities resulting from head injuries.
- According to the American Stroke Association, someone in the U.S. has a stroke every 45 seconds. This cardiovascular disease, which affects the arteries leading to and from the brain, is a major cause of severe, long-term disability. About 700,000 Americans will suffer a stroke this year and about 4.8 million survivors are alive today.
- As many as 1.5 million Americans have some form of autism, states the Autism Society of America, and that number is growing at an alarming rate of between 10 and 17 percent every year. The ASA estimates that up to 4 million Americans could have autism within the next decade.

Thanks in part to mainstreaming in schools and a generation growing up with more sensitive attitudes and greater exposure to people from other cultures, races, and walks of life, prejudice against people with disabilities isn't as prevalent as it once was. Yet, according to a 2003 *Work Trends* study conducted by the John J. Heldrich Center for Workforce Development at Rutgers University, misconceptions about hiring people with disabilities continue to run rampant in the business world. Many entrepreneurs still believe they'll lose money by hiring special-needs workers. Parents and caregivers of disabled kids nearing adulthood often have their own fears. They worry their children will lose valuable Supplemental Security Income (SSI) or Medicare benefits if they earn a real paycheck. Or they want to shield their kids from hard work, intolerance, or the possibility of being hurt on the job.

The Habitat story shows just how wrong these assumptions can be. At this remarkable company, people with disabilities have proven, time and again, that they belong in the workplace, just like everyone else. In the long run they pose no more challenges than do people without disabilities, and they often outpace their co-workers. In fact, they're often the best employees on the payroll.

This book is about gutsy entrepreneurs who opened their minds and hearts by taking a chance hiring people with disabilities, even when the odds were against all of them. It's about dedicated parents who fought fiercely for their children, of teachers who saw the potential in their special-ed students, of business owners and civic leaders who supported this unusual company and its outlandish hiring practices, even when the naysayers said it would never work. This is a story of unlikely heroes: the conservative entrepreneur and his anti-establishment son, the competitors who turned into customers and became part of the Habitat "family," and the employees with disabilities who accomplished far more than they'd ever dreamed. Despite its humble beginnings in Southeast Tennessee, this is a story with a message for the world: Give people with disabilities a chance in the workplace and they'll pay you back with loyalty, unsurpassed productivity, and, most of all, lessons in human goodness and love.

In 1998, Lonnie Jacobs, a kind-hearted Habitat employee with schizophrenia, told a reporter, "Habitat's a company that more or less hires people with distractions, and we work it out together." That statement made such an impact on the company culture that in 2002, Habitat adopted a new slogan—*A Company of Positive Distractions*. When the plant moved to a larger facility in late 2003 to accommodate a boom in orders, a prominent sign bearing the slogan was erected at the entrance.

It would be wonderful if we didn't have to point out the individual disabilities in this book, or call them by name. *Schizophrenia. Autism. Down syndrome.* Such words, say David Morris and the other managers at Habitat, are mere labels for people with various "distractions," nothing more, nothing less. Even the term "disabled" can be misleading because the talented, productive workers at Habitat have *plenty* of ability, and they show it day after day. But because we're human, because we live in a world of specifics, not generalities, we need word pictures—labels, if you will—to help us grasp the challenges they've faced, and to see how far they've come. That's the only reason terms like "mental retardation" and "cerebral palsy" are used in this book, not as a way to pigeonhole people who are visibly different.

Even so, the "distractions" at Habitat aren't always noticeable, at least not at first glance. In 1996, when David was invited to be a torchbearer at the start of the Summer Olympics in Atlanta, a local television reporter came to the plant and spent several hours filming footage for a story. Later he called David back with a question: "Hey, can you help me identify which person has this or that?"

"You tell *me* what the disability is," David replied.

The journalist paused for a moment. "But I can't tell."

One

An Able Workforce

A T THE END OF A LONG INDUSTRIAL DRIVEWAY not far from Interstate 75, gargantuan metal giraffes stretch their necks above sculpted palm trees. Steel panthers crouch beneath the company sign, while a menagerie of critters, from a thick-knuckled gorilla to a fat leaping frog and a regal buck, chase each other around the edge of the parking lot. Inside the gate, red ants scramble to reach the top of a tower, and benches with grass-turf seats and rake-prong backs offer resting spots for visitors at the door. But it's the "Living Fence"—a row of thin silhouettes representing the factory's workers, some in wheelchairs, some with apparent Down syndrome or other disabilities, most holding hands—that really catches the eye.

Once inside Habitat International, Inc., an indoor-outdoor rug manufacturer in Chattanooga, Tennessee, the Living Fence takes on new meaning. Here, real people with real disabilities cut, package, and ship more than 11,000 artificial-grass and needlepunch products a day for large retailers like Lowe's, Meijer, and the Home Depot. Workers with schizophrenia and bipolar disorder drive forklifts next to those with Down syndrome, autism, and cerebral palsy. Recovering alcoholics, employees with hearing impairments, and people with developmental challenges cut floor runners and putting greens alongside co-workers who have sustained brutal head injuries or the loss of an arm. The place hums like a well-run beehive, with no one sitting idly on the sidelines or stopping to take an unplanned break.

Carl Wallace, a successful entrepreneur who suffered a debilitating stroke in 1985, is slow but steady as he folds slate-blue sections of carpet to load onto the bright orange buggies. Not far away, Ryan Lowery scoots stacks of forest-green carpet to the end of the table, where other mentally challenged employees will roll, label, and stand each one upright in the store display cartons. Nearby, Michael Clark, who wears leg braces and has multiple disabilities, works at near-lightning speed.

"Hey, Michael, wanna see who can roll the fastest?" asks the company's playful co-founder and CEO, David Morris. Not one to pass up a challenge, his young employee hoists a 6' x 10' swath of grass carpet onto a worktable, deftly rolls it into a tight tube, and tapes on the tag, while across from him, his boss struggles to do the same thing. By the time David rolls one rug, his protégé has already mastered three. David looks up in mock exasperation. "He was told he'd never be able to work in a setting like this," he whispers. "And just look at him go."

At break time, Habitat's special staff members leave their workstations and congregate around a pool table flanked by a one-armed mannequin with green grass-turf pants and a hodgepodge of signs like "Why Be Normal?" "Question Reality" and "If the People Lead, the Leaders Will Follow." Nearby, a school of steel fish in all shapes and sizes swims just beneath the high ceiling, a huge Styrofoam sunburst watches over the group, and employee photo collages smile down from the cluttered walls. Some workers shoot a few hoops at the basketball court. Others take turns manning the in-house radio station and spinning their favorite CDs. Homeless workers show people with developmental disabilities how to play pool and air hockey. Or is it the other way around?

In fact, it's often a challenge to spot just who is teaching whom. So is finding something that *isn't* unorthodox at this bustling rug factory 30 miles up the road from Dalton, Georgia, the self-proclaimed "Carpet Capital of the World." The eccentric sculptures and whimsical murals certainly aren't run-of-the-mill, nor is the air of contagious enthusiasm that comes from the happy, disabled workers who dance and sing and strum imaginary guitars to the Stevie Ray Vaughan riffs blaring over the intercom. The relationships here are unusual too, with managers hugging employees who do an outstanding job, and the company CEO rolling carpet alongside his staff to help out in a high-volume pinch. Even more unexpected, perhaps, is the fact that Habitat's exceptional workforce out-produces the nearest competitor 2-1.

Looking back, it's hard to believe that, if not for a persistent social worker and a brash young entrepreneur, it might never have happened at all.

Two

The Test

O NCE IN A WHILE a man embarks on an adventure that propels him down his true path. And sometimes he makes a decision that will impact many lives.

On an ordinary day in 1986, David Morris did both.

David and his father, Saul, had been operating their artificial-grass rug business, Habitat International, Inc., for five years when a friend named Joey DeVivo began dropping hints. Joey, a social worker at Orange Grove Center, a veteran agency for people with developmental disabilities in Chattanooga, Tennessee, was fired up about a burgeoning program in which some of her clients were involved. At several "work stations in industry" around town, people with mental disabilities were learning to work outside the agency. An "enclave" of up to eight clients would go into a workplace accompanied by an Orange Grove job coach and complete labor-intensive tasks for the company. The business benefited by paying lower wages and relying on the job coach to supervise the enclave; the clients gained by building their mental and physical stamina, learning new job skills, and becoming productive members of society. Even more important, perhaps, was the obvious boost in their self-esteem. Orange Grove clients had been doing contract labor at the group home for years, but the concept of being mainstreamed into a factory off-site was still new.

"David, I really think this would work for Habitat," Joey told him one night at a dinner party. "We're looking for businesses where our clients can perform and feel good about themselves, without being pressured. You'd be surprised at how well these folks do.

"Then again," she said with a grin, "maybe it wouldn't surprise you that much."

David's sister-in-law, Darcy, had Down syndrome, and he and Joey had often discussed how well she made her own bed or helped with dinner when given a little push and a pat on the back. But this was different—this was business—and David wasn't so sure about bringing people with mental disabilities into the plant. He and his father had just moved their operation to a larger building in Rossville, Georgia; their new line of golf putting greens was outselling the competition; and profits were rising. Maybe this wasn't such a good time to rock the boat. Still, the "experiment" was tempting. An artistic, rebellious type, David liked nothing better than to defy convention, *especially* if the odds were against him. But something like this could jeopardize everything for which he and his father had worked so hard.

"What about workman's comp?" he asked Joey at dinner that night. "How would we pay these people? What if one of the clients is hard to deal with or gets mad at us? How do we fire them? And who's responsible for them while they're at Habitat?"

Orange Grove personnel would oversee everything, Joey assured him. The clients would work as contractors, not employees, so David would be required to do nothing more than fill out some paperwork, set aside tasks for the clients to work on, and report on how they were doing. Orange Grove would bill him for the hourly work each person accomplished. Joey already had a particular job coach in mind, a spunky woman who loved her clients but also knew how to keep them in line.

"I'll make you a promise," Joey said. "If it doesn't work out, if you're not absolutely happy with this, we'll stop."

"I'll think about it," was the best answer David would give her.

For weeks, whenever Joey saw him, she politely brought up the subject. "Come on, there's no reason you can't do this," she'd urge. "You have nothing to lose."

But David and Saul disagreed. When David broached the topic with his father, levelheaded Saul was worried about potential liability problems. "What if someone gets injured on the job?" he asked. "Don't they tend to get hurt more often?" There was one other thing, too. "How will it look to other people—our customers, our suppliers, our friends?" Saul wondered. "Won't they think we've started a charity or something? How will they know we're doing it for the right reason and not to exploit these people and pocket the savings?"

David relayed these concerns to Joey, but she didn't give up. And

David didn't say no. Something about Joey's argument kept nagging at him, and he couldn't stop thinking about what she had said. After all, his father had given *him* a chance, more than once.

Growing up in the mid-sized city of Yonkers, New York, David Morris was quite the paradox, hyperactive and unable to concentrate, but also sensitive and painfully shy. He absolutely abhorred conflict of any kind. The result of this strange blend of qualities was an athletic boy who loved to run and play basketball and couldn't sit still for long, but who would become stone-faced and silent when someone tried to engage him in a difficult conversation. This drove his family nuts. When they disagreed about an issue, Saul and his wife, Joyce, tended to argue, and with great fervor. David's brother, Jeffrey, and his sister, Hope, were also quite vocal when they got upset. But David, the middle child, wouldn't fight, and when tempers flared, he walked away. It infuriated his parents and siblings.

David was so quiet in kindergarten that Joyce decided to talk to his teacher to see whether something was wrong. "Don't you worry about David," the teacher told her. "He likes to observe first, and then participate when he gets comfortable. But believe me, no one can take advantage of him. The other kids have tried, and it doesn't work. He always takes up for himself."

Despite their own emotionally charged lifestyle, Joyce and Saul were extremely tolerant of other people and cultures. Instead of criticizing David when he made a mistake or a choice they didn't agree with, they stepped back and gave him room to think about what he'd done. At Christmas, they decorated a tree alongside their Hanukkah symbols, and didn't force David to memorize his Hebrew when he didn't show an interest. David and his siblings enjoyed a lot of leeway, but there was one thing Joyce and Saul would not tolerate. Under no circumstances were their children allowed to denigrate another human being with prejudice or hate, and they were forbidden to use hurtful labels or names to cut someone else down. "A person's a person, no matter what," Saul would say. "They need to be treated the same." Years later, David would understand why his father was such a non-violent person, and why he never tried to undermine his son's burning desire to fight for the underdog.

While stationed in France during World War II, young Saul and several other rookie American infantrymen stumbled across a horrific scene. There, lined up against a wall, stood 17 Frenchmen with their hands tied, awaiting execution by a group of Nazi soldiers. Saul's comrades froze, but he acted quickly, single-handedly gunning down the Germans

and saving the lives of the French military men. He never talked about
the shrapnel in his shoulder or his Purple Heart or Silver Star, or even
the letter of commendation from then-president of France, Charles de
Gaulle. But he refused to allow guns in the house, and held a strong aver-
sion to people who thought they were superior to everyone else.

Joyce was just as adamant that her children grow up with open minds.
Once, when she was a girl, she had invited a Jamaican friend named
Claire to the family's summer home in Carmel, New York. The neighbors were appalled—a nice Jewish girl inviting a dark-skinned person
to vacation with her!—but to Joyce and her parents, Claire was simply
a friend, and they wanted to spend time with her.

When David was in the fifth grade, Saul closed his paint store in Mount
Vernon, New York, and the family moved to the South to join other
relatives. The Morrises lived in a duplex on Missionary Ridge in Chattanooga, and Saul and his brother-in-law, Seymour, opened a small business selling portable buildings.

By the time he graduated from high school, David had quietly ab-
sorbed a great deal of his father's entrepreneurial spirit. He attended one
year of college but was bored in class so he dropped out and, at age 19,
opened a tropical plant store in Chattanooga. Several times a month he
drove to Florida in his ramshackle Ford bus and brought back a load
of bromeliads and delicate orchids and zebra plants. It was at the plant
shop that he met Hubert Shuptrine, a Chattanooga native and watercolor artist, whose 1974 coffee-table-sized book, *Jericho: The South Be-
held*, co-authored with poet and novelist James Dickey, was selling like
hotcakes. Despite David's long hair and disheveled, hippie appearance,
Hubert and his wife, Phyllis, liked him immediately. They hired him
to travel throughout the Southeast, picking up Hubert's rural portraits
from their owners to borrow for gallery shows. After that, David worked
for his uncle, selling paint and wallpaper, but he felt confined. He knew
this wasn't what he was supposed to be doing. But what?

Saul, on the other hand, was working his way up the carpet-industry
ladder in Dalton, Georgia, a former Confederate hospital town 30 miles
south of Chattanooga and 80 miles north of Atlanta. In the late 1890s a
Dalton craftswoman, Catherine Evans Whitener, had revived the colo-
nial art of tufting bedspreads and triggered a booming cottage industry
that by the 1920s had spread to several neighboring states. On either
side of U.S. Highway 41 coursing through Dalton, brightly colored chenille spreads were hung out for sale, so many in fact, that the area soon

became known as "Peacock Alley." Efforts to mass-produce the popular items, combined with the growing popularity of small "scatter rugs," led to the birth of the carpet tufting machine in the 1940s. Over the years Dalton evolved into the "Carpet Capital of the World," producing first cotton, then nylon floor coverings, and usurping higher-priced goods made from expensive wool fibers at mills in the North.

By the late 1970s Saul had become president of Dalton-based Argonne, a new division of Lancer Industries, a major manufacturer of indoor-outdoor carpet. Where Lancer's primary end-users were boat owners and maritime experts, Argonne focused exclusively on a new but promising frontier: retail home centers. Still in its infancy, the home center industry was just beginning to rival the small hardware stores and wholesale outlets as a source of do-it-yourself (DIY) materials, including long-lasting polypropylene carpet, highly resistant to moisture, mildew, and stains. But the standard method of bundling carpet in cumbersome, 12-foot-long rolls posed a problem for DIY homeowners, who needed a way to buy and transport smaller segments to cover their sun rooms and screened-in porches. "That's ridiculous," Saul's colleagues said when he proposed that Argonne make easier-to-handle 6-foot rolls. Indoor-outdoor carpet was easily spliced and seamed together, he pointed out. So why not sell smaller pieces that DIYers could handle?

Ever the creative thinker, Saul convinced his bosses to give it a try, even as other carpet executives scoffed at the idea. A few years later, 6-foot carpet rolls had become the industry standard. And Saul was a highly respected icon known for his brilliant ideas and pioneering leadership.

David's career, by contrast, was in limbo. He still hadn't decided what he wanted to do; he loved art but didn't feel he was good enough to sketch or paint for a living. And the plant store hadn't been profitable. Saul tried to give David's ego a boost by inviting him to trade shows, secretly hoping his son would take an interest in the more financially sound carpet business.

Despite his success with Argonne and his knowledge of the industry, Saul eventually grew restless. The portable-building venture he'd launched when he first came to Chattanooga from Yonkers hadn't worked out; neither, in the long run, had any of his other independent undertakings. But he still believed he was meant to successfully own his own business —many of his family members, and Joyce's, had done it, so why couldn't he?—and he wanted to try it again.

"Hey, David, what do you think about coming to work with me in the indoor-outdoor rug business?" he asked his son one day. "We'll be partners. We can do both artificial grass and needlepunch. We can set up our own office, have someone cut the rugs for us, and hire the sales force at Argonne to sell them. I think I can talk them into that. It would be a win-win situation for everyone." Saul knew better than to push David, so he said nothing more, at least not right then. He realized David had no experience and might make mistakes, but he also believed that if he gave his son plenty of elbow room, as he always had, David would learn from his blunders, and prosper.

David, however, had his reservations. Working in his uncle's paint store had already shown him that running a family business was tricky, even under the best of conditions. What's more, he and his dad were so different. Would they get along? David was sloppy and unfocused; Saul was a meticulous organizer who kept everything in its place. David was a radical thinker; Saul was a conservative, suit-and-tie businessman. Where David quickly implemented his spur-of-the-moment ideas, Saul needed time to ruminate and look over the plans. While David was visibly awkward around strangers, Saul loved people and had a way of making everyone he met feel at ease. "Hey, lemme ask you a question," was Saul's trademark lead-in when he went on a sales pitch. He had a way of charming even the secretaries; when they moved up the ladder themselves, they often remembered how kind and friendly he had been and funneled business his way. It was hard to say no to Saul, even for David, so he finally agreed.

It was precisely that blend of opposite qualities that made it all work.

The two men found a small, second-floor office in a busy commercial district in East Ridge, Tennessee, a bedroom community on the outskirts of Chattanooga. The price was right. The print shop below had a copier they could use, and since fax machines weren't commonplace yet, they didn't need one. David, a longtime vegetarian, was also a fan of the Seventh Day Adventist-run restaurant a few doors down, and he liked the idea of eating lunch there on a regular basis. He persuaded Saul to rent the space. It was scant, but it would do, especially since Saul wouldn't be on-site a lot.

The new office was made up of two adjoining 10' x 12' rooms, one for David and one for Joyce, who did the bookkeeping. For now, Saul would work mostly in Dalton, overseeing the sales force and cultivating the numerous contacts he'd gained through his years as an industry executive. David would run the office, send out samples, coordinate with suppliers to cut the carpet into rugs, and market the company. The duo worked out a deal with Argonne and, in late 1981, opened for business.

In spite of Saul's eagerness to work for himself, and David's rebellious nature, the Morrises weren't about to go into debt with this venture. In the past, Saul had been prone to pursue business deals far too long, well beyond the point at which he should have pulled out and cut his losses. This time, he would start the business on a shoestring—his startup investment came to a whopping $3,000—and without applying for a bank loan. He would pay cash for expenses instead of charging them, and prod his customers to pay their bills on time. In the future, this precedent would help keep the company financially solvent, even when the economy tanked and other businesses closed their doors. As the years passed and the enterprise grew, David and Saul continued to buy machinery and trucks and paid for expansions without miring themselves or the company in debt.

Even the corporate name was born from a sense of frugality. David's aunt and uncle owned a furniture store down the street called Habitat South. *Hmm*, mused David and Saul. This just might work to their advantage. The word "Habitat" was a perfect fit for the home center industry, their target market, and it was easy to remember. To differentiate it from their relatives' shop, they called their corporation Habitat International, Inc. To save money, they had their calls forwarded to the furniture store, where David's aunt always answered the phone with a friendly "Habitat." To outside callers, it sounded as if their own secretary were taking their messages.

To further bolster their image without spending a dime, David's wife, Katie, a commercial artist, developed slick color brochures and stylish packaging labels, creating the illusion that Habitat was a much larger company. And Joyce, who worried about her husband's past losses, kept perfect bookkeeping records; if her balance sheet was one nickel off, she painstakingly searched until she found the error. If there was one mistake, she reasoned, there might be more.

Joyce didn't say much about her financial concerns or her apprehension about David and Saul running a business together, or her fears that they might bicker too much. She kept most of this to herself because she knew her husband wanted so badly to make it. To her amazement, the two men worked well together. True to his word, Saul gave his son plenty of room to make mistakes. On those occasions when Saul was irritated about an order or a sale that wasn't working out the way they had planned, David knew how to use his conflict-avoidance behavior to smooth the rough edges. "Dad, I'll come back when you calm down," he'd say. "I'm not going to argue with you while you're mad." Other times, David frustrated Saul with his brash stubbornness and unwilling-ness to schmooze with the customers. But somehow their differences fit like complementary pieces of the same puzzle; where one was weak, the other was strong.

However, by 1983 the honeymoon period was over and David's hyperac-tive temperament had kicked into high gear. Sitting in an office all day bored him and he was antsy for more of a challenge. "I think we should start our own factory," David told Saul. "We can do the cutting ourselves and make more money." They already had the customer base—several national home centers that Habitat would, in the long run, outlive—and sales were robust and growing.

David and Saul rented a 3,000-square-foot warehouse, a long narrow building on Jersey Pike in Chattanooga, just off a major highway exit. They purchased two tables, some cutting equipment, and a handful of toggles to hold the carpet in place. David would be plant manager and Saul would continue to sell. Just one thing was missing. David and Saul had partnered with other contract salesmen at the East Ridge office, but until that point they'd been able to run the business themselves. Those days were over. It was time to hire Habitat's first employees.

The owner of the print shop, their first-floor neighbor at the old of-fice complex in East Ridge, told them about a man who had hired some Cambodian labor. They were hard workers, conscientious, and dedicat-ed. They showed up for work every day, with a good attitude, and were grateful for their jobs. The contact was Jim Thomison, vice president of a Chattanooga-based manufacturing company that made rope for the commercial fishing and crabbing industry, and later for mass-market retailers. David invited Jim to the plant, and the two immediately hit it off.

Jim told David about the Cambodian workers, refugees who had fled their homeland during the barbaric reign of the Khmer Rouge in the mid-1970s. A Chattanooga church had sponsored their immigra-tion into the U.S. and helped them find housing. Jim's company had hired several of them, but there was one family in particular, the Tegs, who still needed all the aid they could get, including jobs. There were eight of them altogether, living in one small, cramped house: Chang, the youngest brother and the only one who spoke any English; his sisters Chou, Pik, Cheng, and Y (pronounced EE); his brother, Khang; his sister-in-law, Kiv; and his mother, Ly Siv In.

David wasn't concerned that most of them didn't speak English; if Cambodian employees had worked out well at Jim's company, he was sure they'd fit in at Habitat too. Then he heard the Teg family's story, and he knew he had to give them a chance. It was the least he could do.

Theirs was a tale straight out of *The Killing Fields*. On April 17, 1975, residents throughout Cambodia cheered as black-clad Khmer Rouge soldiers entered the capital of Phnom Penh and promised an end to the bombings and suffering that had taken place during five years of civil war. But all was not as it seemed, and the Cambodians' victorious mood quickly turned to fear as the troops began ordering them to abandon their homes with little more than the clothes on their backs. By mid-afternoon, thousands of people from Phnom Penh, Battambang, and other cities were being marched to the "pure" countryside, as part of the Khmer Rouge's attempt to mold the ideal communist society. Over the next few years, many of the "capitalist" city dwellers—up to 2.5 million by some accounts—would die in the Khmer Rouge camps, some of starvation and disease, others through execution by Angka, "The Organization." When news of the genocide was finally broadcast on television stations in the U.S., it would remind many Americans of the cruel atrocities of Nazi Germany.

One of those uprooted households belonged to the Tegs, a family of merchants who, before their capture, had made a living by selling soap, onions, and other products in the open-air market in Battambang. The Khmer Rouge came without warning. "Come on, let's go!" the soldiers shouted as they burst open the door. "No time to pack. You must come with us. No need to bring anything," they said to the panicked family. "You will be coming back in one week."

This, of course, was a lie. The Tegs, including 10-year-old Chang, the youngest brother, spent the next four years imprisoned by the Khmer Rouge. From sunup to dusk, and sometimes throughout the night, they were forced to work in the broiling-hot rice fields, tend lemon trees, and carry heavy buckets of dirt to dam up the river. The prisoners, including Chang's mother and sisters, were coerced at gunpoint to dig stretches of dirt one yard square and one yard deep. If they didn't finish by the time darkness fell, the soldiers punished them by not letting them eat. Even on days when they were given food, each person's ration was only a handful of rice. At night, the Tegs slept in a tiny, stable-like structure they constructed themselves with coconut leaves for a roof and rice cloth for walls. All around them, their former neighbors were enduring the same inhumane treatment. The Khmer Rouge had enacted new rules in Cambodia; they closed schools and factories, assassinated skilled workers, and banned ownership of private property. Communication with the outside world was abolished. If someone refused to follow the rules, the rebel was shot in front of his family.

One day in 1979, four years after they had been driven from their home, Chang and the rest of his family heard a commotion in the jungle nearby. "The Vietnamese are coming to help us!" whispered one of the other Cambodians in the camp. Then, while the Khmer Rouge soldiers were busy fighting the intruders, the prisoners ran as fast as they could. But when the Tegs arrived at Battambang, they found a ghost town. To their dismay, the Vietnamese Army barred them from entering their house; it might be rigged with land mines, they were told. The family erected a makeshift tent by the lake near where they used to live, and slept on the hard ground. When they felt it was safe, they headed for the Thai border, trudging through jungles and rice fields with no shoes on their sore, tired feet. More than once they heard an explosion and bolted in separate directions, only to find each other again hours later. "Duck!" Chang's father would shout as a bomb whistled past, and they'd plunge nose-deep into the muck for what seemed like days before starting again. The Vietnamese were trying to block their escape.

Finally, after 13 grueling hours, the Tegs arrived at the pitiful refugee camp, which was packed with other Cambodians also trying to enter Thailand. But their ordeal was far from over. Thai bus drivers picked up the Tegs, claiming they were all going to a safe place, but instead drove the unsuspecting family and dozens of other Cambodians to the top of a steep mountain. The only way to get back was to walk through a carpet of mine fields.

The Tegs would most likely die trying to navigate their way through this battleground, but they would certainly perish if they went very long without water. They watched in horror as some of the other Cambodians pushed ahead of them, only to be blown apart when they stepped on the underground charges. Chang and his relatives spent the next several months carefully trekking a narrow mountain path, single file, afraid one of them would step in the wrong place and detonate another land mine. More than once they traipsed across human arms, legs, and carcasses, picking their way to a rare drink of water from a creek polluted with blood and other bodily fluids. Sometimes they would pass the corpse of a baby, wrapped in thin cloth and hanging like a cocoon from a tree. There was no place there to bury the dead.

Chang's father hadn't weathered their 4-year nightmare very well, and he was ill and dying. Chang, now 14 and strong from all the hard labor, often supported his dad on his sturdy shoulders as they walked. Eventually they returned to the river outside their home in Cambodia, and began their second attempt to escape the country. This time the journey was much easier, and they soon arrived at 007, a Thai refugee camp, where Chang's father died. A few months later the Tegs were transported to Khao I Dang, the largest refugee camp in Thailand, and from there they were moved to a succession of other shelters, each one bringing them a little closer to being accepted for relocation to America. Chang's sister, Cheng, gave birth to a son in one of the camps. Her husband was not there; he had been killed in the siege several months earlier. Finally, in November 1981, at the same time David and Saul were launching Habitat in their first tiny office, the Tegs arrived in the United States.

David felt he had no choice but to help these people who had been through so much. Soon after Jim introduced him to the Teg family, Chang's sisters, Chou and Pik, were hired at Habitat, and Chang, who was still in high school, began working part-time. David and Saul also employed two Laotian refugees, a man and a woman, and another Cambodian woman named Moon. For the two big-hearted business owners, there was never any question about whether they should do this, how they would handle the language barrier, or whether they could deal with the repercussions of post-traumatic stress disorder that would haunt their employees from time to time. It was simply the right thing to do. Habitat's practice of hiring people in need had begun.

David bought food and clothing to give to the Tegs, helped them get their green cards, and loaned Chang the money for his first car. When Pik, whose mental stability was forever shaken by what she'd withstood during the insurgency, committed suicide, David arrived at the scene to comfort the family, and he and Saul bought her tombstone. Years later, the day after a tornado tore the Tegs' house to splinters, David and some of his staff showed up unannounced, with pickup trucks, loaded the Tegs' belongings into the back, and stored them at Habitat until they could find a new place to live. The Habitat staff, including the Cambodians, had become a family, and this was what families did.

David had always been fascinated with Eastern cultures and Buddhist philosophies, so he enjoyed learning about the Cambodians' cuisine, religious practices, and customs. It was difficult at first, though, to communicate, since most of the Tegs spoke no English; even though Chang did his best to interpret for his sisters and sister-in-law, there were still misunderstandings. One day David happened to walk by as the Cambodian workers were talking, as usual, in their own dialect. He could tell what they meant from their gestures, so he decided to give them instructions by using his hands. Startled, they thought he understood what they were saying and stopped speaking their native language around him for days.

Compulsively neat and clean, the Tegs usually kept the grass-turf and carpet fibers swept from the floor where they stood. They simply couldn't stand a mess. One February day, all the brooms in the plant disappeared. Puzzled, David began searching for them. When he finally found them, stashed in the closet, he handed one to Chang and motioned for him to clean up the floor. Chang refused, and for three days the floors went unswept. *What in the world?* David thought. *What's gotten into these people?* "It's Cambodian New Year," Chang finally explained. "It's tradition. If you sweep the floor on New Year, you sweep away all your good fortune and wealth. We don't sweep on New Year."

Chang, who would later become plant manager, was still working at Habitat part-time when, quite by accident, David came up with the idea of making his own golf putting greens. Most artificial-grass carpet was fabricated from polypropylene, or plastic, fibers that stuck straight up in the air. When cut and spliced, the seams showed. David was excited about a new product he and Saul were beginning to sell, a non-directional grass that curled in different directions, didn't reveal a seam when two swaths were pieced together, and didn't get crushed as easily when packaged and shipped. The result was a neater, more appealing grass rug.

How are we going to get buyers to look at this grass? David wondered. *How do we convince them to buy it?* Then, as he would do many times in the coming years, he hit on an outlandish idea. He cut a strip of grass turf 18 inches wide and nine feet long, glued a foam wedge to the back, then drilled a 4-inch-diameter hole in it to create a golf-practice putting green. Surely the sample would get the buyers' attention.

There were still only a half dozen workers, including Chang, Pik, and Chou, at the Jersey Pike factory. David showed them his sample. "We need to make lots of these," he said, using gestures to help explain.

The DIY home center industry wasn't yet dominated by Wal-Mart, the Home Depot, and Lowe's but by numerous smaller companies trying to get in on the act. So Habitat would need about 300 samples to send to the various buyers.

With other rugs being cut on the main floor, there was no room to assemble the putting greens after the sections were cut from the rolls of grass carpet. David hired a carpenter to build a raised deck overlooking the plant. Chang filled gallon buckets of glue from a 55-gallon container below, then carried each bucket up to the deck, one by one. There, on the elevated platform, he and Pik spray-glued the foam backing onto the grass putting greens before throwing them onto the table below. At that point, Chou and two other female workers took over and drilled the holes that would cradle the golf ball.

Not long after David sent out the samples, a sporting goods buyer for Kmart called. "I saw the putting green you sent to my buddy in flooring, and I'm wondering where I could get more of these," he asked. "Can you mass-produce them?"

The process of making the practice greens was a pain. It was time-consuming and difficult, and the glue didn't always stick well. David was pleased that Kmart was interested in buying them, but was also smart enough not to jump at the chance without giving it some thought. He and Saul quoted the buyer an inflated price—if making this product was going to take that much time, they thought, at least they should be paid for their efforts—and to their astonishment, the buyer agreed.

Within a few months the Habitat staff was in the throes of filling putting-green orders for the entire Kmart chain. To meet the challenge of supplying every Kmart store in the country, David and the Cambodians worked long hours to assemble the products. They installed a new ventilation system to keep from inhaling the fumes from the glue. By the time they bought the appropriate dye-cutting and gluing equipment to handle the job, they also had orders from Sears and a host of other retailers.

What had, at the time, been merely a clever marketing ploy had turned into the most profitable part of the business. The golf putting greens put Habitat on the national sporting goods map, so to speak, and the company quickly outgrew its factory space on Jersey Pike. David and Saul hired more employees, including Chang's sister, Y, and his sister, Cheng, the one who had lost her husband in the Khmer Rouge massacre. But nothing short of a move to a larger facility would allow them to keep up with the demand.

As usual, David refused to settle for the mundane. He heard about a former chicken hatchery for sale in a residential neighborhood in Ross-ville, Georgia, just across the state line from Chattanooga. It wasn't that large—only about 9,000 square feet—and it had been haphazardly par-titioned into many small sections. It certainly wasn't attractive. Loose wires dangled from the ceiling, the plumbing barely worked, and there was junk piled everywhere. There were no loading docks for shipping the products; those would have to be added. And it was several miles from the interstate. But unlike the rented building on Jersey Pike, it of-fered room for expansion.

"Why on earth would we move here?" Saul gasped when David drove him to see the place. "This is a residential area. It's gonna be hard for trucks to get in and out. And it needs new electrical wiring. It's a mess."

But David, the maverick artist, saw its potential. "We'll have four acres of our own to work with, enough to last us forever if we want to keep adding on. Plus, it's cheap, so it won't be a big risk," he explained. "And the fact that it's not in an industrial area is a plus in my book. This is a beautiful setting. Who says we have to run our plant just like ev-eryone else?" Despite his success at Habitat, he still hated conventional factories. "I just have a good feeling about this place," he told his father. "This is where we need to be."

Saul, of course, was the great compromiser, and he knew better than to argue with David when he made up his mind to do something. If David felt that strongly about this location, if it was that important to him, Saul would have to give his son the benefit of the doubt. In 1986, they moved Habitat to the old chicken hatchery, where they continued to impress buyers with their marketing savvy and product packaging. They began to draw even more attention at industry trade shows. David dressed mannequins in needlepunch jackets and grass-turf berets and positioned the quirky models to look as if they were toting rolls of Habi-tat carpet and slam-dunking a basketball into a hoop flanked by a back-board advertising "The Grass People." Throughout the product displays he scattered novelty items like grass footballs, umbrellas, and soda-can coozies. The strategies worked, and as time passed the company cor-nered 75 percent of the U.S. putting-green market and a hefty percent-age in Europe. When new competitors began to encroach on their ter-ritory, David and Saul teamed up with Spalding, a well-known brand in sporting goods, and made a deal to license the name. For several years every item cut and packaged at Habitat bore the Spalding label, and the secretary answered the phone "Habitat-Spalding."

But David and Saul weren't the only ones looking for opportunities. Soon after Habitat increased its factory space, Joey DeVivo became more determined than ever to convince David to host an enclave of Orange Grove clients. "If it doesn't work out," Joey assured him again, "we'll stop."

David's resistance was starting to wear down. He had initially been concerned about being able to talk to people with mental disabilities or profound speech impediments. Now, he reasoned, that might not be that much of a problem. The Cambodians, after all, spoke little English, and they were among the hardest workers in the plant. Area residents had been underestimating them for years, staring in public and showing their prejudiced ignorance until they got to know Chang, Cheng, Y, and Chou as real people.

There was one other thing, too, a memory David couldn't seem to shrug off.

He had barely had any contact with Darcy, his sister-in-law with Down syndrome, when he and Katie first married in 1976. After a while, Darcy began spending the night at their house once or twice a week. She was extremely overweight, was mentally slow, and had all kinds of medical problems. But she was happy most of the time, and very, very loving. She enjoyed drawing pictures and chatting on the phone for hours at a time. In the mornings, when David asked Darcy to make her bed, more often than not she put up a fight. Sometimes she even pouted, or yelled, "I can't believe you're making me do this!" Later in the day, however, David noticed that Darcy held her head higher and smiled even more broadly. "See what I did?" she'd ask, showing off her smoothly made bed or the table she'd set for dinner. Darcy proved to herself, and everyone else, that she could do more than expected. And after a while, David noticed that having a sister-in-law with Down syndrome didn't seem all that unusual.

Saul was still not convinced about letting the mentally disabled clients from Orange Grove work at the plant, but he remained open-minded. He'd always had a soft spot for people less fortunate than himself. And his wartime experiences had shown him that things aren't always what they appear to be. "Okay, let's try it," he finally agreed.

David picked up the phone and called Joey DeVivo. "Bring 'em on," he told her. At the time, the gutsy father-son team had no way of knowing that such a simple response would change their lives forever, and shape Habitat in a way they'd never thought possible.

Three

"Why Can't We Hire More People Like This?"

THE ENCLAVE FROM ORANGE GROVE arrived in the fall of 1986 with a spitfire of a job coach named Minnie Witcher. A tiny woman with a no-nonsense attitude, Minnie marched into the Habitat plant, her eight protégés trailing behind her like a gaggle of happy geese, and announced, "Hi, my name is Minnie. We're here to help.

"Now here are the rules," she said with her hands on her hips. "If you need my people to do something, please tell me and I'll show them what needs to be done. You will not give them orders directly. If somebody makes a mistake, come to me. You will not give them anything to eat or drink on the job, and they will not ask you for anything. All requests have to go through me. I'm their supervisor as long as we're here. Now. Where do you want us to start?"

David's eyes widened. Chang, now plant manager, grew silent. Neither was used to a woman telling them what to do, and here was this little drill sergeant laying down the law, and in *their* workplace. But as the day passed, it became clear that despite her strictness and take-no-prisoners attitude, she loved her clients and they loved her, and she had a way of coaxing the best out of each one. All eight of them—Anthony, Cecelia, Edward, Colleen, Albert, Vickie, Kenneth S., and Kenneth L.—went to work folding freshly cut rugs and cleaning the floors. Most of them had mild developmental disabilities; they moved slowly and it was sometimes hard to interpret what they were saying. But they listened carefully as

Minnie explained each task, and they followed her instructions without grumbling. David watched them lift weighty rolls of carpet and was surprised at how strong they were. He was also impressed with their eagerness to please.

Minnie drove the small Orange Grove bus to Habitat every day. She was so short she could barely see over the steering wheel. Once they arrived at the factory, the clients would retrieve their boxed lunches from the bus and wait for Chang to fire up the machine that punched the holes in the putting greens. Then they would fold the punched pieces of carpet, insert them into the boxes, tape the boxes shut, and stack them for loading. By lunchtime the boxes were heaped like massive cardboard mountains. And it didn't take long for the Orange Grove clients to become adept at more difficult tasks, like rolling carpet. They worked at the cutting tables, using the dye-cut machines and laboring elbow-to-elbow with Habitat's dozen or so full-time employees.

David found himself falling in love with these good-natured people. There was something about Edward, in particular. He was tall and thin, with long arms and legs, an easygoing personality, and a smile that could melt even the stoniest heart. He had so much natural charisma, in fact, that it was hard to resist hugging him. Colleen, who later competed in the local Special Olympics, was very sweet; so was the lovely Cecelia. It was obvious that some of the clients had developed crushes on each other; at lunch, men and women paired up, ate their sandwiches together, and flirted shamelessly.

But Chang and the other Cambodian workers kept their distance. Minnie was African-American. So were several of the Orange Grove clients, and the Tegs weren't used to being around black people or people with disabilities. Minnie's keen intuition kicked in right away, and she sensed that Chang and the others were reluctant to welcome them. So she decided to make the first move. "Hi, my name is Mrs. Witcher," she offered. "If you want us to do something, please tell me. We're here to help."

Chang mustered a smile. "My English not real good," he politely replied. "If I say something wrong, please forgive me, because I speak my English words like Cambodian, which is kind of opposite."

Still, the Cambodians seemed wary, even jealous, of the enclave. The Tegs cautiously watched the Orange Grove visitors, and at break time wouldn't mingle with them. Minnie was clearly disappointed. She was worried that the Cambodians might say something insensitive or mistreat her clients, and that was the last thing they needed. She decided to talk to her boss about it. "Well, let's try it a few more days," he said. "Let's give it a chance. If it doesn't work out, we'll look for another business to host them."

Chang, meanwhile, was complaining to David. "I can't work with them," he said to his boss.

"Why?" David asked. He had wondered why the Cambodians were reacting so badly, but had hoped they were just nervous about meeting a group of new people.

"Because," Chang replied, "they're mean."

The truth was, the Cambodians were scared. Unlike in America, where socially conscious citizens often tried to incorporate people with disabilities into the mainstream of society, in Cambodia, the mentally challenged were feared. Shunned from birth, with no one to talk to or love them, they often developed antisocial behaviors. Chang remembered walking past mentally retarded people who threw rocks at him. In his country, it was better to just leave them be. He didn't quite know how to say all this to David, so he didn't try. Best to just eliminate the problem right now, before one of these people threw something or hit him, or worse. In his mind, they were all monsters.

"Okay, Chang," David told him despite Chang's guarded explanation. "Tell you what—let's give this two weeks. Why don't you do your best to help them adjust? If you give it a try and still feel the same way in two weeks, we'll get rid of 'em." David didn't want to let Minnie down, or his friend Joey, or these affable people with developmental disabilities. But he had a plant to run, and he couldn't very well fire his best full-time employees over something like this.

The turning point came, as turning points are apt to do, out of the blue. An avid basketball player as a child, David had bought a hoop and set up a small court inside the Rossville plant. The diversion served double duty. It gave him an outlet for burning off restless energy, and allowed his employees to have fun and de-stress during break time. Most of all, it offered a way to digress from the conservative factory atmosphere David loathed.

The clients from Orange Grove took an instant liking to the basketball court. Edward was an especially beautiful player, with a rhythm as graceful as a dancer's. "Watch this, watch this," he'd say, drawing the attention of everyone on the floor. "Watch this." Counting to three, the lanky man would launch the ball from his long fingertips. Inevitably, it would sail through the air, mesmerize the other players as if they had seen a rare bird, and drop through the hoop with a soft swoosh. Despite his athletic prowess, Edward didn't brag about his performance. He simply flashed a charming smile.

One day, about two weeks after Edward and his seven peers arrived at Habitat for the first time, David was strolling by the basketball court when he saw something that jolted him to a stop. The Orange Grove clients were playing a spirited game against a handful of able-bodied employees, and the clients were winning. David dropped what he was doing and jumped in like a puppy bounding after a frisbee. "Go, Edward! Go, Albert!" cheered Colleen and Cecelia from the sidelines as the game gathered momentum. David tried hard to keep up with Edward and the rest of the Orange Grove team, but they couldn't be caught. The next thing David knew, Chang and the other Cambodian workers had joined his team in an effort to give him an edge. But still the clients were winning.

David had an idea. "Hey, let's switch places!" he shouted, divvying up the teams so there were disabled players on both sides. Suddenly, there was Chang, bobbing and weaving and bouncing the ball next to Edward and Albert, and before long he couldn't stop grinning. By the end of the game, they were all laughing and whooping and slapping each other on the back in playful camaraderie.

From then on, the Cambodians and the mentally challenged clients were inseparable. They teased each other at the cutting table and played basketball or shot games of pool during breaks. Sometimes they played a few minutes past their allotted recess, but David didn't mind. His workers were happy, productive, and getting along. They were a family. All of them.

"Well, what do you think?" David asked Chang and the rest of the Tegs. "Do you still want to get rid of 'em?"

Their response set a precedent for Habitat, one that would influence the company's employment practices for years to come. "Why can't we hire more people like this?" asked the same employees who had been so staunchly opposed to the visiting clients. "They're so happy! We need more people like this, who care, do their work with pride, and smile all the time."

At Christmas, David and Saul presented the Orange Grove workers with bonus checks. It was the happiest experience some of them had ever had. That first group worked at Habitat for more than a year, and others came after that. Sometimes there were two enclaves in the building, 16 in all, working on different projects. Each time, the workers with disabilities produced just as much, if not more, than the able-bodied employees.

In 1989, David and his wife, Katie, went through a painful divorce. David was not very good at hiding his emotions in front of the clients with disabilities; they were particularly sensitive to these things, and they knew he was hurting. One day two men with Down syndrome walked up to him, and each one gave him a hug. "It's going to be all right," they assured him. "You've got great friends, a family that loves you, and Habitat. How can you be so sad when you've got us?"

After that, David wanted to hire every Down syndrome person who walked down the street. His personality changed too. Instead of being standoffish, shy, and restrained, he became outgoing and talkative. He still had trouble expressing affection to other people but these kids, well, they were easy to love, and he found himself hugging them back.

Saul was different too. Always the epitome of professional behavior and impeccable dress, the conservative white-collar businessman traded his starched button-downs, neckties, and jackets for a more casual wardrobe of khakis and golf shirts. He smiled more often. He embraced the clients when they came to work, and they adored him. Firm but compassionate, he was a natural father figure.

In 1991, David and Saul hired Jim Thomison, the man who had introduced them to the hard-working Teg family from Cambodia almost a decade before. A self-proclaimed "neat freak" whose spotless desk was the complete antithesis of David's messy workspace, Jim and David had stayed in touch since they met. Jim knew the industry well from his 15 years as vice president of the rope company, where he purchased reprocessed polypropylene and reclaimed carpet backing to make recycled rope fibers. He also knew the ins and outs of manufacturing and of managing a diverse group of employees, so he would undoubtedly be a valuable asset to the company. One of his first contributions was to computerize much of the company's paper-based operations. For years he'd been impressed with Habitat's progressive spirit. By the time he came on board, David and Saul owned warehouses in Los Angeles and Seattle and, long before such automation had become the industry norm, they had set up a sophisticated inventory and invoicing system to link the locations. At the north Georgia headquarters, however, Saul was still doing all his cost accounting on ledger paper and spending his weekends rewriting the figures. At first he was hesitant about changing his tried-and-true system, but when Jim demonstrated the merits of computerization, Saul could hardly believe his good fortune. Where before it had taken him weeks to re-cost the entire product line by hand, it now took him an hour.

Times were changing for the Tegs too. In 1992, Chang was declared an American citizen. At the government office where he passed the test, he was asked if he wanted to change his name. "What?" Chang asked, confused.

"Well, now that you're an American, you have the legal right to use an American name," the clerk said. Chang had never considered this option, so he had no names in mind.

The clerk pulled a five-dollar bill from his pocket. "That's Thomas Jefferson," he pointed out. "How about this one?"

"Okay," Chang replied. "I like that. Give me that one." From then on, Chang referred to himself by his new legal name, Thomas.

For David and Saul, the leaps of faith had paid off. Habitat had grown from a skeletal office to a bona fide factory already seeing its first expansions. The hurried experiment with golf putting greens at the Jersey Pike plant had more than paid off; Habitat had garnered three-quarters of sales in the U.S. and a sizable percentage in the European market. Indoor-outdoor rug sales, both grass and needlepunch, were up. And it was clear that hiring the conscientious Cambodian workers was one of the best decisions they'd ever made.

But the greatest innovation by far was bringing the disabled clients on board. These people had brought to the business an element of warmth, of kindness, and compassion that hadn't been there before. David and Saul had learned so much from them. Even Thomas and his sisters were glad they were there. Instead of being hindered by the disabilities they had all feared at first, they were liberated by the innocent goodness of people who didn't know how to backstab or goof off on the job. And they had helped make Habitat an even greater success.

This was just the beginning of a long journey through triumphs, pitfalls, and frustrating bureaucratic mazes. In the years to come, David would fight so many battles with the disability "system" that at times the free-spirited entrepreneur would feel like Don Quixote, tilting at windmills. But even on the most bewildering days, he would remember that it was the people with disabilities who had unwittingly taught him to see past his own stereotypes and the world's status-quo rules. They had showed him what it meant to be genuine, how to be himself without judging or being judged. Now he had a real cause, and a reason for running a factory.

Here, after all these years, was something worth fighting for.

Four

Bucking the System

A STORM WAS BREWING inside the Habitat walls.

Hosting the enclave from Orange Grove had turned out to be a blessing, both for Habitat and for the agency's clients with mental disabilities. The clients were proud of their job progress, and their innocent candor and unabashed joy had shown David and Saul just how much fun owning a business could be. But that smooth, trouble-free road was about to get bumpy.

Edward and Colleen and the other clients had thoroughly mastered the cutting and packaging process. They knew how to fold the grass and needlepunch rugs and stack the filled boxes for loading without being told what to do. And they loved it there. So when Minnie Witcher's boss, an administrator at Orange Grove, started pulling clients off the job site without notice and replacing them with inexperienced people, David protested. It was bad enough that the awkward switches were taking place when the Habitat workers were in the middle of filling large, time-sensitive orders. Such changes slowed operations and put David and Saul in a bind. But David was even more frustrated when he learned that the clients, who had advanced to a much higher level of work than they'd known at their group home, were now being pulled back into the Orange Grove workshop to assemble ink pens. That, David felt, undermined the success they'd worked so hard to achieve.

"We don't mind training new clients if we have advance notice. We want to give more people a chance to work here," David explained to the agency's administrator. "But we're trying to run a business, and this is not working. And besides, if the people who have been with us a while have fully mastered all the tasks at Habitat, why not help them find real jobs out in the community instead of making them go back to square one?"

"Sorry," the manager replied. "But this is how it's going to be."

David despised red tape, and he hated limitations even more, so in 1987 the partnership fizzled and the clients stopped coming. But from every loss comes a gain, and Habitat would not be without an enclave of cheerful, mentally disabled clients for very long.

Tom Henderson had been looking for local companies to host some of his higher-functioning clients. An employment coordinator at the Walker County Training Center, a state-funded organization serving people with disabilities in northwest Georgia, Tom had been trying, with little luck, to place clients through a new on-site program not unlike the one at Orange Grove. Flipping through business directories borrowed from area Chambers of Commerce, he began calling prospective employers and asking them if they would be willing to participate in the Center's new program. So far most of them had declined. There just wasn't a place in their organizations, they claimed, for people with disabilities. It was just too risky, and it would interfere with the work of their full-time employees. By the time Tom came across a listing for a little-known Rossville rug company called Habitat International, Inc., he was starting to feel discouraged about the whole thing.

"I'd love to do this," David told Tom when they met. "But there's one stipulation. The agency I worked with before kept pulling their clients away just when they got really good at the job. They were always switching supervisors on us, so it was really hard for us to keep up with what was happening, and we kept having to retrain everyone, including the job coaches. If you'll promise me that won't be the case here—if you'll leave the same enclave at Habitat for a while and give us plenty of notice if you plan to take them back—you can sign us up right now."

David's request seemed reasonable enough, so Tom quickly answered, "You got it."

One morning not long after the Orange Grove enclaves had stopped coming to Habitat, a group of eight disabled clients from the Walker County Training Center arrived at the plant. Just like Orange Grove, the state provided a small bus to transport the clients to work. Some resided in group homes, others with a parent or sibling. Few lived alone. Most depended on Supplemental Security Income, or SSI, a federal income source created to help disabled people with little or no income, and they subscribed to Medicare or Medicaid for their healthcare coverage. Now they would also receive a small check from the State of Georgia, funded in part by Habitat.

For the first couple of weeks Tom Henderson accompanied the clients and trained them himself. He was impressed with the unfaltering support David gave the people with disabilities and with how well they responded to him. At break time, there was David, dribbling a basketball, shooting hoops, and laughing right along with them. On the job, he was patient until they learned the tasks and built up their speed. Spending time with his sister-in-law, Darcy, and, later, the enclave from Orange Grove had taught him that the best way to train people with mental disabilities was to break the job down into small steps and give them time to grasp each one. It might take them a while to catch on, but once they did there was no stopping them. Before long they were running not one cutting table, but two, and with supervision were able to perform nearly every task in the plant.

David's interaction with the clients didn't stop at the Habitat doors. A big kid at heart, he started taking the clients and his employees out to dinner occasionally, and to baseball games on weekends. Because he treated them so well, they looked forward to being at the plant every day, and they did their work with pride, and with few, if any, errors. He began hosting special-education classes from the local high schools and even hired one of the vocational students after graduation. He also employed a man with bipolar disorder who turned out to have a phenomenal memory and work ethic. Soon, like the Orange Grove clients before them, they had all become important members of the Habitat family. And it showed.

At first Sharon, who had mild mental retardation, was so shy she wouldn't even look the managers in the eye. It soon became apparent to everyone, though, that she was a perfectionist bent on doing her job well. She wasn't satisfied until the edges of the carpet were precisely matched, and the boxes stacked neatly for shipping. She quickly became a role model for accuracy and speed.

Bright and inquisitive, Ken Jones was particularly observant if something wasn't quite right in the plant, and he didn't hesitate to let David know. Ken was stocky, with premature gray in his hair, a gentle disposition, a moderate form of mental retardation, and a thick-tongued speech impediment often found in people with Down syndrome. A born organizer, he was great at loading and unloading trucks—he developed his own system for knowing what to put on the trucks and what to leave off—and he could assemble boxes with the swiftness of a sprinter. He couldn't read or count or tell time but he knew when to alert his supervisors if the work crew was running low on 4' x 6' boxes. And he could drive a forklift like a pro.

From the outset, Ken and Jeff Brown competed relentlessly to see who could outwork the other. Jeff, whose mental retardation was more severe than Ken's, was also more emotional, and he wore his heart on his sleeve. If a co-worker were having a bad day, he would most likely try to cheer them up with his wise trademark phrase: "It'll be better tomorrow." Where Ken was short and barrel-chested, Jeff was tall and thin, with a long, angular face and a huge grin beneath a thick, dark-brown moustache. While it was immediately obvious that Ken had Down syndrome, Jeff's disability often went unnoticed until he spoke. When he went on an outing with David and the rest of the Habitat gang, he liked to flaunt his big Stetson hat and snakeskin cowboy boots and flirt with the women.

John Moss was just as flamboyant, but in his own way. John's doctor didn't think he could work, and the Walker County Training Center administrators weren't so sure either. But there he was, cutting carpet, dancing right alongside everyone else, and having a blast. The thing most people noticed first about Big John wasn't his slow-moving gait or the slant of his eyes or the flattened facial features of his Down syndrome, an uncommon condition in African-Americans, but his enormous size. He weighed close to 400 pounds, and elephantiasis—a chronic disease caused by an obstruction in the lymphatic system and characterized by an abnormal enlargement in certain parts of the body—was so pronounced in one calf that extra material had to be sewn into his pants leg. To David, he looked like Fat Albert, and he was just as much fun. John coached the local high school football team, and everyone who knew him in his hometown of Ringgold, Georgia, absolutely adored him. It was no wonder. He was one of the kindest people David had ever met. One day the issue of race came up at break time. John looked puzzled. He had never understood what all the fuss was about. "See, David?" he said, turning his big, black hand over to reveal a light-colored palm and placing it next to David's. "We're all the same."

Connie Presnell, an instructor with the Walker County Training Center, couldn't help but be touched by the childlike sweetness of Ken, Jeff, Sharon, John, and the rest of the clients with whom she worked. After the first two weeks of the fledgling Habitat partnership, Tom Henderson

had stepped back to allow job coaches like Connie to take over and supervise the clients. At first she filled in when the other full-time instructor was out, but after a while she became Habitat's primary liaison with
the state program. She had been trained to keep her emotional distance
from the clients, but here Connie found herself acting as nurse, counselor, and, most of all, strong, nurturing mom, a role for which she was
well suited.

Connie had grown up in the small, rural community of Griffith's
Creek in Whitwell, Tennessee, in the mountainous southeastern part of
the state. The ninth of 10 children born to Aaron and Tressie Presnell,
she spent her young days swimming in the cool creek and climbing trees
with her twin brother, Ronnie. Connie was definitely her father's favorite, and she worshipped him. She was just 3 years old the first time she
got up before the sun rose to ride the mule while he plowed the family
garden. With so many kids in the family, dawn was the only time they
could talk, just the two of them. As she grew older she continued to rise
before everyone else and wake her daddy, and together they would build
a fire in the wood-burning stove so it would be ready when Tressie got
up to make biscuits for breakfast. The Presnells were dirt poor; they had
no electricity and no running water. Connie and her siblings were so
proud of the one pair of shoes they each owned that they carried them
down the long path to the school bus to keep them from getting dirty.
But the Presnell kids were happy, and very, very content.

Connie was 9 years old when, in the summer of 1963, that idyllic way
of life came to an end. The year before, on the day after Christmas, a
strike had idled some 600 members of the United Mine Workers Union,
but some of the mines, including the one where Aaron Presnell worked
as a guard, later reopened with non-union employees. Violence erupted
in the pastoral community as the Grundy Mining Company tried to
resume operations in the nearly abandoned coalfields.

One Friday evening in June, two weeks after Connie's father started
pulling the night shift, he was riding to work with another Grundy Mining Company watchman when the driver noticed a car blocking their
way on the unpaved company road. Five men leaped from the Ford
sedan near the loading ramp and began firing their rifles and shotguns.
Connie's father was, according to a flurry of newspaper accounts by
United Press International and the Associated Press, shot "right in the
heart." Panicked, his co-worker stepped on the gas and sped to a nearby
gas station, but it was too late. Aaron Presnell was dead at age 49. Three
weeks later a Grundy County grand jury cleared all five men of charges

in the murderous ambush. The ensuing "lawlessness"—more shootings, dynamiting, and persistent gunfire that put the mine's electric equipment out of commission each night—soon led to the shutting down of all coal mining operations in the county.

Unable to manage the plowing, wood-chopping, and other demanding chores at the farm in Griffith's Creek, Tressie and the seven children who were still living at home moved into a low-income housing project about an hour away, in Chattanooga. In the "big city," in this strange urban environment, the other boys and girls ostracized the Presnell kids for their rural accents, naïveté, and wide-eyed wonder at simple things like running water and in-house bathrooms. They weren't just the new kids on the block; to the street-smart children who had grown up there, they were the Beverly Hillbillies. Something else segregated them from their peers, something Connie couldn't quite understand. A few months after they moved, 9-year-old Connie heard someone make fun of her oldest sister, the family's firstborn. She was confused. Her parents had always treated their 10 children the same, so what was so different about Ann?

"Mama, what's a retard?" Connie asked. "The other kids are saying that's what Ann is. What does that mean?"

"Honey, don't pay any attention to them," Tressie soothed. "They don't know what they're talking about. They don't know Ann and that's why they're calling her names. She's just like everyone else."

Connie was a teenager before she understood what mental retardation meant. As her other brothers and sisters fell in love, married, and left home, Ann stayed behind. But that didn't make any difference to Connie. Ann was kind and helpful and funny and, unlike Connie's insensitive classmates, friendly and easy to be with. Years later, Connie saw this again when she applied for a job as a house parent at a group home for men with severe disabilities. Some were non-verbal, others were in wheelchairs, and all of them required assistance with basic care, from spooning food onto their plates to shaving and taking a bath. By the time she became an instructor at the Walker County Training Center in 1986, the same year the first Orange Grove enclave began cutting and packaging carpet at Habitat, Connie Presnell was primed to help others less outwardly capable than herself. She would soon find her true calling at Habitat.

The first enclaves from Orange Grove had far surpassed David's expectations. So had the ones from the Walker County Training Center. And Habitat had already shown its strong social consciousness at a time when most employers were still too afraid to welcome people with disabilities into the workplace. Many of the other northwest Georgia factories that later agreed to host enclaves didn't allow the disabled workers inside their plants, but instead sent ink pen components or other products off-site, to be assembled at the Center. Compared to those who had "jobs" at Habitat, the clients who put pens together at the Center's workshop were acquiring only minimal work skills, such as identifying shapes, colors, and numbers. All day they labored at small, one-person stations and were discouraged from talking to each other. The clients at Habitat, on the other hand, had learned to interact with the other workers, stay on task while following directions, and keep their work areas neat and clean.

David was aware of all this, and he was glad the clients at Habitat were doing so well, but he still felt that something was missing. What's more, there were conflicts—not with the clients themselves, but with the coordinators at the Walker County Training Center—and they were becoming more frequent. David and Connie discovered they were of the same mind when it came to expecting people with disabilities to excel and grow in the workplace, and they often found themselves bucking a system riddled with red tape and preconceived notions. When the state presented them with formal, written evaluations of the disabled work ers, David and Connie scoffed at the definitions that stipulated what a person with a certain challenge, like Down syndrome or mild retardation, should or should not be able to do. Even the local advocacy organizations seemed to be holding them back with myriad rules, and that angered David and Connie. After all, they knew better. For years they had seen what people with disabilities could accomplish when given the same opportunities as anyone else.

Connie's bosses discouraged her from getting too close to the clients, and reprimanded her when she did. A nurturing mother figure at heart, she found herself doing exactly what she was trained not to do. She hugged the clients, called them after hours to make sure they were okay if she knew they were having problems, even drove them home if they got sick at work. How in the world, she wondered, could she keep from caring about someone like Ken Jones, who hugged her several times a day and called her "Brue Eyes," or Jeff Brown, whose contagious smile could light up a dark room?

Something else, too, was bothering Connie and David just as much as the rules that, by design, appeared to underestimate people with disabilities.

"Connie, what's this?" David asked one day while she was filling out the semi-monthly reports that determined how much each client was paid. For several years he had routinely authorized his secretary to handle the bills from the state for the work the clients had done at Habitat. He knew they were paid by the hour and that they received less than minimum wage, but there, on the desk where Connie tallied their hours, were documents showing a wide discrepancy in compensation for different people from the same enclave.

"Well, they're all paid on a piecework system," Connie told him. "We do a time study to see how fast everyone works and the state pays them according to how many pieces of carpet they can cut or fold or put in a box. Some people work a lot slower than others, so they don't make as much."

On the surface such an arrangement seemed fair enough; after all, in the corporate world, employees who perform best tend to make more money. But it had always bugged Connie to watch the disabled clients work as hard as anyone else in an office or store or manufacturing plant, for a fraction of the pay. None of them were earning very much, but to Connie the time-study scale discriminated against some of them even more. The clients might have mental disabilities, but they weren't stupid. Surely they realized they were doing the same work, in most cases, for less pay than the "real" employees.

David was stunned. "That's just plain wrong," he said to Connie, shaking his head. "Yes, I know," she nodded. She believed things should be different, that the clients should earn more and be more equally compensated, but she also knew this was the way things were done. And it wasn't likely to change any time soon.

From the beginning, representatives from both Orange Grove and the Walker County Training Center had warned David that if the clients with disabilities made too much money, at Habitat or anywhere else, their SSI checks would stop. Connie and David decided to visit the Social Security office to find out more. They were told that although the clients might lose a portion of their monthly cash income if they earned a real paycheck, and that they would have to forfeit the supplement altogether if they made more than a certain amount, their Medicare or Medicaid coverage would stay intact, no matter what. To help ease the growing debate with the Center, David recruited the local chapter of the Arc of the United States, formerly known as the Association for Retarded Citizens, to act as a mediator. A representative from the Arc met with each client in the Habitat conference room, with no one else present, and interviewed them about their goals. "What are your ambitions?" she asked them. "What would you like to see happen when it comes to your work?"

Later, Connie found herself fighting back tears as she read the responses the Arc representative had written down. "I want to learn how to drive," one client had said. "I'd like to have my own job, a real job," offered another. The answers given by John Moss, the overweight man with Down syndrome and elephantiasis in his leg, had been among the most touching. His dreams: "To be able to stay on my feet all day. To stay with Habitat until I die. To be happy."

David showed the Arc report to Center officials as evidence that the clients deserved to be treated with more professionalism and respect. But that didn't help cool the heated dispute with the state, and tensions remained high. It would take one more conversation, this time with someone David didn't even know yet, to push him over the edge and force him to take a stand.

For months David had tried to coax Connie into coming to work for him, but she kept turning him down. She'd been employed by the state for a long time, she explained, and didn't want to give up her hard-earned benefits, which by that time were substantial. Her frustration, however, was mounting. Finally, in the late summer of 1993, she reached a point where it no longer made sense to work for an employer with whom she couldn't see eye to eye. She quit her job at the Walker County Training Center and officially joined the Habitat team. Thomas, the young Cambodian born as Chang, was now working elsewhere, so Connie soon became full-time plant manager. For once she could follow her heart and stop trying to adapt to a system she didn't believe in. However, her new position only seemed to fan the fire with the state, and the arguments over how much the clients were paid and what they were capable of doing at the job site simply got worse.

One day a representative from Partnership 2000, a national business-education program that encourages business leaders to provide financial resources, volunteers, and other aid to local school systems, paid a visit to see what sort of mentoring arrangement might be worked out with Habitat. By this time, neither David nor Connie was very good at keeping their dissatisfaction with the state to themselves, and they mentioned it to the Partnership 2000 spokesman during one of their conversations with him. He didn't act surprised.

"Seems to me that you can't see the forest for the trees," he told them.

"The way I see it, there's only one solution. Tell the state it's over. Tell the parents it's over. It's time to do the right thing."

"But you don't understand," David protested. "If we want to keep providing jobs for people with disabilities, this is the only game in town. We depend on the state to transport the clients back and forth. The parents are already afraid their children are going to lose all their benefits. Without the support of the state and the parents, we'll lose all the clients."

"Well, why don't you throw the ball in the parents' court?" the man replied. "If it's important to them for their kids to keep working at Habitat, then they'll make it happen. All this fighting—it's not helping anyone, not you, not the state, and certainly not the clients.

"Frankly," he added, "I think you should stop fooling with the state and hire these people yourself."

David was fuming. How dare some outsider tell him what he should do!

A few days later, David appeared in the doorway of Connie's tiny, second-floor office. "I've been thinking," he told her, clutching the most recent stack of time studies. "That guy's right. Let's hire them all."

David had finally realized that bucking the system wasn't working, nor was it ever going to. In fact, it was actually hurting him, the business, and the clients. He'd spent so much of his time stubbornly standing by his convictions that he had lost sight of what really mattered: the people for whom he was fighting. It was time to let go of the rope in this crazy tug-of-war battle. Only then would he topple the "opposition" and get what he really wanted: equal rights and equal pay for the workers with disabilities.

"Are you sure?" Connie asked. "We might lose everyone if we do this."

"We'll find a way," was David's reply. "It's the right thing to do."

Connie picked up the phone and called all the parents. Some were upset. Others were excited about the prospect. Most of them wanted to know how this would affect their child's government supplements, and many were fearful of losing the benefits that had helped support their families over the years.

"You want to do what?" the Center's executives said when David and Connie approached them with their proposal. "What do you think you're doing? You'll go broke trying to pay them real wages. There's no way they can keep up with the rest of your employees."

"Well," David said. "They already do."

After a while, the administrators at the Walker County Training Center backed down and agreed to continue providing transportation to Habitat, for a fee to be billed to the clients. There was one catch: the fee was so high no one could afford to pay it.

David and Connie wasted no time inviting the parents to an after-hours, town-meeting-style forum in the Habitat conference room. Tom Henderson, the employment coordinator who had forged the partnership with the Walker County Training Center six years before, was there. He was sympathetic to David's cause but he was just one man working inside a bureaucracy. The special-education teachers who'd seen their students blossom in the vocational program at Habitat came to the meeting. So did three agents from the Social Security office who fielded questions and explained the potential impact on the clients' supplemental government benefits. As expected, that was the parents' greatest concern.

"My son is on several medications," one parent spoke up. "Won't he lose his Medicare benefits if he works full-time at Habitat?"

"No, that's a misconception," said one of the Social Security spokespersons. "Part of the income supplement your son now gets from the government will be replaced by a real paycheck from Habitat, but the Medicare coverage won't be affected. And if the job situation doesn't work out, he can resume the rest of his benefits." David had no qualms about answering even the toughest questions. At this point, none of the people gathered there could afford to sidestep the real issues.

"Change is always tough," he told the parents of Jeff and Sharon and the other clients. "It's not going to be easy for us either. We've got a lot to learn about this. But your children have proven that they can do anything the 'normal' employees can do, and for the most part they've got better attitudes and are more loyal to the company. We want them to work here and we're ready to give this a try."

The meeting ended on a high note. The parents were visibly relieved to learn that their children wouldn't have to give up their economic security to work at Habitat. By the end of the discussion, they were also convinced that their kids should be given the chance to work for a company that welcomed them with open arms. How many factories, after all, would do that? This could be the opportunity of a lifetime.

Since most of the clients couldn't drive, there was still one more hurdle to clear. The parents tackled that one themselves. When they pressured the agency about the exorbitant transportation fee the state wanted to charge to bus their kids to Habitat, the state dropped the

fee to a couple of dollars, or less, per day for each person. Eventually
Habitat and the state organization began working together again, with
Connie's former boss sending job applicants their way and providing a
temporary job coach when a client was having a particularly difficult
time adjusting to the workplace.

Most of the clients were aware of the struggle that had ensued on their
behalf, and they sensed that something wonderful was about to happen.
But David, as usual, wanted to make sure everyone, including his full-
time employees, was privy to the good news. "Hey, everybody, I've got
an announcement to make," he said one Friday, walking into the plant
where the workers were cutting and packaging rugs. The pep in his
voice was hard to ignore.

The clients and staff stopped what they were doing and gathered near
David. "We have some great news to share with you. On Monday, everyone in this room," he said, nodding toward Ken and Big John and the
other clients, "will be an official employee of Habitat International, Inc.
Nobody will work for the state anymore."

An explosion of cheers and high-fives filled the plant. It was hard to
tell who was more thrilled—the clients with disabilities or the people
who had been employed at Habitat for a long time. That day, production
skyrocketed. To Ken and Jeff and the rest of the people with disabilities, it was like winning the lottery. No one had ever offered them a job
before; in fact, most employers hadn't wanted them at all. On Monday
there was an unmistakable bounce in their walks. Jeff smiled even more
than usual. Sharon grinned every time she thought about going shopping with her own money. They all worked faster that day, and the next,
and the quality of their output was even better than before.

On payday, Ken was anxious to open the envelope bearing his check.
He couldn't tell how much it was but he knew there were more numbers on the paper. "How much?" he asked Connie. When she told him,
a broad smile crossed his face, and it stayed there all day. His fellow
employees did the same, and those who knew how to count hurriedly
wiped the tears from their eyes. Never again would they assemble ink
pens for a dollar an hour or bring home less money than the other
workers at Habitat. These were real paychecks, all well above minimum
wage.

Here was the proof they'd been waiting for all their lives: they were
just like everyone else.

Five

Terry:
The Love Builder

WADENE LIVINGSTON HAD HER DOUBTS, serious doubts, that Terry Davis would ever be able to work the full two-hour stretch in the special-ed work program at Habitat. A student in Wadene's class at Ridgeland High School in north Georgia, the chubby, sweet kid with Down syndrome couldn't stand on his feet for more than 30 minutes without complaining bitterly. The Habitat managers placed a supportive rug on the floor so his legs wouldn't hurt when he rolled carpet. Still he whined. When he got frustrated, he'd plop down on the floor and start sobbing. "I can't!" he wailed. "My fingers too short!"

"Okay, Terry, you don't have to," Wadene would say, not wanting to push her student too hard. "Go ahead and take a break." She wondered whether he would ever be able to last a whole morning. But like many of the special-ed students who earned a vocational work grade at Habitat, Terry's stamina did improve over time. He was able to tolerate standing up for longer periods. His "co-workers," Habitat's full-time employees, teased and hugged him and he got the attention he craved without pitching a fit. His attitude changed, and he gained confidence. By the time he graduated in 1998, he could work an entire morning in "Ms. Dene's" class with no tirades.

One day the phone rang at Terry's house, and his mom Betty answered. It was Connie Presnell. "I want to hire Terry," she said. "He is such a joy to have around. And I know he can do so much more."

Betty Davis had known this for almost two decades. In fact, she was aware that people had been underestimating her son since the night he was born.

The morning after she gave birth, the pediatrician came to her room. "Mrs. Davis, I have something to tell you about your baby."

Betty's mind raced, and she feared the worst. "He's not dead, is he?" she whispered.

"No," the doctor replied, glancing around. "Is your husband here?"

"Not yet," Betty said.

"Well, I'll just wait till he gets here," the physician said as he headed for the door.

"Hold on!" Betty called after him. "I don't need to wait on James. You sit down right now and talk to me. Tell me what's wrong. I can handle it."

The doctor continued to argue with her but finally gave in to Betty's demands to see her baby. The nurse brought Terry into the room, laid him in his mother's arms, and peeled back the blanket so Betty could get a closer look. "Your baby," the pediatrician said, "has Down syndrome."

"What?" Betty was puzzled. She had never even heard the term before. She didn't know that Down syndrome occurs in approximately one in every 800 live births, or that people with the condition are born with 47 chromosomes instead of the usual 46, or that it is caused by an error in cell division, not by any mistakes the mother makes during pregnancy. "What's that?"

"Have you ever heard of Mongolism?" the doctor asked.

"Oh yeah, I went to school with a girl who had that." Betty remembered her classmate's flattened features, upwardly slanted eyes, and stuttering speech.

"Well," the physician said. "That's what's wrong with your child."

A strong woman who knew how to handle life's punches, Betty took a deep breath. *Okay, I can deal with that*, she thought to herself. *At least my baby's all right.*

The most unsettling part turned out to be not the news of Terry's condition, but the doctor's unflinching advice. "The best thing you can do is sign him into a home," he urged. "Do it now before you have a chance to bond with him."

Betty bristled. "Oh no. You ain't gettin' *my* baby. I don't care what's wrong; I'm not givin' my son away. No one will raise him but us."

"But you're not going to be able to take care of him by yourselves," the doctor responded. "He'll chill easily and you'll have to wrap him up tight, as if it were wintertime. He can only eat a half-ounce at a time so you'll have to feed him every 30 minutes, around the clock. Even at that, he may not make it. He may not even live through another night."

"We'll do whatever it takes," was Betty's stalwart response.

Two weeks later, Betty and James had just entered the hospital elevator that would take them upstairs for Terry's check-up when they recognized the man standing next to them. The doctor who'd tried to pressure them into placing Terry into a home for special-needs children summoned a weak smile.

"Oh, this can't be Terry," he said. "I sent him home to die."

The Davis family rallied together to bolster Terry's development. A physical therapist came to the home several days a week. Each time, Terry lay on a mat in the living room while the therapist rolled him over a large rubber ball or a log of carpet, then gently pulled him back toward her. Then she'd repeat the exercise. Terry's older brothers Tim and Tony helped "bicycle" his little legs to build muscle tone. So did everyone who came to visit. Betty thought her mother-in-law would surely wear herself out playing with Terry's arms and legs to stimulate circulation.

Betty could see early on that Terry was going to bring the already outgoing, no-nonsense family closer together. They refused to focus on their challenges, choosing instead to live each day to the fullest. It never occurred to them to shun Terry, even in public when people stared, and his brothers seldom took things for granted anymore. Terry and Tony, who was 10 years older than his little brother, were inseparable. To their credit, Tony's friends readily accepted Terry as well, and he often accompanied them when they played. When they went swimming in a neighbor's pool, he sat on the edge and dangled his feet in the water, laughing and splashing right along with them. When Tony started dating, he took Terry too. Tony's girlfriends loved it, actually; to them, Terry was a real-life teddy bear they could cuddle.

As he grew up, area residents stopped staring and he became a welcome sight in the community. With Terry's warm smile, affectionate nature, and lack of pretense, they couldn't help but love him. Total strangers waved at him in the grocery store or Wal-Mart. When the producers of a local cable television talk show invited him to make an appearance, the phone lines jammed with calls from friends, acquaintances, and people who'd seen him around town. In fact, so many viewers called in to chat with Terry that he was asked to come back on the show twice more.

Terry's life, however, was not void of problems. Over the years he underwent four hernia surgeries and the removal of his gallbladder. In 1991, he developed such a severe respiratory blockage between his neck and mouth that doctors had to perform a tracheotomy and create a permanent incision through which he could breathe. The doctors showed Betty, James, Tony, and Terry himself how to care for the tube. Not at all squeamish about the procedure, he quickly learned how to remove the apparatus, clean it with a pipe cleaner or a small brush, and re-insert it into the hole in his neck. His parents helped him clean his "talk box" once a month with peroxide.

By the time Terry began rolling carpet alongside his classmates in Habitat's vocational program, special-ed students from two north Georgia high schools had been working there for a half dozen years. In 1990, Cathy Griffith and her fellow educators were looking for work sites that might be open to helping train special-ed students from their school, Lakeview-Fort Oglethorpe, when they heard that Habitat was hosting enclaves from the Walker County Training Center. Here was a place where the managers had already demonstrated a willingness to work with special-needs people. The teachers approached David, asked if they could bring their classes to work at Habitat too, and the company soon became one of the first in the area to host special-ed youth.

Two shifts of students arrived at Habitat each day. One group could work several hours without getting too tired; the other was made up of severely impaired children who needed more supervision and who could only stay on task an hour at a time, if that much. Most of the other host sites only had room for two kids at most, but Habitat was more spacious and could accommodate up to five. The Lakeview-Fort Oglethorpe teachers brought not only their moderately disabled students, but those with profound challenges as well. The kids rolled carpet runners, bagged putting greens, and assembled boxes by the truckload, earning a grade for their efforts. Many had spent their lives sitting down in a classroom, so standing for long periods of time posed a new challenge. It took most of them a while to build up their stamina, but when they did, their performance improved along with their self-esteem.

One of those success stories centered around a boy named Timmy, a student in Cathy Griffith's special-ed class. He was not only severely mentally disabled; he also exhibited some serious emotional problems. At times he acted like a wild animal. He couldn't speak, so he communicated by grunting, mouthing other peculiar noises, or gesturing with his hands and making up his own form of sign language. He would not sit still and was constantly seeking attention, sometimes by grinning, other times by hitting or kicking or throwing his lunch across the table. Timmy's obsessive-compulsive habits tended to manifest even more when he was aggravated or bored. He liked to peel paper from boxes, or rip it in shreds, and if there were any liquid in sight—a glass of water, an open soda, a bucket of paint—he would dump it out on the floor.

The first day, as the bus was pulling away from the Habitat parking lot, Timmy bolted after it, with Cathy running as fast as she could to catch him. Things only got slightly better as the weeks passed. But Cathy and the Habitat managers vowed not to give up on Timmy. Day after day, Cathy placed her hands atop his as he worked, five minutes at a time. He was easily distracted, and frequently tried to wander, so Connie and the other managers arranged his workstation so he couldn't sneak out. When he did lapse into one of his fits, they simply said, "Come on, Timmy, you can do it."

It took a few months, but the boy who couldn't hold still for more than a few seconds when he first came through the Habitat gate learned to focus his attention on the task at hand. The more positive feedback he received, the better he performed.

Another success story came from a boy with developmental disabilities named Jerry. Like his fellow students, it took him a while to learn how to pack and tape boxes shut, but once he did, he was an absolute whiz. He showed such potential that Cathy set out to help make one of his dreams come true. "Jerry has always wanted to try out for the baseball team," she told the coach at her school.

"Fine," he said. "Let's try it."

Jerry practiced hard that week and gave it his all. He wasn't the best batter or pitcher in the world, but the coach liked his attitude and hired him as a manager. Jerry proudly accompanied the team to every game, later became the school's football manager, and ended up being voted the most popular student in his senior class.

In the mid-1990s, Robin Leventhal, Wadene Livingston, and other teachers at Ridgeland High School started bringing their kids to Habitat too. Byron, a severely mentally disabled boy in a wheelchair, proved to be a champion box-maker and adept at rolling small 2' x 4' rugs. But he didn't start out that way. At first he'd work only 15 minutes at most. "Done!" he'd proclaim, and push the product away. It took almost a year before he could work more than an hour, non-stop, but he did.

Missy, a sociable, dark-haired girl who could work the entire morning with only a 10-minute break, was born with a rare condition that made her bones brittle. She bruised easily and her joints swelled when she fell down. Her hair was extremely thin and her sweat glands didn't function. Like most of the other kids in her class, she began by making boxes, then moved on to more demanding tasks like rolling carpet and using the tape gun. Missy's greatest challenge wasn't the work but the fact that she loved to chat and was easily sidetracked talking to Carl, an older gentleman who'd had a stroke, or one of the other Habitat employees.

When Jerry and David erected the Living Fence at the entrance to Habitat, they included silhouettes of Missy and Byron. Terry's steel likeness would eventually join them.

Betty Davis had been debating where to take Terry to look for a job when the call came from Connie.

"Can you bring him out here tomorrow?" Connie asked.

"Sure can," Betty replied without hesitation. She was thrilled.

Terry, now 20, was very excited to have a real job, even more so because it meant he could go back and work with Connie, whom he fondly called Queetie, David, and the rest of the Habitat staff. The day he was hired, he strutted around with a broad smile on his face.

Like Wadene, Terry's teacher from Ridgeland High School, Connie still wasn't sure Terry could keep up with his co-workers. But she was determined to treat him like everyone else. And she did know one thing: when Terry was around, the other employees brightened, and they seemed to accomplish a lot more. "Hey, Terry!" his co-workers shouted as he entered the plant as a new employee. "Good to have you back!" Terry grinned and went straight to work folding rugs. David remembered the two Down syndrome kids who had cheered him up with their unconditional love during his divorce, and that made him even prouder to have Terry on board.

This time, however, more was expected of Terry. He was no longer a student hanging out for a few hours a day, for a grade. He would have to work hard and produce, just like the other employees. At first he didn't quite grasp the concept of real, full-time work, but Connie was determined to push him beyond what he thought he could do. One day when Terry was falling behind, she slammed a thick roll of tape down on his worktable. "Terry, you are gonna do this right," she said, showing him once again how to roll a long stretch of carpet.

"Don't holler me, Queetie," Terry whimpered, throwing up his hands and heading for the break room. "My fingers too short." Connie thought her heart would literally melt on the spot. But day after day, for more than two weeks, she pushed Terry to keep trying. "Come on, you can do this," she said, showing him how to move a pallet by pushing it with his hands. "Let me see what you can do." Tears would well up in Terry's eyes and his lower lip would quiver. He'd lean across the table so far he was almost lying down. Occasionally Connie let him take a break, but not always. Most of the time, she made him get right back to work. She knew from experience that coddling Terry, or any of the other employees with developmental disabilities, was the worst thing she could do.

Sandra Ball, a temporary worker who had only been at Habitat a few months, was horrified. And angry. She was naturally overprotective of the employees with disabilities, and it didn't seem right to expect so much of them. "Connie, why are you pushing that kid so hard?" she'd ask in frustration. One day Sandra was operating a forklift when, out of the corner of her eye, she spotted Terry. *Wait a minute*, she thought. *I must be imagining things.* As she steered the lift closer to his workstation, a slow grin spread across her face. Terry was rolling carpet, all by himself, and he wore a big smile. His "I can't" attitude had turned into "I can."

Now and then, David loved challenging Terry to a friendly carpet-rolling contest. "Come on, Terry!" David would goad. "Betcha can't beat me!" A few seconds later, Terry would hold up his roll of carpet for all to see while David was still finishing his. And Terry's was more neatly bound.

Granted, his productivity wasn't always that high. He took too much time on certain tasks, and David and Connie playfully teased him for moving at only one speed: *slow.* Terry preferred, above all else, to work on the cutting table. But when deadlines loomed and it took three people or more to get the job done, he'd sometimes get carried away trying to keep up with them and fall down, and it wasn't feasible to leave him on the assembly line.

Terry hated putting boxes together, but he was good at it. One day Connie placed a bundle of the flat cardboard holders in front of him. "Terry, I need you to start making boxes. Okay?" she said, then walked away to attend to something else. "Okay, Queetie," Terry replied. When she returned, Terry was nowhere to be found. In his place stood a fortress of boxes, stacked toward the ceiling. Then Connie heard a slight murmur, and she started to laugh. There was Terry, still working inside the fort, assembling boxes.

He may have been slow sometimes, but in the end that didn't matter. Terry was proud of his accomplishments, he loved going to work every day even when he was tired, and he was the ultimate motivator for the rest of the Habitat staff. He also kept them in line. "Queetie, this guy not working right," he would tell Connie if he suspected someone of goofing off. He'd motion for her when he thought a co-worker was talking too much or not rolling carpet properly. Most of the time, he was right.

Terry was so much fun that, as a rule, the other employees didn't take his criticism personally. If one of them were having a hard day, he'd waddle up, put his arm around the person, and assure them that, "Everything okay." He loved to sing—off-key, of course—and impersonate Elvis with a pelvic wiggle that, his colleagues admitted, wasn't that bad. At company Christmas parties, he wore a Santa suit and handed out presents. And he loved flirting with the female employees—all of them, from Y, Kiv, and Cheng to Queetie and Honey, his nickname for Sandra.

That didn't stop Terry from being brutally honest. One day he presented Connie with a stick figure drawing of herself. In the picture, she was wearing a moustache. "Sandra, why'd he do that?" she asked, puzzled. Sandra just shrugged. A few days later Connie was looking in the mirror when, for the first time, she saw what Terry had seen. "Oh, my God," she said, embarrassed she'd never noticed the dark hair above her lip before. From then on, she went for regular lip waxes. And she posted the drawing on one of the cutting tables. Terry, after all, had seen her exactly as she was, and that was part of his charm.

Despite his exuberance out in the plant, payday was Terry's favorite part of the week. First thing Friday morning, he started asking for his check, initially with sign language, then, if no one was paying attention, with a loud and emphatic, "I want my money!" If that didn't work—and sometimes it didn't, simply because Connie loved to joke around with him first—he'd grab a walkie-talkie and patch himself in to Jim's office. Terry couldn't read or write. He couldn't decipher numbers or dollar figures. He didn't know how much he made, but the amount was irrelevant. For Terry, earning a paycheck each week was simply part of being normal. And that's all that mattered.

Six

What Were We Thinking?

D AVID'S ONLY REGRET was that he'd waited so long to do the right thing. Now there was no stopping him. As the months passed he began to hire more and more people with disabilities; if Habitat had an available job opening and David or Connie or Saul knew of a person with a disability who needed work and could find transportation to Habitat, they did their best to hire him. They employed other special-education students who had been trained in the company's vocational program, as well as people with mental illnesses and those with physical challenges, ranging from autism to cerebral palsy to brain injury. Some of them ran entire departments, assembling putting greens, rolling carpet runners, and loading truckload after truckload for major customers like Wal-Mart and Lowe's. Before long, more than three-quarters of the growing workforce at Habitat had some type of mental or physical disability, or a combination of the two. David was so touched and inspired by what he saw in the plant—a person with a hearing impairment working beside an employee with one arm, someone with schizophrenia packaging rugs with the Down syndrome kids—that he could hardly wait to get to work each day.

Word spread about Habitat's willingness to hire people with disabilities, and referrals poured in from local social service agencies, parents, and churches. If a disabled employee had a sibling who was also physically or mentally challenged, David would try to give the brother or sister a chance too. Connie was now in charge of hiring, and because of her background as a job coach, she knew just what to ask during an interview. If the job applicant still lived at home, it was important, even critical in some cases, for the parents to be supportive of their child and comfortable with the Habitat philosophy. Sometimes Connie would give them a tour of the plant to gauge their reactions. If they were impressed with what they saw, well, that was an excellent sign. If they squirmed or seemed ill at ease, there was a good chance they'd end up pulling their child from the job after a short period of time. Connie's instincts were sharp, too. It usually didn't take her long to sum up an interviewee; more than once she hired someone on the spot, simply because she liked his personality. She turned others away because she sensed they weren't really motivated to work. To her, job performance was secondary. What counted most were a positive attitude and an eagerness to be part of the Habitat team.

Even though the company now hired its disabled workers outright rather than through a state agency, it was still taxing to deal with all the outside attempts to pigeonhole them with stereotypes. The debate continued to rage over limitations imposed by social service groups, medical professionals, even parents. Several doctors gave bleak prognoses for their disabled patients and urged them to stay home all day instead of working. *Why set them up for failure?* they asked. Social service workers tried to define their disabled clients with formal evaluations that categorized the workers and kept everyone "safe." *It's right here in the rules*, they insisted. *People with autism can only do this, this, and this, and no more. An employee with a mental illness shouldn't be expected to show up for work every day. A person with cerebral palsy should sit in a wheelchair rather than stand.* Sometimes the parents were just as narrow-minded. "Johnny has never been able to focus on anything for more than a few minutes, so we're sure he won't now," was a common refrain. The word "can't" came up a lot, but at Habitat, that term was unacceptable. In fact, it was obsolete.

Some parents were also tempted to handle the "kids" with kid gloves. "What if Johnny gets hurt?" they often asked. "What if I'm not there to take care of him?" Even the Habitat managers were guilty of being overprotective at times. At first, Sandra, the temporary worker who later became the company's team shipping coordinator, worried about the disabled employees and tried to stop them from carrying heavy loads or climbing on ladders, just like their able-bodied colleagues were doing. But they quickly set her straight with their bold "I can do it" responses. More often than not, they were absolutely right.

And then there was the ever-present fear of losing SSI benefits, which terrified some parents who had become dependent on their children's government-subsidized income. In some cases it was obvious they had succumbed to a welfare mindset; it was simply easier to keep a disabled daughter at home and collect her monthly check than to drive her to work every day and help her deal with the inevitable ups and downs of real work. Connie and David found themselves explaining, over and over again, that the disabled employees could quickly fall back on SSI payments if the job situation at Habitat didn't work out. It might take a couple of weeks to reinstate the payment process, but the safety net was always there if they needed it. Some things, on the other hand, were not so easily fixed. Instilling a strong work ethic in a disabled worker who'd never been allowed or expected to do anything for himself, for example, required much more patience and time. Sometimes, just like with able-bodied employees, the transformation never happened at all.

The Habitat building already complied with the Americans with Disabilities Act of 1990, so few structural accommodations had to be made for even the most severely disabled employees. Most of the changes were small and required a minimal amount of education on the part of the managers. They learned what to do in case someone suffered a seizure. They occasionally modified a jig or other piece of equipment, or took extra time to train a worker with a developmental disability. Connie had been affiliated with state-funded workshops long enough to know that many of the former clients and special-ed students, like Terry, were used to being seated all day and that it would take them a while to build up their stamina and increase muscle tone. In fact, this was the first time some of the disabled workers had held themselves upright for more than a few minutes at a time. Connie gave them time to adjust by initially scheduling them for just a few hours a week—two days, then three, then four, until they could work 40 hours without exhausting themselves or getting discouraged. Sometimes the adjustment period took as long as a year, and occasionally someone would need to take a sabbatical in a state workshop or other, slower-paced environment until they could return to Habitat. In the end, though, it was worth all the trouble. The employees gradually broke through their own self-imposed barriers and the psychological blockades set by other people who'd previously told them "no way." And Habitat gained loyal wage earners who wouldn't dream of leaving the company to work anywhere else.

Being patient with a slow learner or giving him extra time to adapt wasn't the only concession the Habitat managers made. Early on, it became obvious they would need to install an on-site shower and keep a change of clothes on hand for workers who accidentally soiled themselves. One employee with mental retardation posed a particular problem when he began having bowel movements in his pants every day. As soon as Connie got him cleaned up and back on the job, it would happen again. Such behavior would have been enough to make most supervisors throw up their hands in disgust, but Connie realized that this was the man's way of getting attention. It soon occurred to her that both she and David had been coddling him far too often when he whined or complained about having to work too hard. They agreed to stop babying him, and instead Connie used a motivational tactic that had worked well on her own kids when she wanted them to do something. "You know, they really need your help on the cutting table," she started telling the man. "They can't fold carpet as fast as you can."

"Well…do you want me to show them how?" the man replied. "I know how to do it better." Connie smiled to herself. She had found a way for him to get the attention he craved and be productive at the same time. Almost immediately, he stopped soiling his clothes at work.

Sometimes the workers with mental disabilities vied for attention in other ways too, and they could be fierce competitors. Still, their production was up, they were devoted to Habitat, and they seldom missed a day of work. Absenteeism and turnover were rare. The only real limitation at Habitat was that the company was quickly outgrowing its space. With all the chopped-up partitions and small rooms, the layout of the building was less than desirable, and David and Saul kept knocking out walls to expand and make their operations more efficient.

Even so, things didn't always turn out the way they had hoped, and despite their good intentions, not every employee with a mental or physical challenge was a good fit for Habitat. But then, neither was every non-disabled worker who got a job there. Despite the inevitable disappointments, David, Saul, and the other managers never felt they had failed or done the wrong thing by giving these people a chance. Even the disabled workers who didn't stay very long had, at the very least, tried. Most gained a measure of self-respect and some valuable job skills in the process. But sometimes an employee was so tough to manage that Connie and David found themselves scratching their heads and asking: *What were we thinking?*

In the spring of 1992, a year before the initial enclave of disabled clients was hired from the Walker County Training Center, Lincoln Sottong had become Habitat's first employee with a diagnosed mental illness. The youngest of three sons, Lincoln had inherited bipolar disorder, a condition that affected three generations of his family. As is often the case with the more than 2 million Americans with the disease, also known as manic-depression, the symptoms didn't surface until college. There, Lincoln became restless, irritable, and unable to concentrate. Time after time, he would experience dramatic mood swings, with the pendulum swaying from extreme highs to extreme lows and back again.

Even before the bipolar disorder made its appearance, Lincoln's mental capacity didn't seem normal. He was smart enough, maybe too smart, with a phenomenal memory for birthdays and places and encyclopedic details. He showed such a knack for remembering things that one year, his father, Phillip, took him along to mentally record the names of the people whose hands he shook while campaigning for public office. And Lincoln's distinct, theatrical voice certainly commanded attention. But by the time Lincoln was old enough to attend pre-school, it was obvious he wasn't learning as fast as he should. He quickly lost interest in projects and never seemed to finish anything he started. He was clumsy with his hands and, when interrupted while playing a game or completing a task, he would freeze as if commanded to do so, then be unable to resume or remember what he'd been doing. His parents took him for psychological testing. "Well, you do realize he's retarded," the doctor said matter-of-factly.

"We had no such thought," Phillip answered. "He's a really smart kid, so you're wrong. It's got to be something else."

The next doctor diagnosed Lincoln with attention deficit disorder, which made more sense to his parents. But when they enrolled him in a Pennsylvania school designed to treat people with ADD, the teachers asserted the boy would never be able to do more than twist caps on toothpaste tubes for a living.

Before Lincoln began working at Habitat, he had held down a couple of restaurant jobs as a dishwasher. The Sottongs and the Morrises were old family friends, so David had known Lincoln for a long time and felt he was capable of pursuing more meaningful work. At Habitat, however, Lincoln was easily frustrated, especially when attempting tasks that required fine motor skills, like making boxes. "I quit!" he would boom in his deep, loud voice. All heads would turn toward Lincoln, who could have easily been a Dan Aykroyd clone, both in looks and speech pattern.

Every day, sometimes more than once, Lincoln threatened to quit. Over and over he tried to give Connie a written letter of resignation. "Sorry, Linc. I can't accept this," she'd say.

"Why not?" he'd reply, fidgeting.

"Now, Linc, how can you quit when we still have this big order to fill?" Connie was by now an expert in making the other employees feel needed.

"Okay, Connie," Lincoln would answer. "I'll stay only till that's finished, and then I'm moving on to greener pastures." He would stay, of course, and the next day, vow he was leaving, and the cycle of "quitting" and coming back would start all over again.

Far more challenging, however, was Lincoln's ongoing depression. Some days he would come in so despondent he could barely walk, his clear, resounding voice reduced to nothing more than a weak whisper. During those times, he'd mumble incessantly about killing himself. David knew he had to take drastic measures. Even he, the rebellious nonconformist, would never dream of taking such an extreme stance with most people. But he knew Lincoln well, and he knew Lincoln's parents, and he was convinced there was only one way to stop the suicide threats.

One day when Lincoln was disrupting the workplace with his black mood, David grabbed two shovels from the maintenance room. "Come on," he said to Linc, handing him one of the tools. Lincoln slowly followed him outside, head hanging low like a child awaiting his punishment.

"One, two, three, four, five, six," David counted as he paced off six feet on a spot of ground at the back of the plant. "Okay, you start digging there and I'll start digging here, and we'll meet in the middle."

"What are we doing?" Lincoln asked, looking up for perhaps the first time that day.

David began shoveling dirt. "We're digging a grave," he replied, averting his eyes from Lincoln's. He knew this was radical, perhaps even risky given Linc's mental problems. But it was the only option he hadn't tried. And he had to do something. "Since all you want to do is commit suicide, I thought I'd help you get it over with. When we're finished digging, you can jump in and I'll cover you up. Okay?"

Lincoln stared hard at David, dropped his shovel, and ran back to the plant, grumbling under his breath. "He's crazy, just crazy," was the last thing David heard as Linc headed back to his workstation.

Lincoln never mentioned suicide again. He eventually devised his own system of packing a box or rolling a stretch of carpet, and he worked hard at everything he did. He started socializing with the other disabled workers at break time, where before he had shied away from them. At the end of the workday, he'd head for Jim's office and begin to spout off two dozen creative ways for Habitat to make more money or introduce new products. Then he'd go straight to Saul's office and do the same thing. Instead of ignoring him or closing the door when they heard Lincoln shuffling down the hallway, they stopped what they were doing and welcomed him in for a chat. At Habitat, everybody's ideas mattered.

Always the clever mom, even at work, Connie knew how to use her own brand of reverse psychology. Bart, a young blind man who came to Habitat through a referral from a state agency, had, just six months before, lost his sight to a bacterial infection that spread through his brain and destroyed his vision. He was still a teenager, good-looking, and a bit cocky. He had not yet accepted his disability—instead he fought with it daily—and he was angry, very angry, about being blind. "Connie, I know you don't need him," the agency's job coach admitted. "But he needs you. If you could give him a chance, if you would just allow him to prove himself, maybe he'll stop being so mad all the time."

With minimal assistance, Bart could build boxes, roll rugs, and package them, and after a while he was pretty darn good at it. Jerry Treadwell, the plant engineer, fashioned a special jig to help Bart roll carpet more easily and, after each rug was secure in its box, another employee would step in to tape it shut. As long as the process stayed the same, as long as it didn't veer from the norm, Bart was fine. But if anything changed, if Habitat introduced a new product or box size, or if he was asked to work in a different area of the plant, he would blow up and threaten to quit. Connie could see straight through his frustrated outbursts; he was clearly, and understandably, confused by the changes to his environment, but much too proud to acknowledge that he was scared.

"I quit!" Bart blurted to Connie one day, storming away from his work post. "This is a load of crap."

"Go back to your station," Connie gently chided. "You're not finished yet."

"No!" yelled the young man. "I quit!"

Connie studied him for a moment. It had been a long day and she'd had about all the "I quits" she could stand. "Okay, Bart, just go home," she said, handing him his cane. "If you start walking now, you should be there by dark."

Bart gave Connie a defiant smirk. Then he realized what she'd said.

"Me? You want me to walk home?" he asked. "How am I gonna do that? I can't see."

"I don't care how long it takes you. But you're disturbing the other employees," Connie said calmly. "So you just have two choices: be quiet and go back to work, or head for that door and start walking."

Bart fell uncharacteristically silent. Finally, he nodded. "Okay, I'll stay."

The young man with the chip on his shoulder didn't last long, but David was sure that a visually impaired person would do well at Habitat. Until that point, all of the employees with disabilities worked out in the factory, performing labor-intensive tasks to ready the products for shipping. At the request of one of the social-service agencies, David decided to hire a young woman to help the administrative staff file documents and do data entry. Helen was legally blind. The agency installed equipment to enlarge the type size on the computer, but despite her best efforts, and the determination of the Habitat managers to make it work, Helen just couldn't keep up. The job required speedy fingers on the keyboard, and that just wasn't happening. But the main problem, her co-workers felt, was that she was too needy and lacked the independent spirit that prevailed in many of the other employees with disabilities. David was disappointed but he had to let Helen go.

Sometimes, however, the Habitat managers gave an employee so many chances it nearly wore them out. Despite the temper tantrums, soiled clothing, and other problems that daily tested their patience, nothing compared to the problems they would encounter with John H., an alcoholic with severe mental and emotional problems.

John had been born with fetal alcohol syndrome. His parents, both substance abusers, died at an early age, and he grew up street-smart and conscious of how to manipulate people to get what he wanted. He showed signs of being a sociopath, lying his way through all types of situations and doing whatever he could to survive. One of the first eight workers Habitat hired from the Walker County Training Center in 1993, he posed multiple challenges, but David and Connie and the other managers had high hopes their investment in John would pay off.

Small-framed but with a muscular build, John was strong enough to move heavy equipment and tall stacks of indoor-outdoor rugs. He was particularly adept at spraying the glue and applying the foam backs to golf putting greens, and he seemed to take pride in his job, often working alone in a room just beyond the main part of the factory. But John had a dark side, and as the months passed it emerged with more frequency. He would show up for work obviously intoxicated, with liquor on his breath and a slur in his speech. He made up excuses for being late. Sometimes he even faked seizures to divert attention away from a reprimand.

John's personal hygiene was terrible; in fact, it was virtually non-existent. He smelled bad and would go for long periods of time without brushing his teeth or changing his clothes. Connie and David decided to take John under their wing and visit him at home to see how they might be able to help. What they found there made them nauseous.

John's apartment was a literal rat hole. It was obvious he hadn't used the shower in weeks, maybe longer. The bed sheets were dirty and soiled, like they'd never been washed, and when Connie and David lifted the mattress to change them, hundreds of cockroaches scurried from where they'd been nesting. The disgusting insects were living elsewhere, even inside John's refrigerator. Oddly, in some areas of the house, John was compulsively organized, with neat stacks of magazines or dishes or clothes. At least it seemed that way, until Connie or David removed one of the stacks to clean around it. Underneath it all was nothing but filth, grime, and more bugs.

Always ready to crusade for the underdog, Connie and David and the other Habitat managers found John a nice duplex, bought him a new bed and other furniture, with their own money, and recruited their staff to help him move. They took him grocery shopping, taught him how to select nutritious foods, and showed him how to keep his place neat and clean. He had never had a driver's license, so they signed him up for driving school and practiced with him in the Habitat parking lot after hours. It took John about 10 tries, but he finally passed the test for his license, and David bought him his first car. John learned how to read, earned his GED diploma, and began paying his bills on his own. He even contributed to his 401K plan and stashed away a few rainy-day bucks in a savings account.

Most of the employees who were hired when they were down on their luck were grateful for the generosity shown them at Habitat, but John seemed only to siphon more and more—more time, more money, more patience—from his co-workers. Unlike the other people with disabilities, John didn't meet them halfway, nor did he appreciate what they did for him. But Connie and David kept trying. To most people, he was just another drunk bum. To them, he was a lost, broken soul who had never been loved and who needed someone to show him they cared.

One winter day it all came to a head. With a layer of snow blanketing the ground, Connie called and asked Jim to pick her up for work in his four-wheel-drive truck. In her usual motherly style, she also phoned the employees to see if they were snowed in or needed a ride. John didn't answer. "I'm kind of worried about him," Connie told Jim. "His duplex is on the way to the plant. Let's stop and make sure he's okay."

When they arrived, they spotted tire tracks in his driveway but there was no sign of John. He didn't show up at work that day, or the next, or the next. Determined to find out what was going on, Connie and David recruited another employee to spy on John's duplex. Each night, about 3 or 4 in the morning, he would leave. He'd be gone all day, then come back about 10 o'clock that night to crash for a while before starting the routine all over again. It was well past dark when one night Connie called David's house. "John's at home," she said. "We need to get over there right now before he leaves again."

David met her at John's duplex, and together they knocked on the door. "John, what's going on?" they asked, almost in unison. "You haven't shown up at work. You're never home. We were worried about you at first. Now we're just puzzled."

"Well, you won't have to worry anymore," John said with a touch of sarcasm. "I quit."

Maybe he knew they were going to fire him anyway, that this was the end of the line. Maybe he didn't. But David and Connie had given him all the second chances they could muster. In later years, when friends and colleagues asked them why they went to so much trouble to help John instead of firing him, they simply replied, "Because we're Habitat and that's what we do."

One of the greatest trials the Habitat managers ever faced was learning to work with people with autism. Connie, in particular, was a demonstrative, nurturing type for whom hugging came naturally. Most of the Habitat employees, especially those with mental disabilities, loved it. Some even thrived on it and looked forward to the times when Connie would give them a fond atta-boy pat on the back or drape her arm across their shoulders and give them an affectionate squeeze. Not so with Jason Cook.

Like many of the 1.5 million Americans with some form of autism, Jason couldn't stand to be touched. A neurological disorder that affects brain function, autism is often characterized by, among other things, an inability to communicate or interact well with other people. Unlike most kids, children with autism may cringe when cuddled, and they sometimes make little or no eye contact with their peers. Most can hear normally, but are often unresponsive when someone talks to them, as if they were deaf, and they may talk at other people, in monologue style, rather than talking with them.

None of the managers at Habitat had ever known a person with autism. They had long since learned how to relate to someone with mental retardation or bipolar disorder or Down syndrome, but this was a totally new frontier. So it came as a shock to Connie when, a few days after Jason came to work at Habitat in the summer of 1995, she gently touched his hand and he stiffened as if she had jabbed a knife into his back.

At first he only worked three days a week. He was very withdrawn and for a while wouldn't mingle or talk with the other employees. It took him a few minutes to learn a job task but when he did, he remembered the steps. In fact, he turned out to be the fastest box-maker in the plant and highly skilled at rolling carpet. And he was extremely focused in everything he did. That, however, was part of the problem. When Connie tried to steer Jason from one task to another, he pitched a fit. If she moved a box away from his workspace, he would stare at the empty spot on the floor where the box had been, and keep staring. Connie had worked with mentally challenged employees who needed the security of repetition, but this was unlike anything she'd ever seen before.

About a year after Jason was hired, Connie's niece gave birth to a son with autism. In an effort to better understand her new grandnephew, Connie talked to her niece and checked out some books from the local library. *Ah*, she thought, flipping through page after page. *So this is what's going through Jason's mind when he acts up.* Connie learned that, like Jason, many people with autism don't deal well with change. She also realized that when he obsessed about getting a driver's license or going to college like his brother had done, he was simply expressing his frustration over wanting to be like everyone else.

Like a turtle that, after a while, senses it's safe to come out of hiding, Jason eventually poked his head out of his shell. Eventually, he would let Connie touch him without squirming. He became much more relaxed and outgoing, even singing and dancing at his workstation when one of his favorite tunes played over the intercom. He showed an unexpected flair for computers and, after one of his tantrums, would sometimes type up an apology. When visitors came to the plant, he walked up to them without hesitation and began asking a barrage of questions: "What's your name? How old are you? Are you married? How many kids do you have? Where do you work?" He liked to flirt with "yellow-haired" women and jokingly referred to Saul, with his Bob-Keeshanstyle moustache and stocky build, as Captain Kangaroo. One day when David walked out in the plant, there was Jason singing "Jesus Loves Me," in Chinese, and holding Y's hand. David assumed Jason was ad-libbing the song, but later learned he really had learned it at church.

But Jason still had a quick, uncontrollable temper, and eventually it got him in serious trouble. If Connie tried to correct him or tell him no, he would grab a pool stick and threaten to hit her. More than once, he shoved her to the ground. He pinched her arm. He would act as if he were going to choke her, and she'd respond by firmly clasping his hands in her own and lowering them away from her throat. Most of the time, that was enough to make him stop. Sometimes it wasn't. "I'm gonna kill you!" he'd scream if things didn't go his way. A few minutes later, he would say he was sorry and give her a hug. By the end of the day, he'd be pounding his knuckles on the side of the building until they were bloody and swollen.

One day Sandra rushed to Connie's defense and before she knew what was happening, Jason had twisted her hand in a painful contortion. By the next day Sandra couldn't move her thumb, and it was swollen. When the doctor asked her how she sprained her hand, she shrugged and told him she'd pulled a muscle at work. It took a long time for the injury to heal.

Even with their near-saint-like patience, Connie, David, and the rest of the management team couldn't keep putting up with Jason's violent outbursts—after all, he might hurt one of the other employees next—so Jason was fired from Habitat. But they never stopped caring about him, and continued to welcome him at company picnics and parties. Despite his distressing behavior, they were still proud of how far he'd come since the early days when he couldn't stand to be touched and wouldn't get near the other employees. To David and Connie, to Jim, Sandra, and Saul, there were no failures, only varying degrees of success.

After that they hired three more people with autism. And Jason returned to work at Habitat part-time.

Through the years, some of the company's greatest challenges came not from the people who worked at Habitat, but from those outside its walls. Over time, most of the truck drivers and buyers who visited the plant on a regular basis grew accustomed to seeing the company's unusual workforce. But some were uneasy at first, and others were downright prejudiced. Occasionally a temporary worker who was brought in to help handle a large order acted as if he might "catch" a disability like a cold or the flu. A few of the temps were even afraid, the way Chang and his sisters had been when the first enclave from Orange Grove came to the plant. Sooner or later, most of them let their guard down and warmed up to the employees with disabilities. A few never did.

Terry, a big strapping guy who came to Habitat through one of the temporary agencies, was a hard-working perfectionist bent on doing everything well, right down to his neatly stacked boxes of carpet. But he was a bigot. He didn't like the Cambodian workers, hated the African-Americans, and definitely wanted nothing to do with the "retards." David and Connie decided to leave him alone, at least for now; he wasn't ridiculing the disabled workers to their faces, and besides, he was a temp, which meant he'd be gone when the current order was finished. One day David accidentally witnessed something he never thought he would see. Another temporary worker was picking on one of the mentally retarded employees.

"Hey!" Terry shouted to the newer temp. "What do you think you're doing?"

"None of your business," the man replied.

"Damn right it's my business," Terry shot back, ready to fight. "Don't you go putting these people down. They can work circles around the likes of someone like you."

Terry had not only learned to tolerate people with disabilities, but to love and take up for them. They had shown him the importance of compassion, just by being themselves, and he was a better man for it.

In spite of his open-minded nature and willingness to overlook just about any foible, at least once, even David was prone to underestimate the disabled workers at times. He returned from a floor-covering trade show in Chicago to discover Ken Jones, one of the workers with Down syndrome, running a 25-ton press designed to stamp holes in golf putting greens.

"You can't let him do that," David told Connie, pulling her aside. "He might get hurt."

"There are plenty of safety devices on that machine," Connie assured him. "Just leave him alone. He's doing fine."

David walked closer to where Ken was working and inspected a few of the putting greens. "You're not doing it right," he told Ken. "Why are they folded like that?"

Ken's thick speech impediment was so pronounced that David had trouble understanding him. He tried to explain, but his babbling made no sense to David, who could only make out a word here and there.

Connie held up a stack of the putting greens. "Look again," she told David. "Look at what he's doing."

David peered at the flat pieces of carpet and the circles Ken had punched out with the press. To David's surprise, Ken had found a way to fold the carpet so that he could cut not one rug, but two, at the same time. While David was out of town, one of his favorite employees had doubled his speed and production.

"Now," Connie said, with hands on her hips. "Are you still going to tell him he can't?"

Seven

Martin:
Mr. Determined

M ARTIN ARNEY WAS JUST 10 YEARS OLD when, during a
routine cerebral palsy exam, an insensitive doctor made a star-
tling prognosis in front of him.

"Your son's condition is serious," the physician told Martin's mom,
Lisa Blair. "Because of the way it's affected his muscles, he'll end up in a
wheelchair by the time he's an adult."

Not one to mince words, Lisa began to rebuff the doctor's words but
Martin interrupted.

"Watch me," he said with a grin.

"What did you say?" asked the doctor, puzzled by what he'd heard.

"I said 'Watch me,'" replied the no-nonsense boy with the sandy
blonde hair, sky-blue eyes, and charming smile. "There's no way I'll live
my life in a wheelchair."

Lisa laughed. This wasn't the first time she'd witnessed her son's determination and refusal to accept the limitations of his disability.

"Well," the doctor said, softening. "With *that* kind of positive attitude, you just might be right."

A first-time mom at 18, Lisa didn't know quite what to expect when Martin was born. But it wasn't long before she could tell that something was
wrong. He lacked coordination when he rolled over, and didn't crawl
much. He delayed sitting up on his own for a long time and when he

finally did, he perched in a "W" position, knees bent, legs splayed behind him. For two months after his birth, his chin would shake when he cried, and his movements were jerky. The doctors prescribed Phenobarbital for the small seizures, but Martin slept so much that Lisa finally stopped giving him the medication. Despite these early signs, the pediatricians never mentioned the possibility that her son might have cerebral palsy.

Martin was nine months old when the doctors finally diagnosed him and told Lisa that, like 20 percent of people born with congenital cerebral palsy, her son's disorder was probably caused during the birthing process—in Martin's case, they said, by a brief lack of oxygen. No matter the reason, one thing was for sure: the motor areas of his brain had been damaged, disrupting his ability to control movement and posture. According to the United Cerebral Palsy organization, about 8,000 babies and another 1,200 to 1,500 preschool-age children are diagnosed with the condition each year, and more than 750,000 people in the U.S. manifest one or more symptoms. Lisa, a food-service worker for whom challenge and hard times were nothing new, started educating herself about what to expect. She learned that Martin's cerebral palsy could not be cured, but it could be managed. There was never a question that Lisa would do all she could to help. Each day she exercised Martin's short legs to stretch his calf muscles. He underwent physical therapy to learn better balance and to minimize his frequent falls. Finally, at 19 months, he started walking on his own.

As he grew older he still fell a lot, often banging his knees or his head as he hit the floor. One time he got dizzy and toppled backward in the shower, an accident that required surgical staples to close the gash in his head. When he walked, he shifted his weight to the balls of his short, wide feet, which he turned inward. His classmates made fun of his shuffling and slurred speech, and he frequently heard them taunting him behind his back.

Because of his dragging gait, the police sometimes tried to arrest the teenager for public drunkenness. Martin was often too proud to explain his condition and simply took the sobriety tests, defiantly proving there was no alcohol in his system. One day Lisa heard a commotion in the grocery store where she was working. A customer had called the cops to report a young man who, despite the lack of alcohol on his breath, looked like he'd been drinking. Lisa immediately knew what had happened, and she rushed to the scene.

"Ma'am, that's my son," she said, approaching the woman. "He's not drunk. He has cerebral palsy."

Despite his challenges, Martin had inherited something much more powerful than any disability: his mom's stubbornness and unwillingness to accept the word "can't." Over the years, Lisa gave birth to three more boys, but to her, her oldest child, the one with the big heart and the fun-loving nature, was no different from his brothers, and she simply would not treat him as if he were special. "Martin," she told him, "there are people who are far worse off than you. Just because you have to find a different way to do something doesn't mean it can't be done."

Lisa was right. Early on, Martin had been placed in special-education classes because he couldn't keep up with his writing assignments and other tasks that relied on fine motor skills. But he excelled at typing, partly because it allowed him to hold his wrists steady. He developed a thick emotional skin and when someone at school bullied him, he swung right back. And despite his clumsiness, at one of the special vocational schools he attended, Martin fell in love with horticulture. He later landscaped his mother's yard and kept the lawn trimmed with a non-powered push mower, a safer option than the gas-fueled kind for someone whose limbs wouldn't always cooperate. Perhaps most importantly, he developed a zany sense of humor that sustained him when other people put him down.

By his late teens, Martin had already held down jobs at several fast-food restaurants. He worked as a custodian and later learned to flip burgers without burning himself. He cooked deep-fried chicken and cleaned tables and washed lots of dishes. But sometimes it was hard to keep up, and his last job at a bakery had proved especially frustrating. He was expected to wash the pans quickly, and without making a mess, but the harder he tried the slower he got, and the more he dropped things.

Not long before his bakery job ended, Martin and a friend drove by the Habitat International, Inc. property and spotted the weird, eye-catching sculptures outside. "What in the world is that?" he asked his buddy. "I don't know," the friend answered. "But it doesn't look like any business *I've* ever seen." Perhaps it was coincidence, or fate. But a few weeks later, a social worker at Signal Centers, a local agency offering supported employment and other services for people with disabilities, was encouraging Martin to apply for a job at Habitat.

Connie sized him up right away. The young man was skinny, with long hair and a bit of a cocky demeanor. Underneath it all, though, she could tell he was a sweet person, and incredibly proud. And there was a confidence in his wobbly stride that Connie found irresistible. "Do you think you can keep up?" she asked him during the interview. She already knew the answer.

Martin grinned. "Of course."

In March of 1996, 11 years after he'd caught the doctor off guard with his spunk and contagious "watch me" attitude, 21-year-old Martin went to work making boxes at Habitat.

To Martin, the place was just as odd inside as out. There was Lincoln, a man with bipolar disorder who was spiraling into one of his depression cycles and barely spoke. And Lonnie, who had schizophrenia and was, on Martin's very first day, talking to the carpet. *What am I doing here?* Martin thought to himself. *Do I really want to do this?*

But he kept his promise to Connie, and to himself. Martin's hands shook from the cerebral palsy but that had never stopped him before, and it sure wasn't going to stop him now. He quickly learned how to roll carpet, bind the rolls with the tape gun, and ready the packaged products for shipping. He was so loyal that for more than five years he never missed a day of work, even when he was visibly sick.

"Martin, what are you doing here?" Connie would ask when Martin showed up with a fever or achy cold.

"I'll be all right," he replied, never missing a beat at his workstation.

"Come on, Martin, you're going home," Connie insisted. But Martin would shake his head no, and more often than not, he won. Giving up, for any reason, was simply not an option.

Martin was very proud, almost macho, in his work ethic. In the days before Habitat began using pallets, he would stack four boxes on top of each other, slide a hand truck beneath them, and, despite his quivering hands, balance the seven-foot tower for loading onto a truck. Sometimes he dropped the haul, but when that happened, he simply started the process all over again. He wasn't about to be defeated by a bunch of boxes, even if it took him 10 tries to get it right.

Sandra, who would later be promoted to team shipping coordinator, came to Habitat as a temporary worker two years after Martin was hired. She underestimated the young man at first, and was tempted to baby him. One day she saw him climbing a ladder to get to a batch of product. "No, Martin, you might fall!" she yelled out. "I can do it," he said, without looking her way. And he did. No matter the job, Martin would give it a shot; if he fell he got back up and tried it again. Nothing, not even cerebral palsy, would stop him.

Occasionally, however, Martin showed a vulnerability that touched the hearts of even the toughest Habitat managers. One day not long after Sandra came to work at Habitat, she noticed that Martin was particularly frustrated about something.

"What's wrong?" Sandra asked him.

He mumbled a few words she could barely hear. "What was that?" she asked again.

Martin looked at her with his disconcerting blue eyes, then replied, "I hate the way I walk."

Sandra suddenly had trouble fighting back tears. She remembered how she'd looked askance at Martin when she first started at Habitat, how she'd stared at his gangly form and the fists he held together to mask the trembling. She recalled her initial awkwardness around him, and she was ashamed.

"Now, Martin," she said, swallowing the lump in her throat. "You're a special person and it doesn't matter how you walk. You know how I sometimes have to come in early, *really* early, to get things going here?"

Martin nodded.

"Well, you're the one I can always call on when I need someone to come in early and help me," Sandra said. "I know you won't let me down."

Martin's loyalty and hard work were often rewarded in more ways than one. When David heard that Martin wanted to learn how to drive, he arranged for him to attend driving school through a special human-services grant. On days when painful arthritis stiffened Martin's hands, the Habitat managers subtly pulled him away from the cutting table and assigned him an easier task. One day Connie inspected Martin's new-looking shoes and discovered holes in both heels, evidence of Martin's club-footed stance on the unforgiving concrete. She immediately made sure Martin got cushioning pads for his shoes, then set about researching the possibility of braces to help correct his posture and alleviate the pressure on his sore feet.

Thanks to the physical demands of his job, Martin's muscle tone improved and he grew stronger and stronger. After a while, his lack of co-ordination wasn't nearly as noticeable. And like many other employees, Habitat gave him the social outlet he'd never had.

Still, Martin remained a bit cocky. He was an emotional guy, but patience was not his forté. He was critical of slackers and could be downright tactless when he thought a co-worker was doing something the wrong way. He had little tolerance for temporary laborers who didn't work as hard as he did. Sometimes his high expectations were both a blessing and a curse.

It took Martin more than six months to feel comfortable in this new, wacky workplace. Despite his determination and pluck, he was naturally shy, seldom made friends right away, and wouldn't talk much until he really got to know someone. Gradually, he opened up and befriended some of his colleagues, including Daniel Johnson, a slight young man who was hired two months after Martin.

Daniel had sustained major brain and facial injuries in a near-fatal car crash. He too was a paradox of innocent goodness and don't-mess-with-me edginess, and the two were about the same age. Before long the young men had forged a strong bond. After Martin earned his driver's license, he often drove Daniel to work and back, and they hung out at each other's houses at night.

In the summer of 1999, Daniel had his first grand mal seizure. During the violent episodes, he turned blue-black and foamed at the mouth, and every muscle in his body jerked uncontrollably. His hands drew and he drooled. He convulsed and bit his tongue. When this happened, there was nothing anyone could do but make sure Daniel didn't hit something and hurt himself even more. Eventually he would wake up and be unaware of what had occurred or where he was.

The seizures were horrifying to most people, even to Martin, but he wasn't about to let that stop him from helping his friend. During one of many surgeries, Daniel's doctors implanted a Vegal nerve stimulator, a sort of pacemaker designed to normalize the rhythm of the brain's intricate circuitry, in his chest. Daniel's family, friends, and coworkers learned how to swipe a special magnet across his chest to double the strength of the stimulator's signal and lessen the severity of an attack already underway.

Martin kept one of the small oval magnets in his pocket and when he and Daniel got in the car each day, he placed it on the dashboard, just in case. He stashed another one beneath the worktable where he and Daniel rolled carpet together. The Habitat managers knew how to use the magnets, and were sometimes forced to, but it was Martin who often came to Daniel's rescue. More than once, Connie looked up to see Martin catch Daniel in mid-air, lower him gently to the floor, and run the magnet across his heart, all the while cradling Daniel in his arms until the seizure stopped. Martin never said a word about how much the fall had hurt his own body. The only thing that mattered was that his friend was safe.

One Friday after work Martin drove Daniel to the bank so the two could cash their paychecks. Suddenly, as they sat at the drive-through window, Daniel lapsed into a seizure. Without hesitation, Martin reclined the passenger seat, jumped on top of Daniel, and held his convulsing friend until the crisis had passed. When he finally looked up, bank tellers had clustered at the window and were staring, wide-eyed, at the two men. "Thank you, ma'am," Martin said, crawling back into the driver's seat and driving away.

The duo arrived at Daniel's house a few minutes before Sherry Taylor, Daniel's mom, got home from work. "Oh, my God," she said as soon as she saw her son, who was still obviously shaken from the seizure. Martin explained what had happened, and he and Daniel started to laugh about what the bank tellers must have thought.

Sherry didn't see anything funny about the ordeal, so she responded by giving Martin a hug. "Thank you, Martin," she said. "Thank you so much for helping Daniel."

"Hey, it was nothin'," Martin said with a shrug and his familiar wry grin. "I just didn't want him to bust the window and mess up my car, you know?"

Eight

We Are Family

H ABITAT WAS RICH WITH SURPRISES. Ken Jones had found a faster, more efficient way to punch holes in the golf putting greens, a revelation that embarrassed David when he realized how much he'd underestimated the young man with Down syndrome. Terry, the big, burly temp worker had, all on his own, been able to conquer his prejudice against people with disabilities, even coming to their defense when someone else put them down. After a while, Jason Cook, the man with autism, not only tolerated physical touch but welcomed it from his co-workers.

Something else was happening, too, and neither David nor any of his managers had seen it coming. By now the workers with even the most noticeable challenges, like Terry Davis and Martin Arney, had mastered most of the tasks in the plant. If another person with Down syndrome arrived at Habitat, Terry would walk up to him and say, "Hey, do you want me to show you how to roll carpet?" If Habitat hired someone else with cerebral palsy, Martin was right there, helping the newbie learn how to cut holes in the golf putting greens. There was little, if any, negative competition, and the veteran workers with disabilities didn't seem to feel threatened or worried that someone might accomplish more than them or try to steal their jobs. To them, this was just another nice person in the building, a new friend who needed their help. The more established employees, of course, gained just as much from the mentoring partnerships as the new hires. They were no longer the trainees; now they were the teachers, and they loved it. When Terry or Martin or Sha-

71

ron were able to share what they'd learned with someone else like them, they just seemed to glow, and their production went up even more. And their disabled protégés benefited enormously.

A few years before he began working at Habitat, a young man named Joe had been watching television at home one night when a buddy knocked on his door. "Hey, Joe, wanna go for a ride?" the man asked. Off they went in the friend's four-wheel, all-terrain vehicle, speeding through open fields and scaling dirt slopes. Suddenly, one of the ATV tires veered into a patch of loose gravel, and the four-wheeler flipped over. The friend broke his shoulder; Joe, on the other hand, sustained a devastating brain injury that permanently impaired his motor skills and caused him to shake and have little control of his muscles.

Just like many of the other employees with disabilities, Joe found Habitat through word-of-mouth "advertising." Joe was a handsome man, with perfect white teeth, a sweet disposition, and the ability to charm everyone with whom he came into contact. He was married to a woman in a wheelchair, and they had two children. In addition to his lack of coordination and jerky movements, the accident had left him with a limp and a speech impediment, a sort of slow stutter that could only be understood by those who listened closely. And his hands wouldn't do what he wanted them to do. In the plant, it was obvious that rolling carpet was very difficult for Joe, but he was determined to do it.

An unlikely mentor, a man from a temporary agency, taught Joe how to compensate. Where Joe had two arms, the other man only had one. One day the temp worker saw Joe struggling to roll the indoor-outdoor rugs for packaging. "Watch this," the man said, twisting his shoulders and torso to lift and bundle the carpet as well as anyone with two hands. "You always have options," the man said, never mentioning their respective so-called disabilities. "If you want to do something bad enough, there's always a way."

Before long, Joe was rolling carpet as fast as the rest of the Habitat workers, including the man with one arm.

Habitat's impromptu mentoring "program" paid off in another way too: without even trying, the employees with disabilities became role models for the special-ed students who were earning school credit in the vocational program at Habitat. Terry Davis was an anomaly of sorts; unlike many of his disabled peers, he had won the hearts of many in the community who had never before been around someone with Down syndrome. And his brother, Tony, and the rest of the Davises had, from the beginning, selflessly included Terry in their daily activities. He was family, so why treat him any differently from everyone else? But not all of the special-ed kids had known such warm-hearted acceptance. Many of them had spent their lives dreading trips to the grocery store or church or the shopping mall because other people stared so hard or made fun. In some cases, their families had shunned them in public and ignored them at home. And the "normal" kids at school, the ones with the perfect hair, rock-star attitudes, and beautiful faces, well, they weren't always friendly to people in wheelchairs. At Habitat, the special-needs students could be themselves, without being judged for their looks or their clothes or even their mental abilities. When they came through the Habitat doors, they saw people just like themselves, many of whom had graduated from special-ed programs, working beside their able-bodied colleagues without being stereotyped. In fact, no one seemed to notice if a person had only one arm or stuttered a lot or used a cane when he walked. At Habitat, almost everyone was "different." How could they not fit in?

Here, the invisible, societal lines that divided people out in the real world had simply disappeared.

"Hey, lemme show you how to do this," the employees with disabilities often said to their young counterparts in special-ed. "It's not that hard." David, Connie, and the teachers watched in amazement as, time after time, the permanent workers helped make the students feel at ease and showed them that they too could exceed expectations, even their own. The school kids were thrilled. At Habitat, other people knew just how they felt.

The special-ed students and the newcomers weren't the only ones who learned something from the employees with disabilities. When the Teg women first came to Habitat, they didn't speak very much English, and understood even less. They had attended classes for Asian immigrants, but hated the lessons and ended up dropping out. English, with its maze of odd words, colloquialisms, and accents, was confusing to Y, Cheng, and the others. So they often relied on their brother, Chang, who was younger than them and had picked up the American language more easily, to translate what David and the other managers at Habitat were saying.

One day David noticed that Y was beginning to speak a few more words in English. Curious, he decided to find out why, and his detective work led him to Linda. One of the original workers hired from the Walker County Training Center, Linda was very outgoing and loved to talk. But to most people her sentences sounded, at best, like gibberish. One day David was out in the plant when he overheard what appeared to be an English lesson. He stopped what he was doing to listen.

"What she say?" Y was asking her brother. "What Linda say?"

Chang nodded toward Linda, who was mouthing one word at a time. "Just listen. Talk back to her when she says something. If you talk back to her, you'll learn."

Y picked up a mop. "Linda, what this?"

"Mop," Linda said slowly. "M-ah-p."

"M-ah-p. Oh—mop!" Y exclaimed, then touched a chair at a table nearby. "What this, Linda?"

"That chair," Linda replied. "Ch-air. That chair."

David could hardly believe what he was hearing. Y hadn't done very well in her English class. She hadn't even retained many of the words the Habitat managers had tried to teach her. But here she was, taking instruction from a girl with mental retardation whom no one else understood. And it was working.

The employees with disabilities ended up teaching the Tegs a lot more than just language skills. When they first arrived at Habitat, Chang and Y and the rest of their family members were very serious people. Maybe it was because of the horror they'd endured in Cambodia and Thailand during the reign of the Khmer Rouge. Or perhaps it was just their cultural upbringing. But for several years they kept to themselves and, although they were polite when addressed, for the most part, they were much more reserved than David and the rest of the Habitat staff. All that changed when Ken and Jeff and the others were hired from the Walker County Training Center. These fun-loving guys had a way of bringing out the best in other people, and it was next to impossible to stay uptight around them. When Jeff made a joke or a funny face, Y couldn't resist laughing out loud. When Lincoln danced in the aisle, she moved her feet too. And when Jason sang along with the radio, Y sometimes chimed in. Before long, the Cambodians had softened up and lost a lot of their initial reticence. How could they be solemn when the disabled workers around them were always happy and saying nice things?

The spirit of camaraderie spreading throughout the company touched Saul's heart too. He began finding excuses to slip out of his office and into the plant for a hug and a laugh with one of the employees.

"It's Captain Kangaroo!" Jason would exclaim, as if overjoyed to see his boss.

"I have some more ideas for you," Lincoln would add in his deep, resonant voice. "Let's talk after work."

"Dad!" Ken would say, giving Saul a bear hug. "How are you today?" Then he would lapse into his favorite Hulk Hogan imitation, flexing his muscles and grimacing like a pro wrestler. Pretty soon, he'd have everyone around him howling with laughter.

Saul, who didn't miss his suit-and-tie days at all, ate it up.

Every once in a while one of the disabled workers got the last word on David, and the other managers would tease him about it for weeks. True to his artistic nature, he was a very visual person. And like many visually dominant learners, he often didn't discern the tiny nuances of sound. Even though Connie instinctively knew how to listen to someone with a speech impediment and pluck out the pertinent information, David sometimes had trouble understanding one word. All he could hear was "blah-blah-blah-blah-blah." So when Ken, whose thick-tongued speech patterns masked much of what he was saying, asked David a question, more often than not David responded with a standard nod and a "yes."

"David, you're gonna get in trouble doing that," Connie warned. "You better find out what he's saying before you say yes to something you'll regret." She knew how smart Ken was; after all, he had sweet-talked her many times into doing something by bribing her with a cold Dr Pepper, a smile, and a "Pwease, can I do it, Brue Eyes?"

David, of course, ignored Connie's advice. One day Ken walked up to David and struck up a conversation, but David, as usual, heard only "blah-blah-blah-blah-blah" with an inflection that sounded like a question mark at the end.

"Sure, Ken," he replied. He was in a hurry and didn't have time to get someone to interpret. "Okay. Whatever you say."

Connie, who'd been standing nearby, burst out laughing.

"What's your problem?" David asked, puzzled. He'd never seen Connie laugh so hard.

"Not a thing," Connie said, doubling over as if she'd just shared a hilarious insider joke. "You just agreed to give Ken his own office."

And he got it. Not one to renege on a promise, especially to his employees with disabilities, David cleared out a small room next to Connie's, declared it Ken's office, and equipped it with a desk, a chair, a calculator, a note pad, and a handful of ink pens. Ken was ecstatic. Each Friday afternoon at 3 o'clock he proudly began to take "inventory." Never mind that he didn't know how to read or do math. Wearing a hard hat with the word "supervisor" emblazoned across it, Ken strutted around the factory, carrying a clipboard, surveying supplies, and marking a series of x's and o's on a legal tablet. At the end of the day, before he went home, he handed his half dozen sheets to Connie or David. The markings didn't make much sense, not even to Connie, but Ken's remarks did. "We low six by nine," Ken would say, and Connie would check. Sure enough, every time, there would be just a short pile of boxes left for the 6' x 9' carpet rolls, which meant that in a day or two they would be completely out. More than once, Ken's astute observations helped the company save face and valuable time.

But David hadn't yet learned his lesson with Ken, especially when words were involved. One day not long after Ken set up shop in his new office, he approached David with another request. And again, "blah-blah-blah-blah-blah" was all David heard.

"Okay, Ken, okay," he shot back, unaware that Connie was eavesdropping a few paces away. "Whatever you say, buddy."

When Connie started to chuckle, David knew he'd duped his own self once again.

"What now?" he asked, a sheepish grin crossing his face. "What did I agree to this time?"

Connie grinned. "Business cards."

In a few days, Ken was walking around with a handful of jangling change in one pocket—a practice he'd adopted when he started earning real paychecks—and a wad of business cards in the other that read:

Ken Jones
Assistant to the assistant to Connie

Just like he did with the boxes, Ken notified Connie when his supply of cards was running low. Because he handed them out to everybody he met—strangers at the supermarket, shoppers at Wal-Mart, family members—this happened quite frequently.

After that, David knew better than to grant Ken's requests without verifying what he was saying yes to.

Partly because of the unorthodox way some of his mentally challenged workers communicated, and partly because of the language barriers that were present when he hired the Cambodians—and later, other wartime refugees from Laos, Vietnam, and Bosnia—David felt that hiring a person with a hearing impairment would be a piece of cake. He was right.

Like many other supporters who learned of Habitat through word-of-mouth channels, a woman in a small northwest Georgia community found out about the company's dedication to hiring people with disabilities. She brought her niece, Tammy, in for a job interview and interpreted for the young blonde woman, who was deaf. During the course of the conversation, Connie learned that except for her hearing impairment, Tammy was "normal." She was married. She drove a car. She and her husband lived in a nice house in the country. Connie liked her instantly, not because she was so independent, but because she smiled a lot.

When Tammy first came to work at Habitat, Connie knew only one sign-language sentence, which she had picked up when she was employed at the Walker County Training Center: "Stop looking around and go to work." At first, if she didn't understand what Tammy was trying to say, Connie would hand her a pencil and a slip of paper, and Tammy would write it down. During the five years she worked at Habitat, Tammy taught Connie more and more words in sign language. Not only were the two women able to "talk," but Connie learned how to communicate with other hearing-impaired employees and special-ed students, making it easier for them to glean the information they needed to do their jobs. And much to her credit, Tammy was able to keep up with Sharon Adams, one of the first mentally challenged workers hired from the Walker County Training Center and a stickler for speed and accuracy on the cutting table.

Habitat had become a workplace where people facing the most difficult of circumstances could flourish and where even the most outlandish ideas were considered. Lincoln, the man with bipolar disorder and the first person with a diagnosed mental illness at Habitat, was extremely creative, especially when it came to music and art. His voice was highly animated and strong, well projected but not offensive, as if it were meant for much more than just everyday conversation. One time in college, he played the part of Romeo, and he took ballroom dance lessons. His fellow Habitat workers loved to watch him work; if a catchy song came on the radio, he would spin and turn and step with a natural-born rhythm. Occasionally he would partner with one of the female workers and wow everyone with his Fred Astaire moves. And despite his serious nature and ongoing battles with bipolar disorder, there was a ham-it-up side to Lincoln.

David was out of town on a business trip when Lincoln confided to Connie about his dream of becoming a radio disc jockey. "I want to quit

Habitat so I can be one," he told her. "I've always wanted to do that. My talents are wasted here."

"Now, Linc, that is out of the question," Connie gently scolded. "You cannot quit Habitat to become a DJ. We need you."

But the more she thought about it, the more Connie felt there might be a way to help Lincoln do both. She rifled through some old cast-off junk at home and urged the other managers to do the same. Together, they came up with a couple of speakers, a compact disc player, an audio-cassette tape deck, and an odd collection of music. Then they assembled everything in an old office near the break room and added a desk and a chair. When David returned and heard about their idea, he commended them for what they'd done. He promptly went out and bought the one missing piece: a microphone.

From then on, Lincoln practiced his DJ skills each day at break time. He became the "Voice of Habitat," reporting the daily news, weather forecast and sports updates, and playing a few carefully chosen songs before going back to work. As the days passed, he loosened up even more and began to announce birthdays and comment on David's up-coming travel itinerary. His memory for details was sharp, and he frequently knew more about his boss's airline reservations and meeting plans than David did.

However, a few of Lincoln's co-workers were jealous. "How come Linc gets to be a DJ and we don't?" they asked, needling Connie and David. Before long the managers had come up with another creative solution: a radio schedule that would allow all the DJ wannabes to have their own 15 minutes of fame. After that, the in-house "station" was open four times a day: first thing in the morning, at mid-morning break, during lunch, and on afternoon break. All broadcasts lasted 15 minutes except for the half-hour lunch spot. Since Lincoln worked mostly in the afternoons, Connie would pencil the other disc jockeys in for the mornings and lunchtime, and if they were particularly productive, the gabby crew might be rewarded with a fifth broadcast that day. Lincoln's co-workers ended up enjoying the radio station as much as he did. It allowed the spunky DJs to express themselves and, since music calms some people with mental illnesses and mental retardation, it became a way for the listeners to de-stress.

The station was later named WLINC, in honor of its founder.

David had an artistic side too, but for the first few years of the company's history, and even after he and Saul moved the plant to Rossville,

Georgia, his talents remained mostly hidden, except for the occasional design of an eye-catching tradeshow mannequin or a new packaging concept. Sometimes, in the middle of the night, David woke with dreamlike visions of sculptures and paintings and sketches. He didn't have the patience to sit still and painstakingly work on an art project, but he could see the end result in his mind, and was good at recruiting other people to help him work toward it. David loved what was happening at Habitat—people with Down syndrome driving forklifts next to co-workers with cerebral palsy and schizophrenia, recovering alcoholics cutting floor runners with colleagues who had learned to cope with severe head injuries, disabled employees mentoring special-ed students who were following in their footsteps. A sense of joyfulness pervaded the air, and visitors noticed it too. But much to David's chagrin, the place still looked too much like an ordinary factory. At home, he reasoned, most people covered their blank walls with photographs and art prints, and crowned their tables, counters, and desks with decorative objects that not only expressed who they were but lifted their spirits as well. Why not do the same thing at Habitat?

One Saturday morning, a group of adventurous employees, special-ed students, and family members showed up at Habitat and clustered around a work area in the plant. There they found 40 gallons of paint in assorted colors, several cases of canned spray paint, and dozens of brushes in all shapes and sizes. Cranking up the music, they rolled up their sleeves and set about transforming the walls, doors, ceiling, and floors into one huge piece of art. Some played tic-tac-toe with rollers poised on wooden extensions that reached 20 feet in the air. Others drew colorful racecars, self-portraits, and psychedelic designs that echoed the tie-dyed look of the 1960s. Employees and special-ed students in wheelchairs brushed the concrete floors with swirls of chartreuse, magenta, and cobalt blue. Even Connie's young granddaughter, Coty, got in on the act and wielded a pint-sized paintbrush. When David wasn't supervising the party or splattering rainbows of paint alongside his employees, he walked around snapping photos. By the time they were finished, the factory's interior was one big tribute to sensory overload.

Saul was glad to see everyone having fun but he wasn't so sure about the outcome. "Well, how does it look?" Joyce asked when her husband came home that day. She loved the idea of infusing the plant with bright colors.

"It looks very different," Saul said with a shrug.

"But how does it look?" his wife asked again. "Give me the details."

"Very different," Saul repeated. Then he took a deep breath. "I just hope the buyers don't think we're nuts. What's The Home Depot gonna think?"

Saul was worried, really worried, that the sales representatives, buyers, and customers who visited the plant would stop taking Habitat seriously and, at worst, funnel their business elsewhere. But his fears proved to be unfounded. In fact, the buyers for the Home Depot and other major retailers loved the eccentric artwork. Saul was so relieved that he asked David for copies of the photographs to send to his other business contacts.

After that, the wacky artwork took on a life of its own. David encouraged the employees to paste together collages of their favorite photos from special events. Then he reduced the collections on the copier, turned them into laminated placemats, and gave one to each worker. Vividly hued, primitive folk art punctuated the break room. Mannequins sporting artificial-grass haircuts and coats made of Berber carpet ushered visitors into the front office. Throughout the factory, hallways, and office areas hung inspirational posters—"Question Reality," "The most important tool for success is the belief that you can succeed," "More than a workplace...a care place"—that, once again, defied convention and played up the Habitat message.

Jerry Treadwell, the company's engineer, was also a visionary, and knew how to make just about anything if given a piece of metal and a welding torch. From steel he cut out the shape of an artist, complete with color-dabbed palette, and perched the figure atop a narrow ladder. He fashioned a one-of-a-kind conference table from conveyor belt parts. For the foyer, he created a bench with a rake-prong backrest, rake arms, and garden-tool legs. Now it was time to do the same thing outside. Up went a steel archer, aiming his arrow at the sky. An oversized metal woodpecker appeared in the parking lot, tapping at a tree. A rusty vulture kept watch from its perch on the roof. Just past the woodpecker, a gurgling koi pond beckoned from "Who's Happy? Park," a covered patio for stir-crazy employees who needed a breath of fresh air at break time. Oversized steel silhouettes—a man hauling boxes, kids pulling a wagon, a secretary filing her papers, a golfer, a basketball player dunking a ball in a real hoop—paraded across the factory's façade. A menagerie of jungle animals, from towering giraffes to swinging monkeys to mighty lions, guarded the front of the building.

David, who had wanted to build an airplane since he was a child, talked to Jerry about constructing a mock aircraft and attaching it to the exterior of the building. The more they discussed the idea, the more they liked it, so they agreed to meet at 8 A.M. one Saturday morning and get started. By the time David pulled into the parking lot, just before 8 A.M., Jerry had already affixed what looked like an old Army bomber to the side of the almond-colored building and had almost finished painting it. Nearby hung a sign that read: "Thanks for dropping in."

"I couldn't sleep," Jerry said with a boyish grin. Sometimes, even for a grown-up with a sophisticated knowledge of mechanics, it was fun to be a big kid.

It was Jerry who brought another one of David's internal visions to life. For a long time David had had the idea for a steel fence that would depict his employees, all holding hands. When he mentioned this to Jerry, the talented engineer immediately knew what to do. One by one, the Habitat workers and special-ed students posed in front of 4' x 8' sheets of steel while David traced their shadows directly onto the metal with chalk. Then Jerry cut out the forms. The "models" were delighted. "I'll be there forever," said one man in a wheelchair. "How many times does a person get to have a sculpture of himself next to his family and friends?" Over the years more silhouettes took their place on the Living Fence, and Habitat supporters, from neighbors to teachers to parents of the disabled employees, were invited to join the ever-lengthening row of steel figures.

David and Saul had always understood the importance of family. After all, they had started a successful family-owned business. What's more, since the day they hired the first Cambodian refugees, they had tried to include the employees' relatives in everything from job interviews to company parties. Habitat had become a family of diverse human beings who did what they could to take care of each other, both on and off the job. And the extended family grew to include a hodgepodge of unlikely members. The Living Fence had proven that.

Truck drivers who stopped at Habitat to pick up orders were often so touched by the "kids" that they ended up buying everyone a round of Cokes and shooting hoops with the workers on the basketball court, or playing a game of pool with them at break time. Even before Habitat was using pallets to transport its products, when the employees were still loading 53-foot trailers via hand trucks piled high with teetering boxes, the drivers looked forward to going to this unusual plant where everyone seemed to smile. The buyers did too.

The Habitat family wasn't made up of fair-weather friends, either. The day after the Tegs' house was demolished by a tornado, a truck-load of staffers pulled up in the driveway, rolled up their sleeves, and proceeded to load what was left of the Tegs' furniture and clothing onto a truck for storage at Habitat. When Chou, one of the Cambodian sisters, was sick and dying of cancer, she didn't want to stop working, so David and Saul brought a bed to the plant so she could take fre-quent rests. Each fall they paid for on-site flu shots. When necessary, they called in a dentist to treat employees with bad teeth, and a podia-trist for people who'd been wearing ill-fitting shoes so long their toes had been permanently damaged. If insurance didn't cover the doc-tor visits or if the physician didn't offer to donate his time, the other employees would chip in to cover the balance. Often, David and Saul paid the difference from their own pockets, sometimes to the tune of thousands of dollars.

The practice of welcoming "friends of Habitat" into the fold gathered steam over the years, especially when it came to celebrating the com-pany's success. Mothers and fathers, brothers and sisters, husbands and wives and children were invited to the company's "Field of Dreams" pic-nics, open-house luncheons, and employee recognition dinners where, sooner or later, just about every Habitat worker received an award for his efforts. At Christmas, David and the other managers hosted a week of festivities including an open-house luncheon, a more formal din-ner, a trip to see a holiday movie, and an after-dark drive to scout out the showiest neighborhood light displays. There were bowling parties and field trips, Halloween dress-ups, and dinners out on Friday nights. When profits were up, every employee received a year-end bonus that far exceeded anything they'd ever imagined.

For several years in a row one of Habitat's insurance agents took Da-vid, Jim, and Jerry, along with John Moss, Jeff Brown, and Ken Jones, out on the lake in his cabin cruiser. After a while, the female workers protested their exclusion from the "guys only" fun, and they started go-ing out on the boat too. No one, however, was ever left out of the trips to the ballpark. On weekends, David loaded the entire gang, and their family members, into a caravan of vehicles and headed for the stadium where the Chattanooga Lookouts, the local minor-league team, were playing. "Yay, team!" cheered the employees with Down syndrome. "Go go go!" screamed the Cambodians. Sometimes there'd be so much yell-ing and clapping that no one knew who was winning or losing, much less what the person next to him was actually saying. They couldn't have cared less about the details; to them the important thing was that they were all having fun together.

Such leisure-time camaraderie strengthened their loyalty to each other and to the supervisors who appreciated their efforts and did such nice things for them, all year long. Employee turnover was rare, and absenteeism was virtually nonexistent. Several employees even tried to sleep in their cars when it snowed so they wouldn't miss work the next day. David and Connie would have to tap on their windows and make them go home.

Now and then, David and Jim would take some of the guys with them to Kmart or Sears or one of the other retailers that carried the Habitat rugs. No one could have been prouder of the company's store displays than Ken and Jeff and the other disabled workers. "Hey, this is ours!" they shouted to customers who happened to pass. "We made these!" And they would beam as if they owned the whole store.

So it came as no surprise to David when, in early 1996, his employees couldn't wait to celebrate his good news. Earlier that day a local Chattanooga television reporter had called to congratulate him and set up an interview. "For what?" David asked, mystified by the call. Despite the strength of the Habitat "family," both inside the walls and out, the company's presence in the community was still low-key, and David had refused to do media interviews for fear the reporters might treat the disabled employees as helpless or pitiful. The last thing he wanted to do was unravel all the hard work his staff had done to prove just how independent they were.

"We got your name off the list," the reporter told him. "Didn't you know you were a Community Hero for the Olympics this year?"

David was dumbfounded. "No, I didn't know anything about it. How did this happen?"

"You were nominated by someone in the community," the reporter replied. "He wrote an essay praising your work at Habitat. Because of that, you were named one of the 5,500 Americans who will carry the Olympic flame."

"Who was it?" David asked. The reporter told him, but the name didn't register. As it turned out, a man named Glenn Vaughn, a longtime civic leader in Catoosa County, Georgia, where Habitat was located, had toured the plant with a local leadership group the previous year. Glenn had been so impressed with what he had seen that, when he came across a nomination form for "Community Heroes" to participate in the torch relay just before the 1996 Summer Games in Atlanta, he immediately thought of David Morris. That very day, Glenn sat down at the computer and described his visit to the special workplace where people with disabilities were given a chance to succeed. Then he printed the letter and dropped it in the mail without ever telling a soul except for his wife, Kaye.

David didn't remember anyone named Glenn Vaughn, but then he had never been good with names, especially when he met several new people at once. By the time the Summer Olympics began, however, the two men had become friends.

Since Habitat's post office box was still in Chattanooga, where it had been located since the company opened for business in 1981, David ran in Knoxville, Tennessee, instead of Georgia. On the day of the event, the managers shut down the plant and locked the doors, the employees piled into a large rented bus, and the whole group traveled to Knoxville, two hours away in the eastern part of the Volunteer State. Thanks to Saul's ingenuity and big heart, everyone wore a shiny, campaign-style badge that read "Habitat Hero."

David was nervous, and very emotional, that day. Despite his hyperactive nature, he wasn't used to being in the limelight and didn't like drawing attention to himself. At the starting line, he and the four other torchbearers braced themselves for the run. As they shoved off amid cheers, holding their torches as high as they could, David looked back to see the Habitat gang waving him on. There were Ken and Connie and Jeff, holding a "way to go" banner and looking as if they had just won a million bucks. The other employees were clapping wildly, just like they did when a player hit a home run out of the ballpark. But David's most treasured memory of the torch relay wasn't that snapshot of his "fan club," or even the media coverage or the party his Habitat colleagues threw for him later that evening. It was the sight of Martin, the young man with cerebral palsy, trotting alongside the road, trying his best to keep up with David and smiling a big, crooked grin.

Nine

Lonnie:
The Encourager

YOUNG LONNIE JACOBS wasn't just bright or popular or a whiz kid at sports. He excelled at everything he touched. He made the honor roll. He was always the first one in line to sign up for a new team at school. And he showed such enthusiasm for everything he set out to do that it was hard not to get swept up in his passionate energy.

He had always been this way. One day when he was 4, he hopped on his brother Rick's full-size bicycle, unable to sit on the seat because he was too small. That didn't stop Lonnie, who began pedaling through his family's suburban neighborhood, shocking the residents who ran after the tike to stop him. He was just as fearless at the swimming pool, where his mother, Phyllis Schwarz, kept a watchful eye as he scrambled up the ladder to the high dive. She wasn't worried. He had already done this many times—the precocious pre-schooler had even won a number of competitive titles—and she knew he could do it with ease. "Oh, God, somebody grab that baby!" a bystander would inevitably yell. "He thinks he's gonna go off that diving board!" Phyllis would grin, and off her little daredevil would go, sailing through the air, only to land a perfect, clean dive to the amazement of the wide-eyed onlookers.

As a teenager, Lonnie was every teacher's dream student. On Friday afternoons when school let out, the other kids couldn't wait to run outside and enjoy the start of the weekend. Lonnie, on the other hand, came home, went straight to his desk, and began tackling his homework. "Why don't you go out and socialize with your friends?" Phyllis would ask. "It's the weekend. It's okay to have a little fun."

"No, Mom," he'd reply. "I want to finish it now so I have the rest of the weekend to do what I want to do. I want to make sure it's done." Lonnie was so far ahead of his classmates that he finished high school at age 16.

But something happened that year, something that no one, not even Phyllis, could have foretold. At first Lonnie just wasn't himself. He stayed in his room most of the time and wouldn't come to the door if someone knocked. He no longer wanted to talk to his friends. Phyllis hoped it was only a phase, an adolescent mood that would soon lift. It was almost time for him to start college, and that would surely make everything better. One day Phyllis noticed something protruding from the top of the garbage can. She opened the lid, and her heart sank. Lonnie had thrown away his favorite music albums.

"Lonnie, what's wrong? Why did you trash your record collection?" she asked, softly tapping at his door.

"I don't want them anymore," was all he would say. "I don't need them now."

Phyllis, who was studying for her degree in social work, recognized the signs of suicidal depression, and tried not to panic. She decided to keep a watchful eye on her son, while at the same time rallying the aid of her ex-husband. "Honey, when you're ready to talk, I'll listen," she told Lonnie. "It doesn't matter what's bothering you—you can tell me. I'll just listen."

A few days later he emerged from his room. "Mom, I've got something to tell you," he said. He wouldn't look her in the eye. "There's something wrong with me."

Phyllis sat down with her son and prepared herself for the worst. But nothing could have readied her for what she was about to hear. "Mom," Lonnie began, "there are voices talking in my head. And I can't get them to stop."

Thus began a 20-year ordeal to bring Lonnie's schizophrenia under control. The disabling brain disease, which affects approximately 1 percent of the population at some point, had surfaced right on cue. For men, the primary symptoms—frightening delusions, internal voices, hallucinations, an inability to concentrate, feelings of detachment or anxiety—most often appear for the first time during the teen years. Phyllis and her ex-husband did all they could to find help for Lonnie, and for a while they hoped for a cure. This could be fixed, they reasoned. But the prescribed medications merely sedated their son, and he spiraled downward into a state of near-catatonia. He sat and stared into space, more dead than alive, and sometimes he didn't even know who he was. He was unable to care for himself and could barely eat or talk. When the doctors tried to alter his medication, the voices returned.

Phyllis didn't tell her friends what was happening. How could she explain? This was, after all, the 1970s and most people didn't understand mental illness, much less know how to respond to it. She had no idea there were countless other parents just like her, searching, hoping to find the right magic pill.

Eventually Phyllis remarried and she moved with her new husband and Lonnie to Atlanta. The mental health association there was much stronger and larger than the one in Chattanooga, and Phyllis soon got involved. She also switched her career goals and became a mental health counselor. An advocate at heart, she started a support group for families of people with schizophrenia at a time when nationwide deinstitutionalization had dumped thousands of patients out of mental hospitals and armed them with only prescriptions for Thorazine, an antipsychotic medication that, if used long-term, could lead to tardive dyskinesia, a serious neurological disorder characterized by uncontrollable shaking. There were virtually no community programs to help people like Lonnie deal with their illnesses, and many ended up living on the streets.

During regular meetings of Phyllis's group, which she named ROSI (Relatives of Schizophrenic Individuals), frustrated parents would tell their own stories and cry. They screamed out in anger and despair. "My daughter is wild and uncontrollable," one mother said, wringing her hands. "She's not violent toward me, but I'm afraid she's going to hurt herself."

"My child's behavior is so bizarre I think *I'm* going nuts," another offered.

"I was in a concentration camp," one woman spoke up. "And to me this hell is far worse."

Similar support groups began to emerge across the U.S. Phyllis launched several more in Georgia, then another in Knoxville, Tennessee, when she and her family moved back to that state. She aligned herself with a fledgling organization called the National Alliance for the Mentally Ill and began testifying at legislative sessions, pressuring lawmakers to fund the programs her son, and others like him, so badly needed. She often felt as if she were racing the clock to restore Lonnie's sanity, and her own.

A professor at the University of Tennessee at Knoxville told Phyllis about a new medicine being tested in Europe. "It won't be here for a few years," he cautioned. "But it shows a lot of promise." Before long, Phyllis and her fellow support group members were part of a growing movement to bring the drug to the U.S. They wrote letters. They made phone calls. They lobbied incessantly. The federal Food & Drug Administration finally approved the treatment, but Tennessee was one of the last states to make it available to the public. In 1992, two decades after Lonnie was diagnosed with schizophrenia, he began taking Clozaril, the new anti-psychotic drug. The change wasn't rapid; in fact it took almost a year before he seemed more like his old self. But as the months passed he regained some of his energy and became more physically active. He carried on intelligent conversations and started taking better care of himself. Lonnie would never again be the same as before the onset, but he was back.

The medication had transformed Lonnie's life, and he was ready for more independence. When the family moved back to Chattanooga in the early 1990s, he joined the AIM Center, a local "clubhouse" that mimicked New York's nationally acclaimed Fountain House by giving members a chance to learn or regain the work and social skills they needed to become productive citizens. Lonnie moved into a mental-health housing development, a sort of group home, where he functioned on his own with the help of a caseworker. The AIM Center, however, wasn't structured enough to keep Lonnie as busy as he wanted to be. But he did enjoy its on-site work programs, in which members were paid real wages while learning job skills at various companies around town. One of those businesses was Habitat International, Inc.

Beginning in early 1995, for three hours a day Lonnie and nine other severely mentally ill AIM Center members worked at Habitat, cutting, rolling, and boxing the company's grass rugs and indoor-outdoor carpet products. Thanks to the Clozaril, he was functioning at a much higher level than before, but there were still problems. When Lonnie first arrived at Habitat, he wore a bandana, his hair hung down in his eyes, and his clothes were disheveled. He was withdrawn and quiet.

But David saw a spark of potential in Lonnie that no one else saw, and with good reason. He had known Lonnie since they were about 10 years old, and David had been high school pals with Lonnie's older brother,

Rick. Lonnie was a jokester back then, and a bit goofy at times, David recalled, but there had been no sign of mental illness. One day after the onset of Lonnie's schizophrenia, David ran into him at a shopping mall. With his sloppy dress, scraggly hair, and incoherent rambling, Lonnie hardly resembled the perfectionist kid with whom David had grown up.

David couldn't help but recall this discovery when Lonnie visited Habitat with the other AIM Center members. Lonnie had been so vibrant when he was a kid, before his illness, and maybe, just maybe he could be again. "I want to hire Lonnie," David announced to Connie in his usual I've-made-up-my-mind-and-don't-try-to-change-it fashion. Connie had her doubts, and so did Phyllis. Lonnie had come a long way, but a real job? That was a different matter entirely.

Connie finally agreed to hire Lonnie, but only under certain conditions. First, he had to get rid of the bandana. And he had to cut and comb his hair. Shortly before he started working at the factory he called "the Habitat," Lonnie left the mental health housing system and moved into a little cedar duplex down the street from his mom's house, marking the first time he had ever lived alone. He was 39. Phyllis went with him to open a bank account and taught her son how to balance his monthly statements and budget for expenses. Still, both Phyllis and Lonnie were apprehensive about whether he could manage a full workload.

As they suspected, things didn't always go well. In his early days on the job, Lonnie rolled carpet and occasionally helped unload the trucks. Despite their effectiveness, the Clozaril and other medications slowed him down, and he tired easily. His mind wandered and he needed close supervision. By the time he got home each afternoon he was limp with exhaustion.

One day Connie approached him in the plant and said, "Lonnie, come with me, we have a job to do." She pointed to a wall of stacked boxes. "We need to move all these boxes into the next room."

"You mean all in one day?" he asked, frowning. Physical labor was a new concept for Lonnie, and he wasn't so sure he wanted any part of it.

"David, I just don't know if I can do this," he later told his new boss.

"Tell you what," David replied. "If something starts bothering you, come see me. Otherwise, just relax and go with the flow. You can do it."

The hurdles, however, had just begun. Stress still triggered the voices in Lonnie's head. Sometimes he talked to the rolls of carpet, or to imaginary spiders or purple elephants no one else saw. It might take him two dozen cuts, instead of one, to slice the protective plastic wrapping from one of the rolls. And sometimes he simply zoned out.

One hot summer afternoon, Lonnie kept falling asleep. "Wake up, Lonnie," Connie nudged. He roused himself, worked a few minutes, then drifted off again. Connie kept waking him up. All of a sudden she remembered how heat could adversely affect Lonnie's energy level and production; when he perspired, his much-needed medication literally seeped out through his pores. She fetched him a bottle of water and a fan to cool him down, and he worked without incident for the rest of the day.

Like many people with schizophrenia, Lonnie was a heavy smoker, and when he got frustrated he'd head for a smoke break. (Statistics show that the prevalence of nicotine addiction among people with schizophrenia is about three times higher than the general population, perhaps because the symptoms of withdrawal can cause a temporary worsening of the condition.) He constantly looked at his watch to gauge the time for his next dose of "meds." Sometimes this habit was so disruptive that Connie would ask for his watch, adding it to a drawer already full of confiscated timepieces. Lonnie also had a hard time adjusting when new temporary workers were brought in to handle rush jobs and large orders. When the changes were too confusing for Lonnie, he would find an excuse to go home early.

But over the years, the man who had once been too shy to speak emerged from his emotional shell and grasped—even embraced—the importance of teamwork. He loved the company parties, picnics, and playing pool at break time. David teasingly called him the Lonster. Jerry, the plant engineer, called him Lawnmower Man. Lonnie smiled each time someone gave him a new nickname. His self-esteem soared, and so did his sense of belonging.

To his co-workers, Lonnie was a source of encouragement. He frequently told the female managers how pretty they looked and how nice they were. "Cheer up. It's not that bad," he said to co-workers who were having a tough day. When Lincoln sank into a depressed mode, Lonnie worked hard to lift Linc's spirits. He helped train new hires who were nervous about what was expected of them, and calmly introduced himself to salespeople and truck drivers, setting them at ease with his friendly "Hi, welcome to the Habitat." His compassion and tender spirit prevailed, and he intuitively knew how to bring out the best in everyone.

Lonnie was such a positive influence that by 1998 he had become the "official Habitat poet and philosopher." He started writing his own two-liner jokes and spouting them off in the plant. "Hey, Lincoln!" he'd say. "Why did the frogs celebrate New Year's Eve? Because it was leap year!" Everyone laughed, including Lonnie.

"Hey, why don't you start writing those down?" David asked him. "Maybe we should do a book."

"Okay," Lonnie said with a grin. Week after week he brought in a handful of jokes and when there were more than 100, Patty Gregory Keith, Habitat's national/international sales coordinator, typed them up, bound them into a slim booklet, and distributed the collection to the employees and their families. Lonnie eventually "published" four editions of his "short line" jokes.

Lonnie would continue to hear voices and see things his co-workers didn't. He couldn't work as quickly as some of the other employees. And he would withdraw when he felt overwhelmed. But the work helped keep his mind off his problems. He was eventually given more responsibilities and since his forté was unloading carpet, that became his primary task.

Lonnie had no idea he was about to create the company's new slogan when, in the summer of 1997, he thoughtfully answered a reporter's question about Habitat. "What's it like working here?" the writer asked.

Lonnie paused for a moment. "It's freedom to do what I want to do— have a job. I didn't think I could do it. Habitat's a company that more or less hires people with distractions, and we work it out together."

The "distractions" word stuck. It was, on all levels, an appropriate term for the mental and physical challenges many Habitat employees constantly battled. It slowly became part of the company culture. David and Jim mentioned it in their presentations to customers and the term showed up in other magazine articles. In 2002, five years after Lonnie made that introspective comment, Habitat adopted the new slogan, *A Company of Positive Distractions*. When the company moved to a much larger facility in late 2003, a prominent sign bearing the offbeat motto was erected just outside the gate. Twenty-five years after being diagnosed with schizophrenia, Lonnie had proudly shown that a "distraction" wasn't necessarily such a bad thing after all.

Ten

David and the Goliaths

FTER A WHILE MOST OF THE BUYERS and truck drivers and temporary laborers who were initially prejudiced against the company's disabled workers realized that what they were doing was wrong and stopped making fun. Some even became allies, taking up for the employees when someone else showed their intolerance. Many of them became part of the extended Habitat "family." But there was one holdout, and it was a big one.

Like most companies that manufacture consumer products, Habitat relied on independent sales representatives to serve as liaisons with the buyers, who work under contract to purchase goods for the retailers. As late as the mid-1990s, sales reps not only sold Habitat's rugs, putting greens, and other products, but were also responsible for everything from keeping an eye on store inventories to straightening the product on the shelves. In return, the reps, who generally worked as a team to service one or more accounts, earned commissions from Habitat or, in some cases, the retail customer.

Since day one, David and Saul had relied on a large, Seattle-based sales rep agency to handle one of their biggest accounts, a major home center chain with locations throughout the Northwest. The sales reps were extremely good at what they did, both in service and sales, and they held a powerful monopoly on all purchasing decisions made by this particular home retailer. They were also arrogant and cocky, often belittling the Habitat managers with subtle comments and sideways glances. David, Saul, and Jim didn't dress to their standards. They ran a company with no name recognition outside the industry. And their little factory was located in an obscure, backwoods town in the hills of north Georgia. So it came as no real shock to David and Saul when the sales reps, especially one man with a super-inflated ego and a sarcastic tongue, failed to treat their disabled employees with respect.

Most of the time, three or four reps from the agency would fly east to meet with the Habitat executives and discuss a new product or display or marketing idea. For years David and Saul, and later Jim, stifled the temptation to say something about the holier-than-thou attitudes and condescending remarks. They just kept their mouths shut. But the one thing they wouldn't overlook, under any circumstances, was overt narrow-mindedness about their disabled employees.

It didn't happen very often at first. But after a while the sarcastic salesman couldn't seem to control his offensive comments when he and his colleagues were out in the plant. "Hey, look at that retard over there," he would say to the other reps. "Look at that dummy go." Although they never repeated his words, his colleagues would smirk as if in agreement. When David or Saul or Jim overheard such remarks, they brought them to the salesman's attention and politely but firmly asked him not to do it again. They never caught him criticizing the disabled workers to their faces, but it was obvious from the employees' body language and the way they lowered their voices around him that they sensed his contempt and were trying to stay out of his way. No matter how many reminders he was given, he never stopped making his cruel observations in front of David.

It reminded David of the utter disdain a few of the truck drivers had, in the past, shown toward the Asian workers. One day a driver yelled out to Jim, "Hey, buddy, what do you pay these gooks? They look like slave labor to me."

"Well, that person walking across the parking lot there is making about $58,000 a year," Jim replied without hesitation. "Now. What do you make?" The truck driver didn't say another word that day, and he never made another derogatory remark about the Cambodians.

The problem with the prejudiced sales rep, however, was not so easily fixed. By early 1996, the tension between the Habitat staff and the sales representative group was so thick that the agency's owner came down from Seattle to meet with David, Jim, and Saul. He apologized for his staff's behavior, and promised it wouldn't happen again. It did. Before long, the Habitat managers met with the group again, and explained their position. They weren't as diplomatic this time. "Look," David said. "We're sick of the way you treat us, and we absolutely will not put up with the way you treat our employees. You need to cut the crap. We've had enough of your attitude."

"Hey, business is business," said one of the reps. "It's all about money, so why do we need to get along anyway? And why should you care what we think about your retards? What does it matter?"

"Hey, it matters a lot," David replied, struggling to stay calm. "These people are important to us. This is what Habitat is and what we stand for. You're messing with the wrong people on this one. It's not a fight you can win."

The Habitat managers were faced with a thorny decision, one of the toughest they'd ever encountered. At that point they enjoyed a 100 percent share of the roll goods and indoor-outdoor rugs in the Seattle-based chain. The retailer had been carrying their products since they opened for business, and was still considered the best in the industry in sales of DIY products. And the rep group was Habitat's only real link to the home center chain. If David and the other managers looked the other way, if they stayed with the powerful sales team, their relationship with the retailer would remain secure. If they did something drastic, they would probably lose the important account they'd had for the past 15 years and throw away 10 percent of their orders $1 million in annual sales. The prospect was hard to swallow.

"Are you nuts?" Saul said when David finally told him he wanted to fire the sales reps. "That's a lot of revenue for us to give up."

"But, Dad, we've always tried to do the right thing," David replied. "And this is the right thing to do. These people have no respect for us or our employees."

Saul sighed. From a moral standpoint, his son's argument made absolute sense. But from a business aspect, giving up a longtime customer they'd worked so hard to keep, well, that was going to hurt. Jim was worried too. He knew the lost business would be hard to replace. But the insensitivity of the sales group made his blood boil, and it didn't look like things were going to get any better. Like David, Jim had no use for bigots.

Prolonging the relationship with the sales group would only throw fuel on an already-dangerous fire. The unsettling conflict had gone on far too long, and Jim and David knew what they had to do. As they prepared to fly to Seattle, they typed up a letter to give to the arrogant sales rep who'd frequently treated the employees with such total disregard.

"Dear XX, We will no longer be needing your services. We can't work with you any longer," the note read. "Thank you." David tucked the letter in an envelope and slipped it into his pocket.

As was often the case when they met in Seattle, the sales rep picked David and Jim up at the hotel on his way to meet with the buyer. This time they rode in awkward silence. At the door, David turned to the salesman and handed him the letter. "Read this," David said. "Do not come with us into this meeting. We do not want you there. When we come out, we'll be glad to discuss anything you want to talk about."

Inside, the buyer welcomed them as she always did. She had often told David and Jim how much she admired what Habitat stood for. But, they knew, she was also a good friend of the sales rep, and that relationship would most likely outweigh their own business connection.

"We realize we're going to jeopardize this account with what we have to say," David told her. "But we just can't work with the sales rep anymore. He is extremely prejudiced toward our employees with disabilities, and he looks down on us. We've tried to talk to him and his boss about it several times, but that hasn't worked and things have just gotten way out of hand."

David took a deep breath and continued, "We just gave him a letter saying he no longer represents us. And we're coming to you without him because we know we can still do the job. We know you like us, you like what we do and we see no reason why we can't keep the account. We just can't work with that sales rep anymore."

The buyer smiled. "No problem. It's okay," she assured them. "This shouldn't affect your relationship with the retailer one bit. And you won't have to work with him anymore. We'll be sending more orders your way in a few days." She hugged them both as they left the conference room. The three of them even had dinner together that night. "Don't worry," she said again. "It'll be fine."

Back at the hotel, David and Jim should have been celebrating their coup, but something about the situation didn't feel right. It had just been too easy. Jim, especially, had a sense of foreboding, and he knew better than to ignore his keen intuition. "Mark my word," he told David. "In the morning she'll be making arrangements to switch vendors. And in a couple of weeks our account will be gone."

At first it appeared that Jim might have been wrong. For the next couple of weeks, Habitat received standard rug orders from the reassuring buyer they'd met with in Seattle. Soon, however, the orders began to dwindle. Then the buyer stopped returning their phone calls. It didn't take David long to figure out that the $1 million account, the one he and Saul had cultivated so many years before, the one that had been a sure thing for so long, was a thing of the past.

The disabled employees never knew what their bosses had done for them. Blissfully unaware that Habitat had given up a major account to get rid of a prejudiced sales group, they happily kept rolling carpet and packaging rugs and taking turns being radio DJs at break time. It was seven years before Habitat sold the last of the inventoried remnant mats made exclusively for their Seattle-based customer, but David, Jim, and Saul never regretted their decision to fire the sales rep. In fact, they were relieved they no longer had to deal with his condescension and arrogance. And, since what goes around generally comes around, even in the business world, it wasn't long before one of Habitat's other DIY customers acquired the big Northwest chain and began working with sales reps who were more socially conscious. Within two years, Habitat was doing business with the retailer again and had fully recovered the loss.

After their ordeal with the insensitive salesman, the managers stopped cultivating business relationships with executives who showed an extreme lack of respect for Habitat's disabled employees, or for that matter, their own workers. If they knew for a fact that a major retailer was taking advantage of its laborers, if the corporation used low-paid illegal workers in the U.S. or outsourced orders to documented sweatshops in poverty-stricken countries, David, Saul, and Jim took their business elsewhere, even if it meant losing money. To them, the thought of exploiting someone just to make an extra buck was simply unconscionable. The essence of Habitat, after all, was people—living, breathing human beings who differed in so many ways, but who all deserved to be treated with dignity. They were the ones who had made the company strong. They were the ones who had made Habitat "more than a workplace—a care place."

Slaying the giants who posed a competitive challenge, on the other hand, called for more ingenuity. During the 1980s Habitat had practically owned the sporting goods market in golf putting greens, with approximately 75 percent of U.S. sales to athletic shops, major mail-order catalog companies, and mass merchandisers like Kmart, Wal-Mart, and Sears. European sales were robust as well. The accidental success of the putting green, a product born in the early days when David and Saul were seeking a way to hand out carpet samples to buyers, had catapulted their business to a higher level than they'd ever thought possible.

Habitat's annual revenues had topped $12 million a year and were still growing. For a tiny, two-person shop launched on a shoestring with the modest goal of selling a few indoor-outdoor rugs and generating enough income for Saul and his family to live on, that wasn't half bad.

But the days of coasting on their good fortune were over. The sports market had matured and become more sophisticated, with consumers demanding not just one golfing accessory, but 10 or 15. Almost overnight, other companies began manufacturing golf putting greens in the U.S. and Asia. Old hands at predicting industry trends, Saul and David clearly saw the writing on the wall; it wouldn't be long before they'd be edged out as the market leader. It was time to switch gears and take a more proactive stance. At trade shows, they began approaching the sporting goods distributors instead of the retail buyers. "We're aware of what's happening in the industry, and we're changing our strategies too," they said. "We can beat the pricing that's coming out of the Asian countries and we can ship products to you much faster than they can. We'd like to work with you instead of selling everything direct to the retailer." Back at the plant, they would follow up each trade show spiel by sending a packet of information that included not only their product lists, but told the Habitat story and emphasized the company's strong work ethic. Then, in a few weeks they'd send another friendly note, then later, another. Before long the distributors felt like they'd known the Habitat managers for years.

The strategy paid off. A number of golf-accessory distributors ordered products from Habitat, and the company began packaging greens, driving mats, and putting cups under other private labels, such as Top Flite, Izzo, and Gold Eagle. In 1992, Habitat became an authorized licensee for Spalding, a high-profile supplier of athletic equipment. For six years most of the products made at Habitat, including the entire collection of indoor-outdoor rugs, bore the Spalding name.

The company was changing in other ways too. Looking back, Saul and David realized they should have already unburdened themselves of the roll goods division. Selling large rolls of grass and needlepunch carpet to home centers was cumbersome, not to mention financially draining, especially for a small company like Habitat. With the increasing demand for the smaller cut rugs, golf putting greens, and other accessories, it was no longer feasible for them to serve as the roll goods middleman between the large carpet manufacturers and the retailers. It was time to sell the roll goods.

In 1996, Habitat's owners began taking bids. Executives from Chattanooga-based Dixie Yarns were interested. So were the decision-makers at General Felt Industries (GFI), a Pennsylvania flooring manufacturer, maker of Foamex carpet cushion and padding, and, at the time, Habitat's chief source for roll goods in both needlepunch and grass turf. Since GFI was already manufacturing and warehousing the product, it seemed like the likely winner. But there was another candidate too, a Goliath named Beaulieu of America, the third largest carpet manufacturer in North America and a formidable competitor just down the road in Dalton, Georgia.

The Morrises had crossed paths with this industry giant more than once over the years. From time to time, Saul would run into Carl Bouckaert, the Belgian founder of Beaulieu, at carpet trade shows, where the two men chatted and enjoyed a non-competitive working relationship. Occasionally Carl came to Saul with his industry questions, and Saul served as an older mentor, just like he had with his own son. It was little wonder that they hit it off. They had several things in common: both owned family businesses. Both were shrewd entrepreneurs who knew the industry well. And Saul had once worked for Conquest, a major Beaulieu division that included the Argonne home center branch, before starting Habitat. Carl was impressed with Saul's sales expertise and ability to win over customers with his irresistible charm. Saul admired Carl's ambitious nature, generosity, and drive to succeed, even in the face of tremendous adversity.

Carl and his wife, Mieke, had established Beaulieu in 1978 and, with the financial backing of Mieke's father, built the Dalton-based carpet company from scratch. At first they focused on manufacturing polypropylene 9' x 12' Oriental rugs at a time when most were still made of wool. Later, Beaulieu became a true vertical company, making its own yarn from resin to fiber to finished product, eventually evolving into an industry leader that generated most of its revenue from sales of residential floor coverings. Along with Shaw, Mohawk, and Interface, by the 1980s Beaulieu dominated the market in the U.S. But achieving success had been a bit of a roller-coaster ride. The company had lost a lot of money during the three years it took to fine-tune the complex yarn-making process. To make matters worse, the dollar value had spiked from a record low in 1981 to a record high in 1984, which meant that much of Beaulieu's inventory was seriously devalued. Sales were being outpaced by aggressive European imports, which were priced at one-third the cost of Beaulieu's. Ironically, the greatest threat came from Belgium, Carl Bouckaert's native country and a major exporter of inexpensive rugs. Before long, Beaulieu was in deep trouble.

An articulate, charismatic achiever, Carl wasn't about to sit idly by and watch all his hard work go down the drain. His executive team installed a special heat and humidity conditioning unit that helped the yarn plant run more efficiently and resulted in a higher-quality product. Then they redesigned the rug collection and introduced a new palette of pastel hues. The selection was brand new to the market and posed a threat to the European manufacturers, who had historically made rugs in rich reds, deep blues, and other traditional colors. Thanks to the overhaul, Beaulieu pulled back from the brink of near-bankruptcy, introduced more innovative machinery, and created what quickly became a must-have for homeowners wishing to carpet their family rooms, porches, and sunrooms: low-pile Berber carpet. Over the years there were more ups and downs, with Beaulieu sometimes teetering on the edge of disaster due to a bad investment or an unpredictable surge in oil prices or interest rates. But each time, Carl and his colleagues found a way to get back on course, reduce the company's debt, and maintain the firm's status as an industry trailblazer.

By the time David and Saul decided to sell the roll goods segment of their business, Beaulieu had become a friendly but worrisome opponent with more than 7,000 employees and over $1 billion in annual revenues. The Dalton-headquartered Goliath was now going head to head with Habitat in roll goods. What's more, Beaulieu had started a division called Citation, which competed directly against Habitat in packaged grass-turf and needlepunch rugs. Habitat was still widely known for its quality products, outstanding service, and imaginative marketing ideas. But when it came to the size of their staff, the physical plant, or the company's financial resources, they were eclipsed by the giant Beaulieu. It could, at times, be quite intimidating.

Little did David know that Carl Bouckaert thought the same thing about Habitat. In fact, for a long time Carl had considered Saul Morris his only serious competitor. Saul was a true people person, with a long track record of sales in the home center industry and a knack for sweet-talking buyers into a deal. He was old enough to be Carl's father and he'd had far more experience in the field, especially when it came to finding creative ways to keep customers happy. It took a lot of energy to keep up with Saul.

The three carpet companies that were set to bid on the roll goods division sent representatives to Habitat to talk to David and Saul and inspect the plant's operations. Carl Bouckaert sent himself. Dressed to kill in a tailored designer suit and silk necktie, the trim, wealthy Belgian entrepreneur arrived at the outlandish factory guarded by whimsical steel giraffes and elephants. He walked into the office area, past the rake-prong bench and the grass-hair mannequins, and shook David's hand, as the two men headed back to the conference room to meet Saul. It was there that Carl leaned forward and finally asked the question he'd been dying to ask: "How do you do it?

"I don't understand," he continued. "I mean, you guys have this small plant, you don't even make the carpet here, and you still split the Home Depot account with us on the west coast. I know you're great marketers and Saul, you're a genius when it comes to selling. But your staff isn't that large, so there must be something else going on. What's your secret?"

"Do you really want to know?" David asked with a gleam in his eye.

"Of course," Carl replied in his distinguished European accent.

"Come on," David said, scooting his chair away from the table. "I'll show you."

The Habitat managers had recently installed a doorbell at the front loading dock so the truck drivers could gain quick access to the prepared shipments, without having to walk all the way through the maze of offices in the front of the building. Carl followed David into the plant, where he met several of the employees with various disabilities and struck up a conversation with a group of Bosnian workers. Each time he was introduced to one of the disabled people, he was greeted with a smile, a genuinely cheerful "hello," and sometimes an unforeseen hug. He couldn't help but notice that everyone seemed to be working much faster than the "normal" employees in his own plant in Dalton, and they weren't making any mistakes. Before he even had time to protest, two employees with Down syndrome had grabbed him by the sleeve of his expensive jacket and were steering him outside to see the new bell. "Look, Mr. Carl!" they exclaimed. "Mr. Carl! Come look at this!"

Carl was an emotional man, and he found himself fighting back tears. He didn't even know these people, but they had welcomed him with open arms, as if they were old friends. To top it all, they actually enjoyed their work and obviously wanted to share their joy, even with strangers. There was nothing choreographed about their "presentation," a truth that touched Carl so deeply he could hardly keep from sobbing right there on the spot.

David saw what had happened, and he gave Carl time to regroup. "Are you ready to go back in and talk some more?" David finally asked.

Carl clearly did not want to leave. "No, I think I'd like to stay out here a while and spend some time in the plant," he said. Then he took David aside and made a statement David found hard to believe. "Whether we buy the roll goods division or not," Carl said, "I want to be part of this. One way or another, we're going to do something together."

Beaulieu didn't win the bid. The best offer came from General Felt Industries, which was equipped to automatically assume Habitat's roll goods inventory because it was already stored in their warehouse. Because of the sale and the subsequent decrease in revenue, Habitat's profits were down for a few years after that. So was the stress factor. More than once, David and Saul had seen that for every loss there is a gain, so they knew that it wouldn't be long before Habitat would be embarking on a new, better venture, one that was well suited to their labor-intensive workforce. They just didn't know exactly what it would be.

Still, they were surprised when, not long after the sale of the roll goods division, Carl gave them a call. He was closing Citation, his company's rug-cutting division and the only industry segment where Beaulieu and Habitat still competed directly. Would David and Saul like to buy their roll goods from Beaulieu and, together, supply the rest of the Home Depot stores? *Yeah, right*, David thought to himself. *Like that's really going to happen.* But Carl's offer was real, and before long, the men were shaking hands over an agreement that would ultimately benefit everyone.

The partnership did make sense. Beaulieu was already producing the carpet rolls Habitat needed at a more cost-effective rate than Habitat ever could. Habitat, on the other hand, was well known for its quality products, personal service, and prompt delivery. While Beaulieu was highly mechanized, Habitat was labor-intensive. To David, that meant only one thing: an opportunity to hire more people, especially those with disabilities.

A few months after they sealed the deal with a handshake, Beaulieu was channeling millions of dollars to Habitat in orders from the Home Depot. David could hardly keep from pinching himself. It all seemed too good to be true. There were skeptics at Beaulieu as well. Not everyone there was as convinced as Carl that this was a profitable move, at least not at first. In fact, they were worried. David Bagby, bypass distribution manager, had actually worked with Saul at Argonne years before, so he had no qualms about Saul's character. Hans Bakker, director of product management, knew Saul as well. But to forge a partnership with a competitor, and one that was fairly low-key, not to mention under-funded compared to the Carpet Capital's "big boys"? The financial officers, too, were dubious and they quizzed Carl about Habitat's solvency. "How do you know if they're financially stable? What if they run out of money and can't fill the orders?"

"It's okay," Carl assured them all. "They won't let us down. You'll see."

Kim Brown, Beaulieu's customer relations manager, was curious about the little dynamo of a rug factory that had impressed Carl so much. So was David Bagby. Why was their boss willing to take such a gamble, and after all the company had been through? Kim and David drove up to Habitat, about 20 miles north of the Beaulieu headquarters, to meet David Morris and see the place for themselves. Like Carl before them, they were met by a jungle of quirky steel characters. Inside were more of the odd sculptures. Motivational posters and folk art plastered the walls. Out in the plant were boxes stacked floor-to-ceiling with carpet products. Workers were busy cutting and rolling the rugs. But it wasn't the most organized-looking place in the world, and it was hard to take in all the murals and paintings and color splashed on the walls. And what was the deal with that radio station, and the indoor basketball court?

"There's no way," Kim whispered to her co-worker, David. "There is no way this place can keep up with the Home Depot's demands."

By the end of their visit, however, the Beaulieu visitors had seen what Carl saw the day the employees with Down syndrome showed him the new doorbell. Instead of bizarre sculptures and crazy artwork and a plant that appeared to be much too small and chaotic, they saw people who took great pride in their work and inspired just about everyone with whom they came into contact. Just like Carl, the Beaulieu executives found themselves wanting to do business with such a socially responsible company. And before long they and their colleagues considered themselves part of the Habitat family. They began attending the company's annual picnics, and the Habitat employees came to Beaulieu's social events. Kim even took her kids to the Habitat parties so they too could see how people from so many backgrounds, and with so many different challenges, could make a company a great place to work just by being themselves.

At one point Carl asked David to help the human resources department at Beaulieu set up its own disability-hiring program, but it never quite got off the ground. Unlike the labor-intensive Habitat plant, Beaulieu was extremely mechanized, with lots of high-speed equipment. In the end, the HR executives felt it was just too risky for people with physical and mental disabilities to work in that environment.

The Beaulieu-Habitat partnership turned out to be one of the best moves both companies had ever made. Beaulieu manufactured the grass and needlepunch carpet and trucked it up the road to Habitat, where the workers cut and boxed the rugs under their former competitor's label, then shipped them back to Beaulieu for transfer to the Home Depot. David and Jim, the masters of creative marketing, designed all the artwork for the packaging and point-of-purchase displays. In addition to "sharing" the Home Depot account, Beaulieu supplied Habitat with grass and needlepunch carpet that was then cut into rugs for Habitat's other private-label and major retail customers. For years Habitat had sold roll goods and area rugs to the Home Depot, but mostly in certain regions of the country. By 2004 the DIY titan accounted for a large percentage of Habitat's sales growth.

The collaboration paid off for Beaulieu as well. Unlike Habitat, the company wasn't set up to painstakingly teach employees who didn't catch on the first time around. And the workers there weren't nearly as productive as Habitat's when tackling laborious jobs like cutting and rolling grass rugs. In fact, when it came to efficiency, Habitat could teach the giant a lesson or two.

Carl had promised to maintain an open line of communication between David and the Beaulieu executives, including himself. This open-door policy was nothing new for Carl, who encouraged employees and customers to come directly to him if they had a problem. David admired this trait in Carl; after all, he and Saul had always made themselves accessible to the Habitat workers, no matter what. But Habitat's owners also believed in running a tight ship. On days when David was expecting a truckload of roll goods from Beaulieu, he cut his supplier no slack on the schedule. If the carpet was supposed to be there at 8 A.M. it had better be there at 8 A.M., not 8:05 or 8:10. If it was late, David didn't hesitate to pick up the phone and call Carl or one of the other Beaulieu executives. "Where's my carpet?" he'd chide. "The machines are set up and I've got people waiting to work."

Despite the importance of the Beaulieu-Habitat partnership, David's top priority was, first and foremost, his employees. He didn't want them standing around with nothing to do. He didn't want to have to send someone home because there wasn't enough work to go around. And he didn't want to spring too many changes on them at the last minute. Sometimes the Beaulieu executives would roll their eyes at David's demands. Most of the time, though, they were grateful he cared enough to keep the process on track and look out for their best interests. They were glad he made sure they didn't look foolish in the eyes of the retailer. In fact, thanks to its top-notch workforce, Habitat made Beaulieu look *very* good.

Once again, the workers with disabilities had shown they could keep up under pressure. Even when large orders came in at the last minute—and that was often the case—the employees stepped up to the challenge and cranked out every last rug. David would never have dreamed of asking his hard-working staffers to give up their weekends, but when deadlines were tight, they stepped forward and volunteered to work Saturdays and Sundays. On weekdays some of them arrived at the plant as early as 4:30 A.M. so they could get started on the day's quota. The once-skeptical Beaulieu executives were blown away by the loyal attitude and unwavering work ethic of the Habitat workforce. So were the Habitat managers.

And David and Saul learned a priceless trade secret: that sometimes, the best way to beat the competition is not to keep fighting but to join forces. Instead of trying to go head to head with Goliath, Habitat had handed him a slingshot. Or maybe it happened the other way around. Either way, Habitat and Beaulieu were no longer wary competitors. Now they were each other's customers. Now they were allies.

From time to time, David's thoughts flashed back to the spring of 1996, the day of the Olympic torch run in Knoxville, a few months before he invited Carl to the plant to meet his disabled employees for the first time. An accomplished equestrian who owned several championship venues in north Georgia and was scheduled to compete on the Belgian horseracing team that year, Carl was also nominated to carry the torch in Dalton. A reporter for the same television station that had originally aired the torchbearer segment on David phoned to see if David would do a commentary at Carl's torch run in Dalton. Was it coincidence? Perhaps, or an omen of good things to come.

On the day of the Dalton torch relay, as the two men signed autographs together, David was struck by the irony. Here they were, two very different men who hailed from two very different countries separated by hundreds of miles and an ocean. Here they were, two steadfast competitors, united in a single cause, just like the Olympic hopefuls.

Eleven

Daniel:
Man of Courage

S HERRY TAYLOR WAS HOME that Sunday morning when she got the call. A neighbor had been traveling on a busy road about five minutes away from Sherry's house when she came upon a fresh automobile accident and recognized the car. It belonged to Daniel Johnson, Sherry's 18-year-old son.

"How bad is it?" Sherry asked, grabbing her keys.

"Well, he's got a cut on his face and he's bleeding, but I think he's okay," the neighbor replied.

Moments later Sherry was standing at the scene of the wreck. Daniel was still inside the vehicle, and the emergency medical technicians were working to stabilize him and stop the bleeding. Sherry tried to get close, but the EMTs steered her away from the car. "Daniel, hang in there! It's going to be all right," she yelled from a distance, not knowing if he could hear her or not. "You're going to be okay."

A handsome teenager with striking blue eyes and blonde-streaked hair that grazed the top of one brow, Daniel was, understandably, a popular kid. Smitten girls kept the phone tied up with their calls. His friends rambled in and out of the family's house in Ringgold, Georgia, almost as much as he did. Like most teens, he had a mischievous side, but his active participation in church programs kept him, for the most part, out of trouble.

Around 9:30 A.M. on May 29, 1994, six weeks before Daniel's 19th birthday, he was on his way to Sunday School when, for reasons he would never remember, he lost control of the car and ran off the road. There was no shoulder, no strip of land where he could regain his bearings, and he careened down a steep drop-off and slammed into an unyielding concrete culvert. Daniel's torso struck the steering wheel and, although it didn't fully eject him, the seat detached from its post. His ankle was cracked and dislocated, and he had a broken back. Far more serious, however, was the head injury.

Sherry caught a glimpse of Daniel as he was being wheeled into the emergency room, and her stomach lurched. His eyes were swollen shut and his head was already enlarged to the size of a basketball. His face was so full of fluid that there were no delineations where his nose or cheeks or chin were supposed to be.

The nurses whisked Daniel into a treatment room and warned Sherry and her husband Dick not to follow. Dick had been mowing his mother's grass when he got the news and dropped everything to join Sherry at the small north Georgia hospital. Charged with adrenaline and nervous energy, Sherry stepped outside to thank the ambulance drivers for taking care of her son. "Well, ma'am, we're not finished," one of them said. "We're taking him to Erlanger."

Erlanger Medical Center in nearby Chattanooga offered the region's only Level I trauma center. Critically injured patients were often sent there from other hospitals in 50 counties within a 150-mile radius. Sherry was both heartsick about the severity of her son's injuries and hopeful he would get the care he needed at the larger facility.

But the emergency room physician at the first hospital did nothing to bolster that hope. "Mrs. Taylor, you need to say goodbye to your son," he told her.

"What are you talking about?" she replied. "I'm going with him."

"No, I mean you need to say *goodbye*," the doctor said matter-of-factly. "He probably won't make it to Erlanger."

"No, you're wrong. I know my son. He'll be fine."

The physician grabbed Sherry by the shoulders, spun her to face him, and looked her straight in the eyes. "Lady, you don't understand. If you don't say goodbye to him, you're not going to get to."

"Well, I'm not," Sherry said firmly. "I'll be at Erlanger when he gets there."

It was the first of many times Sherry Taylor would challenge the doctors' predictions for her only son.

In the operating room at Erlanger, the surgeon removed the bone from Daniel's brutally battered frontal lobe and immediately saw that the damage was much worse than he had thought. The doctor sewed him back up, instructed his assistant to move Daniel to the intensive care unit, and told Sherry and Dick that their son had only a slim chance of making it through the night. A week later, Daniel was still unconscious, and the doctors said he'd probably never wake up. If he did, they asserted, he would remain in a vegetative state for the rest of his life. And if by some miracle their son did recover partial use of his body, he would be blind. He'd never walk again. With each piece of bad news, each bleak prognosis, straight-shooting Sherry responded with, "Well, you're wrong."

Daniel remained in a coma for 11 days. One morning Sherry walked across the street from the Ronald McDonald House, a temporary "home" for families of seriously ill children being treated at Erlanger, and a familiar male nurse answered her call when she tried to buzz herself in for the day. "Wait right there," he said. "I've got something to show you." Sherry's first thought was, *Oh no, what now?*

"Now don't panic," the nurse said as if reading her mind. He met her at Daniel's door.

"Okay, Mama, you can come in now," said the kindhearted nurse. Daniel was sitting up in his bed, eyes still swollen shut, surfing TV channels with the remote control. Sherry could hardly believe what she saw, and she was ecstatic. She had no way of knowing that this mindless channel flipping would go on for weeks. And Daniel had no clue what he was doing.

But he did know her voice. "Hi, buddy," she ventured. Her son couldn't talk so he waved. When the swelling finally began to subside, Daniel communicated by writing notes. "What's your name?" Sherry asked. It took him a while, but he penned the word D-A-N-I-E-L on a pad.

"Who am I?" she asked next. M-O-M, he scribbled. M-O-M. Sherry knew then that Daniel was going to make it.

Dr. Larry Sargent, a renowned craniofacial surgeon who practiced at Erlanger, began repairing Daniel's many facial fractures. The left eye orbit was the only bone left intact; every other one, from the jaw up, was either fractured or crushed. The complex reconstructive surgery began early one morning and lasted well into the night. Soon after, Daniel developed his first staph infection, which required another operation and additional rounds of strong antibiotics. Doctors continued to tell Sherry there wasn't much hope. But over and over, she fought for Daniel's survival and his return to a normal life. "This family doesn't accept the word 'no,'" she told those who dared to challenge her positive attitude. Dick, a mild-mannered man with a big heart and a burly physique, told them they'd better back off. Sherry was a fighter and it would be in their best interests to stay out of her way.

Daniel's birthday gave Sherry and the rest of the family a good excuse to forget about their problems for a while. On the morning of July 18, Sherry's sister and brother-in-law smuggled water pistols into the hospital. The head nurse was in on the surprise; so were two more male nurses, including the one who'd been so anxious for Sherry to know that her son had emerged from his coma. Sherry handed Daniel a gun, and the nurses armed themselves too. Before long, they were all squirting each other with thin bursts of water, and giggling and squealing with childlike glee. Daniel hid his toy pistol under the covers and when someone entered the room, he would shoot them and laugh. Eventually a stern, by-the-book nurse busted them all and rounded up the guns. But, the partiers later agreed, it was worth getting in trouble for.

Two months after his accident, contrary to what doctors had told Sherry that horrific day, Daniel walked out of the hospital, able to see and talk with his family. But the road to recovery would be full of abrupt twists and turns. For some reason, the parts of Daniel's skull that had been surgically fused wouldn't heal, and he developed "breakthroughs" in the skin of his head from which liquid would ooze. He was besieged with staph infections and underwent several more surgeries. During one procedure, the surgeon removed one of his sinuses, which had completely deteriorated due to the penetrating staphylococcus. Finally, in February of 1995, nine months after Daniel's car smashed into the culvert, the infections were under control.

The physical injuries and ongoing setbacks were heartbreaking for Sherry and Dick; with each one came a slight decline in Daniel's mental capacity and ability to communicate. Far more unsettling, however, was the drastic change in the person Daniel had been before the wreck. Because his frontal lobe had been irrevocably damaged, Sherry would never again know the son to whom she gave birth. His personality, as she knew it, was gone.

Despite the months Sherry and Dick had spent with the doctors, nurses, and other healthcare practitioners, no one had explained the lasting effects of brain trauma on someone like Daniel. According to the Brain Injury Association of America, each year at least 1.5 million Americans sustain a traumatic brain injury. And 5.3 million—a little more than 2 percent of the U.S. population—are currently living with a disability due to brain damage. Like Daniel, they often exhibit reduced cognitive thinking, behavioral changes, and emotional problems.

The new Daniel was very different from the old one. His inhibitions and self-control had all but disappeared. His once-amiable disposition was often eclipsed by anger and frustration. He cursed. He pouted and threw tantrums. He lashed out at his parents. Even so, he seldom wanted to let Sherry out of his sight. It was kind of cute when, as a toddler, Daniel hovered outside the bathroom door, anxious for Mommy to come back out. But Sherry never imagined her 20-year-old son would one day do the same thing.

Little by little, Daniel's health improved, he grew stronger, and he regained some of the weight he had lost. For almost two years Daniel had accompanied his mother each day to the flower shop she owned and operated not far from the house. Sherry was desperate for a much-overdue break from the constant demands of a disabled son, and she felt it was time to see if he could accomplish more. Most importantly, Sherry and Dick wanted Daniel to feel good about himself again, to tackle responsibility, and enjoy a sense of accomplishment, just as he had before his accident. They arranged for a psychiatric evaluation to help gauge Daniel's intellectual level and ability to perform certain tasks. After the exam, Daniel waited outside the doctor's office while the evaluator shared his analysis with Sherry and Dick.

"Your son will never work," the psychiatrist said. "He'll never be able to do anything, period. His life is pretty much over and this is all you can expect. Now if you'll bring Daniel in here, I'll tell him the same thing. He needs to know his limitations."

"No way," Sherry said with a don't-try-to-hold-me-back glare. She was fuming. "Neither you nor anyone else is going to tell my son that he has no future."

Sherry and Dick stormed out of the meeting, led Daniel out to the parking lot, and vowed to keep looking for options.

One day the family's accountant and close friend told them about an unusual workplace in Rossville, Georgia, and the company's big-hearted owners, David and Saul Morris. Many of the employees were disabled, and the managers were patient when somebody needed extra time or attention. Maybe Daniel could get a job there. Sherry picked up the phone and called to set up an appointment and a few days later, the Taylors met with David in the Habitat conference room. "Daniel has problems," they told him. "But he has a good heart and he's willing to work."

Later that week Sherry brought Daniel back to Habitat for an interview. Connie could tell right away he was angry, and easily confused. It was obvious he had a chip on his shoulder, but she knew it came from frustration, and she empathized. Before the wreck, he had been one of the most popular kids in town, frequently going to ballgames and church events with his friends. He could no longer do those things, and his old friends had long since disappeared. There was something else about him, too, a sort of childlike innocence that made it easier to overlook his attitude problem.

It was also hard to say no to Sherry. She was determined her son was going to work around his disability, not give in to it. Connie was impressed with her dedication to helping Daniel feel normal, an important quality that seemed to be lacking in some of the parents whose grown children interviewed at Habitat. It wasn't enough to just land the job; the parents had to step back and allow their children to take risks and make mistakes. They had to break away from their own preconceived notions of what their kids could do. Most of all, in order for their children to be successful in the workplace, they had to believe in the impossible.

Partly because Sherry and Dick fit this description so well, Connie shrugged off her own nagging doubts and hired Daniel, Habitat's first employee with a brain injury, in the spring of 1996. In the early days, Dick dropped him off at 8 A.M. and Sherry picked him up at noon, but eventually Daniel could master a full shift. As Connie had suspected, the young man wasn't easy to work with. He wandered off task and needed constant reminders of what he was supposed to do. "Now get back to work, Daniel," Connie would nudge. "Come on, you can do it. I know you can." And he would, at least some of the time. He loved to cut carpet and he especially looked forward to helping Sandra unload heavy cargo from trailers on Wednesdays. That was a man thing, and it made him feel proud.

Many days, however, it was as if he had regressed into the moody rebellion of adolescence, only worse. No one could tell him what to do. If they tried, he'd make an obscene gesture, curse hatefully, or stick his tongue out in sheer disobedience. He referred to David as "warden."

He was abrasive, outspoken, and opinionated with his co-workers, and, like a hyperactive, out-of-control child, he didn't know when to stop. When he smarted off, Connie would banish him to the ledge outside her second-floor office, where he would sit in plain view of the other employees. More often than not, he'd give them all the finger.

On the days they were tempted to give up on Daniel, the Habitat managers remembered the ordeal he'd been through. They knew that the accident, not his natural personality, made him act hostile and mean-spirited. They realized that Daniel's frustration over losing his friends and his old life, at times, was almost unbearable. He simply wanted to be like everyone else. And they had to admit that most of the time he apologized when he calmed down. "I'm sorry," he'd say, giving Connie or Sandra a hug. "Are you still mad at me?" Even when his antics made them want to pull their hair out, he still touched their hearts. And they always gave him another chance.

Eventually Daniel ran out of chances. One day in early 1999 he was particularly obnoxious, shouting vulgarities, and Connie ordered him to sit on the ledge, facing the wall. Once there, he spun around on his perch, made obscene gestures with both hands, and cursed Connie like he never had before. It took a lot to get fired at Habitat, this workplace where the managers bent over backward to be tolerant of even the most troublesome behavior. But Daniel was disrupting the entire plant and interfering with the other employees' ability to focus and get their work done. It had been going on far too long, and the managers' patience had been stretched way too thin. It was time to let Daniel go.

Daniel was away from Habitat for almost a year. Sherry and Dick enrolled him in a community re-entry program at the Chattanooga-based Siskin Hospital for Physical Rehabilitation, Tennessee's only not-for-profit hospital dedicated exclusively to physical rehab. He spent the next few months in the program, where he exercised in a gym, participated in volunteer projects, and prepared for job interviews. The vocational consultants also worked with Daniel to improve his behavior, and the destructive conduct eventually stopped.

That didn't last long.

With the help of the specialists at Siskin, Daniel got a job as a greeter at a local retail home center. It was soon obvious that this wasn't such a good match. Even though Daniel's harsh attitude had softened, he had little patience for the customers and, when asked for directions to hardware or lamps or appliances, was more likely to say, "I don't know, ask somebody else" than to smile and be pleasant and helpful. Before long there were other problems too. Each day as soon as Sherry dropped him off at work, he waited until she drove away, then exited another door, where his friends were waiting for him. At the end of the day they dropped him back off at the store; by the time his mom arrived to take him home, he was exhausted from "work." To make matters worse, one Friday night Daniel got mad at one of his friends and shoved his fist into a brick wall, breaking his hand.

A few days later, in July 1999, Daniel had his first grand mal seizure. Sherry and Dick came home from work and noticed odd markings on Daniel's stomach and arms, the sort of skin flush that results when blood rises to the surface. Then they noticed his hand cast was broken. And his tongue was bleeding where he had bitten it.

"Daniel, what in the world happened to you?" Sherry asked. "Did you get in another fight? Is that a rash? What happened to your tongue?"

The doctor knew right away what had transpired, and when he told Sherry and Dick, they braced themselves for yet another bumpy ride. In September Daniel had his second seizure and was placed on daily medication to curb the attacks. The drugs worked for a while and by the end of the year Daniel was yearning to go back to Habitat.

"Daniel, are you ready to work this time?" Connie asked when she conducted the re-hiring interview. "Can you do what we ask you to do? And without mouthing off?"

"Yes, ma'am," Daniel answered.

Connie had sensed a transformation in Daniel, a shift away from the hostility that had hindered him in the past, and she agreed to let him come back. Besides, she wanted to believe he had changed. There were still problems—Daniel was nicer now but he was no angel—but the progress was noticeable. Most of the cursing had stopped. He often hugged Connie, and not just when he messed up; when he left for the day, he told her he loved her. She and the other managers guessed that Daniel had missed Habitat and the people who accepted him for who and what he was. Several lawyers and doctors, all friends of the Habitat family, insisted the seizures posed too much of a risk and urged David and Connie to let Daniel go. As usual, they steadfastly refused.

At the "Peaceful Warriors" holiday dinner in December 2002, David surprised Daniel with a "True Grit" award for his perseverance and courage. "Life has challenged Daniel with many hardships, but Daniel's determination and drive have allowed him to fight and continue to conquer whatever life's next challenges may be," David read from the special plaque he had crafted for Daniel. Above the words, a dove perched on the blade of a double-edged sword. "All of us at Habitat feel privileged that Daniel is a part of our lives and look forward to many more years of sharing our friendship with this true peaceful warrior."

Instead of heeding the advice of others who cautioned them about liability issues, Connie and David stashed special magnets in various parts of the plant—the refrigerator in the break room, beneath Daniel's work table, in his friend Martin's pocket—in case Daniel had one of his seizures. Daniel's doctors had implanted a Vegal nerve stimulator in his chest to help normalize his brain and slow down the attacks; the device's strength was heightened by swiping one of the small, oval-shaped magnets across his heart. Several Habitat employees, including Martin and Connie, quickly learned how to use the magnets in case of emergency.

They also bought Daniel a bicycle-style helmet to keep him from cracking his head if he did have a seizure and fall. They remembered his penchant for law enforcement, so they glued a police symbol on the side, along with the Habitat logo. But the helmet was uncomfortable and hot, especially on summer days. It also made Daniel stand out from the other employees. No one else wore a protective head covering, and the last thing he wanted was to be different. Many days he argued about it with Connie, but she wouldn't budge. "No, Daniel, you can't work without your helmet," she'd gently but firmly remind him. It was a company rule, she said, and breaking it could prove disastrous for everyone.

To better educate themselves on Daniel's condition and how to handle the seizures and mood swings, David and Connie started attending meetings of the Chattanooga Area Brain Injury Association. At the first gathering, people who had sustained brain injuries, and their parents and caregivers, shared one heartfelt story after another. Many of the tales sounded eerily familiar to Connie and David, and they were touched by the courage of people whose lives had changed radically, often in a single instant. They left with an even clearer perspective of what Daniel had been through and what he continued to battle. In 2002, the Chattanooga Area Brain Injury Association awarded David its annual Public Service Award for his support of people like Daniel.

None of this, unfortunately, stopped Daniel's seizures, which were caused by scar tissue from all the surgeries and usually came with no warning at all. He could be anywhere when it happened—at the cutting table, in the office, in the car on the way home. During an episode, his lips turned dark, he convulsed, and his body jerked uncontrollably. Connie or Martin or one of the other employees would hold Daniel close while someone else grabbed a magnet and some blankets to make him more comfortable when he woke up. When he finally came to, he couldn't remember the seizure at all. Afterward, he'd have to take two or three days off from work to recover, sometimes sleeping for 24 hours after an episode.

Eventually the seizures became much more common, with Daniel sometimes sustaining two or three in one day. "Connie, Daniel's having one!" was a frequent call from the plant floor. The attacks had happened so often by now that the other employees no longer feared them, and they knew what to do when one started, but even Connie and David had to admit it was just too risky, especially for Daniel, to keep him at Habitat. In September 2003, Daniel underwent his 10th surgery, this one to halt the life-threatening seizures. When he healed enough to get out of the house, Sherry sometimes took him to Habitat to have lunch with David or hang out with Connie. He was, after all, a part of the Habitat family. And he always would be.

Twelve

Doing Well By Doing Good

B Y THE MID-1990S, Habitat had become an industry force to be reckoned with. The Beaulieu partnership, in which Habitat bought its roll goods from the Dalton carpet giant and Beaulieu closed its rug-cutting division to shift that labor-intensive task to Habitat, had paid off for both companies. Thanks to more than a half dozen expansions, the 9,000-square-foot former chicken hatchery in Rossville, Georgia, now spanned 42,000 square feet. And more than 1 million Habitat rugs and golf putting greens were now selling each year in stores across the U.S., Canada, Europe, Asia, and South America.

The success of the company, of course, could be chalked up in part to the shrewd business sense and marketing savvy of its gutsy owners. When they launched the company in 1981, David and Saul had made a pact to keep themselves out of debt, and they never reneged on that vow. Even when they invested in new equipment or structural renovations, they quickly paid off the bank notes. They handled their bills with the same professionalism, paying invoices not just on time, but early, a practice that strengthened their working relationships and negotiating power with vendors. In spite of the less-than-desirable layout of the Rossville building, the plant ran smoothly and orders were filled on time. And the lack of corporate bureaucracy made it easy to implement change. More than once, Habitat's top-heavy competitors were still waiting to get an idea approved months after David and Jim had already introduced a new marketing strategy or product display. Even more impressive was Habitat's ability to meet with a buyer on Monday

117

and be able to follow up with concrete product samples on Tuesday. It was enough to make a rival's head spin.

One of the main reasons for Habitat's enviable position in the carpet industry, of course, wasn't as apparent to outsiders, or as measurable to the bean counters. Despite their creativity, knowledge of the industry, and knack for making quick decisions, David and Saul knew that the real key to their success was the people who helped make it all happen. Habitat's unique workforce had become not just a team that pulled together to get the work done, but a family of people who looked out for each other off the job too. In stark contrast to many of the larger manufacturers, whose employees never veered from their own workstations, everyone in the Habitat plant, including the managers, was cross-trained on every task. David was often seen driving a forklift. Connie and Jim never hesitated to cut carpet alongside the other employees. Over there was Saul, organizing boxes of rugs for shipment to the mass merchandisers. The cross-training approach served another purpose as well. David knew for a fact that if he stood in one place all day, working on one task without being allowed to vary his routine or have any fun, he'd go bonkers. Why should he expect his workers to be any different?

There was also no reason to implement a formal quality-control program at Habitat. With Terry Davis pointing out co-workers who were goofing off, Martin Arney refusing to hear the word "can't," and Sharon Adams teaching new hires how to be quick and accurate, who needed to nudge the employees to stay on course or watch for errors? It just came naturally.

The number of employees gradually increased over the years, from a handful in the early days to about 70 by the mid-1990s. The majority had a disability of some sort, and sometimes more than one. During slow years, when Habitat lost an account or orders slacked off, David and Saul refused to lay any of them off. Even when times were lean and they were forced to grapple with ways to save money, letting employees go was simply out of the question. "You can't play God with other people's lives," they agreed. "They've still got to put food on their tables, just like we do. And besides, they're family. How can we fire our own family just because profits are not as strong as last year's?" Time after time, they stuck to their convictions and when necessary, trimmed expenses, pounded the pavement for new accounts, and devised ways to out-market their competitors—whatever it took to keep their workers busy and taking home a paycheck each week. No matter what, the employees came first. Not surprisingly, there was always a waiting list of people, both disabled and not, who wanted to work at Habitat.

The employees, of course, benefited from the fierce loyalty of business owners who kept their welfare at heart. But David and Saul, perhaps, reaped even more. They had undergone tremendous personal growth since they opened the tiny office in East Ridge, Tennessee, in 1981. Saul, the suit-and-tie salesman who had resisted the prospect of bringing the first mentally challenged clients into the plant, had learned that in business, it's people, not money, that matter most. And David, the painfully shy boy who fled from conflict as a child, was now willing to do battle with anyone who didn't respect his disabled workers. Like many of the employees, he had also emerged from his protective shell and become a more affectionate, outgoing person. He had always hated the selling aspect of his business, but now that he had a philosophy—not just a product—to sell, all that had changed. He just couldn't seem to stop telling the Habitat story.

Even so, when David was asked to run in the Olympic torch relay in the spring of 1996, Habitat was still keeping a low profile in the Chattanooga-north Georgia community, just as it had for the previous 15 years. Since Habitat was a business-to-business supplier, not a retailer selling goods directly to the end user, there was no need to advertise in consumer publications or on TV or radio. Many area residents were totally unaware of the company's socially conscious hiring practices. Even Connie had lived in the community for 10 years before she learned about Habitat through her role as a job coach at the Walker County Training Center. Some of the company's buyers and retail customers still didn't know. And David and Saul had deliberately shied away from reporters.

Wary of drawing attention to Habitat for fear the journalists would portray their employees as weak and dependent, and the public would feel sorry for them, they had shrugged off all requests for media interviews. Even though times were changing and people with disabilities had become more visible as front-of-store greeters and busboys, there was still a stigma associated with having Down syndrome or schizophrenia or cerebral palsy. "Oh, those poor people," some visitors said when they met Habitat's special workers. "Look at that pitiful retarded person over there. Look at that poor kid in the wheelchair." Others praised David and Saul for supporting such a "charitable" cause, oblivious to the fact that the employees with disabilities were just that: real employees, earning real wages, week in and week out. Acquaintances often assumed that Habitat hired people with mental and physical challenges because they could be paid less than their "normal" counterparts, thereby reducing labor costs. David and the other managers rolled their eyes each time they heard that one. Many of the employees with disabilities actually earned *more* than their able-bodied co-workers and, like everyone else, were awarded regular raises through hard work, ambition, and commitment to the company.

But David couldn't shield himself from the press forever. In 1996, when the Olympic committee invited him to represent the Summer Games in Knoxville, Tennessee, they gave one stipulation: David was required to answer the media's questions and allow reporters to follow along on his torchbearer journey.

When she heard that a local hero would carry the torch, a feature writer for the *Chattanooga Free Press*, the city's evening paper, called David about writing an article. "I'll agree to the interview, under one condition," he told her, mindful of his promise to the Olympic Committee, but even more aware of his commitment to the Habitat employees. "You have to focus mostly on the people here, not me and my torch run. And you can't portray them as pitiful or as people who need sympathy. If you can't assure me of that, then I can't agree to the story."

"No problem," she said.

On May 12, Jan Galletta's story ran on Page 1 of the newspaper's "Weekend" section with a headline that read, "People Are Its Most Important Products." Eight color photographs depicted the employees at work, rest, and play. There was Lincoln, broadcasting factory bulletins from the in-house radio station. And Jason, proudly wearing his Habitat t-shirt. And Martin, sizing pieces of grass carpet for golf putting greens. It was difficult, if not impossible, to detect their bipolar disorder and autism and cerebral palsy just by looking at the pictures. And that suited David just fine.

He soon discovered that his fear of media scrutiny had been unnecessary. The response from the local community was overwhelmingly positive, and the coverage only accelerated the bond between Habitat's socially conscious business partners and the "kids" who worked there. Some asked, "Why didn't you tell us before? This is great!" A Kmart buyer started hanging around to shoot hoops with the Habitat guys on the in-house basketball court. A local Coca-Cola distributor donated a case of sodas for the company picnic. "No, you don't have to do this," David protested when he heard about the Cokes. "We're a for-profit business. You need to give these to the non-profit agencies, not us."

"Well, you guys are doing a good thing," the distributor replied. "And besides, you're helping these people earn money so they can be productive citizens and buy our products just like everyone else. The way we see it, you're doing us a favor. And we want to show our appreciation."

Before long, one of David's retail contacts was encouraging him to tout the Habitat story on the company's rug boxes. "But isn't that a bit much?" he asked. Saul thought so too. "Won't that exploit the people with disabilities? Won't customers think we're using that as a ploy to get people to buy our products?"

"Absolutely not," replied the customer. "David, what you're doing is so rare. The public needs to know about this. They need to know it can be done."

David and Saul did a lot of soul-searching. *Maybe, just maybe,* they thought, *our message will reach another business owner out there and light a fire under him to do the same thing. Maybe somebody with a disability will get a job who never had one before.* They agreed to give it a try, and before long, added a "Did You Know?" message to the side of each boxed product sold under the Habitat brand. Now, when a homeowner bought a 6' x 8' grass rug, she could also read about the company's inspiring workforce:

"At Habitat International, Inc., people make the difference—"special" people, that is. The people are special because most are disabled in various ways.

"For years, Habitat has employed the mentally challenged. And, in recent years, the company has added to its crew of workers the physically challenged, the mentally ill, recovering alcoholics, the brain injured, and those with autism.

"Habitat has shown that these special people, when treated with dignity and given a real chance to develop job skills, return valuable assets: superior workmanship, team spirit, loyalty. And those assets are not all they return: they touch the hearts of the 'normal' people at Habitat and inspire tolerance and genuine caring.

"Habitat encourages individuals, businesses, and communities everywhere to do likewise. The returns are the difference the special people make."

The *Chattanooga Free Press* article had also created a ripple effect, triggering subsequent stories in *Southern Living, Nation's Business*, and other high-profile magazines. A local cable talk show invited David to speak on the program, and a CNN film crew drove up from Atlanta to shoot a short documentary about Habitat. The employees with disabilities beamed when they spotted their names in print or saw themselves on television; in the supermarket, they often approached people they didn't know, told them about the stories, and proudly offered to sign autographs. David couldn't help but grin at the sight of Terry Davis, the jovial young man with Down syndrome who had far exceeded the expectations of his special-ed teachers, or Daniel, the courageous worker who had sustained a life-altering brain injury, drawing a curious crowd at the newsstand. In the main hallway of Ridgeland High School, Terry's alma mater, the special-ed students hung a huge color copy of an article that showed them playing pool with the other Habitat workers at break time. "Hey, you may be in the newspaper all the time," they teased the school's macho football players. "But we're in *Southern Living.*"

Letters poured in from all over the country, and the feedback from readers outside the community was almost overpowering. Disability advocates from across the U.S. commended David and the other Habitat managers for their support of special-needs workers. Business owners were curious about their "trade secret." Parents of grown children with disabilities called from as far away as California and Maine. "How can I find a company like Habitat near me?" they asked. "Where can my son find work like this in our town? Why don't more business people do what you're doing?" Like many parents who had struggled to help their children find meaningful work before they were hired at Habitat, they too worried their kids might never find acceptance in the business world. They wanted nothing more than a few words of reassurance from someone who understood.

"In a time like now, especially, it helps one so much to read about people like you," wrote a psychotherapist in Arkansas, also the mother of a daughter with mental retardation. "Thank you, David, for taking a chance and for listening to your heart!"

"I would like to commend you on the work you are doing for special-needs people," penned a Rhode Island woman seeking information to help start a support group for parents of children with learning disabilities and autism.

"We wish to give you accolades for all you do! If more businesses followed your leadership, the world would be a better place!" wrote the executive director of a Texas residential community for adults with functional disabilities.

"David Morris is a hero because he views 'the people no one else wants to hire' as able, not disabled," an Indiana professor said in a published letter to the editor of *Southwest Airlines Spirit* magazine, which ran a profile of David and Habitat. "His insight [into] the abilities of the special-needs population has brought business success and proven business acumen."

The vice president of a Baltimore medical company sent David a letter about his brother, a former senior nuclear safety engineer suffering from epilepsy and the early onset of Alzheimer's. According to the letter writer, his sibling could no longer "hold a job as a stock clerk at a grocery store or at the front desk at the local gym...Because there are no people like you in our area, he is forced to take odd jobs without security and rely upon my mother and me for help. What you have done for similar people is both good for your business and for people like my brother; it gives them the pride of a job well done and regular income."

Each time a new magazine story came out, the Habitat mailbox bulged with letters and the phones rang off the hook. For weeks, David did little else but return calls and answer written requests for more information. But he didn't mind. At times, he even regretted he hadn't consented to media interviews 10 years earlier. Maybe he could have hired more people with disabilities. Perhaps he could have spurred other business owners to do the same thing. Then again, he wondered, would readers and viewers and listeners have so readily accepted the idea of hiring special-needs workers back then? A decade can make a big difference when it comes to social change and awareness. Maybe this was happening at just the right time.

Habitat's newfound exposure also triggered an enormous response from the national business community. Human resources directors called for advice on how to set up their own disability-hiring programs. Out-of-town entrepreneurs flew in to tour the north Georgia plant and see its unparalleled workforce firsthand. David even received complimentary letters from customers he hadn't heard from in years. And executives from big-name retailers lauded the example set by David, Saul, and their employees.

"The greatest thing that we as human beings can do is to add meaning and value to each other's lives. You have certainly done that," wrote a former competitor. "I want to personally thank you for caring enough about people to see past their difficulties and emphasize their abilities. Thanks for giving good people a chance."

"As I have known for a long time, you are a shining example of what

people should be," wrote the marketing director of a large home im-
provement retailer. "Your courage in offering opportunities to those who
may not otherwise receive them is highly commendable. You give our
industry a great example of leadership into those areas often ignored."

One of the most heartfelt compliments came from a high-ranking
executive at Beaulieu of America, the carpet Goliath that had previously
been a competitive threat and was now a "partner" of Habitat: "I admire
tremendously what yourself, your father, and your management team
have been able to create and achieve and I am proud to be able to call
you not only a business associate but a friend."

Before long, David and the other Habitat managers were being asked
to speak to disability, business, healthcare, education, and civic groups
throughout the country. David delivered speeches at Chamber of Commerce and Kiwanis Club meetings. He and Connie were asked to serve
on the Governor's Committee on Disabilities, and they helped lead state
and federal disability-hiring seminars. At Constitution Hall in Fort
Oglethorpe, Georgia, Connie sat at a long conference table, next to her
former co-workers from the state, and fielded questions from parents.
As always, the audience wanted to know: "How does the program work
at Habitat? How can my daughter get a job there? Do you know of anyone else who hires people with disabilities?"

In neighboring Southeastern states, the University of Tennessee at
Knoxville and Virginia Commonwealth University in Richmond were
conducting a joint study on people with disabilities in the workforce. The
researchers wanted David to be the closing speaker at a conference at the
UT campus in Knoxville. In the audience would be dozens, maybe even
hundreds, of state agency employees—the very people who, in David's
opinion, often underestimated their own clients and tried to make them
adhere to placement guidelines that restricted their progress. They, most
of all, were the ones who needed to know just how far the employees with
disabilities could go if their wings weren't clipped. *These people don't need
to just hear my story*, David thought to himself as he made plans for his
speech. *They need to hear it from somebody else.* So he decided to ask one
of his disabled employees to accompany him to Knoxville.

Johnny K. was a tall, lanky young man with dark wavy hair and a
natural curiosity about the world around him. His developmental disabilities stemmed from malnutrition caused by a lack of food when he
was a baby. He had subsequently been removed from his birth mother's
home, placed in foster care, and later adopted by his loving foster parents. Johnny was highly emotional and slow at times, but very smart. At

Habitat, he had excelled on the cutting table and had become one of the star disc jockeys for the in-house radio station.

At the symposium, David took his seat on a stage high above the crowd. When it was his turn, he spoke for only about 10 minutes, first sharing Habitat's history, then urging the state attendees to stop classifying people with disabilities and holding them back from their true potential. "One of the problems is the bureaucracy of state programs," David said, not afraid to scold the workshop participants if that's what it took to get their attention. "You've got to see these people as people, not numbers. And Johnny here is one of the people I'm extremely proud of. He's not Number 202 or 203. He's Johnny. He's done a great job and he's really grown. Now I'm going to step back and let him tell you about his experience at Habitat, in his own words."

Johnny carefully made his way to a table jammed with microphones. He looked wide-eyed, almost frozen, like a deer caught in the headlights of an oncoming car, and his hands were shaking. As soon as he touched the mike, he started to cry, not softly, but in loud, heart-rending sobs. The audience members quietly waited for him to regain his composure. Some sat spellbound. Others shifted nervously in their seats. "Sorry," Johnny finally said, pulling himself together. "I've never given a speech before.

"I just want to thank David for giving me a chance to work at Habitat," he began. "I never thought I could do this. I was always told 'no.' This has been a great opportunity for me and it has shown me just how much I can achieve." Then he paused, fighting back more tears. "You guys need to listen to me. If you just give people like me a chance, if you stop trying to tell us what we can't do, we can do anything. You'll see."

By the time he had finished with his remarks, even the participants who'd been fidgeting uncomfortably at first were drying their eyes. "Oh, and there's one more thing," Johnny added. "I have one more thing to say."

He looked at David, then at the sea of faces below him, then back at David. "Do you agree that I'm a hard worker, that I do a good job?" David groaned. His instincts told him Johnny was about to put him on the spot. "Yes, Johnny," he answered. "You work very hard."

Johnny turned away from David to focus again on the audience. "Well then. Don't you all think I deserve a raise?" The participants stopped dabbing their eyes and grinned at Johnny. They laughed and nodded their heads. Then Johnny handed the microphone back to his boss amid loud applause. David gulped. Once again, he had underestimated one of his favorite employees.

Not every presentation invoked tears, nor was it designed to jolt the audience out of complacency. In fact, because David and the other managers spoke from the heart and not from prepared speeches, each lecture was different. Connie preferred to respond to questions from the audience. David was the visionary motivator who talked in generalities, while Jim filled in the blanks with important details. Sometimes they tag-teamed the speeches; on other occasions they attended a meeting solo or with one of their most productive, disabled employees. When they talked to educators or parents or state agency workers, they discovered a captive audience of people tackling similar issues. Sometimes they even found themselves preaching to the choir. Speaking to business executives, however, was much, much tougher.

When he first began lecturing to other entrepreneurs, David tried to appeal to their generosity by urging them to "do the right thing" and help others less fortunate. "If you hire one, just one, disabled person," he told them, "you can help break down the walls of prejudice and fear." Unfortunately, the "right thing" approach was frequently met with blank stares. But when he changed his tactic and started showing them how they could improve their company's profits, they sat up and paid attention. "Look, this is not a charity. If you want a charity project, take out your checkbook and send a donation to your favorite non-profit cause," he told his peers in the business community. "What I'm talking about is hiring people who care about their work and have a good attitude, who make few, if any, mistakes, and who are willing to get the job done no matter what. It's a win-win situation. This *will* improve your bottom line, and the reason is simple: if you encourage teamwork, if you help your employees become more productive, if they feel good about what they're doing, you will in essence be building a company where everyone profits. *They* benefit by having real jobs rather than sitting at home, and *you* benefit because there is so little absenteeism, turnover, and general laziness. Besides, how many business people can walk out of their offices and into a place where they're greeted with smiles and hugs from people who want nothing more than to make them look good? There's an able workforce out there with all of these qualities, just waiting for you to hire them."

One day in the summer of 1998 David received a call from a San Francisco-based organization called Business for Social Responsibility. He had never heard of the group before, so he didn't think much about it when the caller asked him to speak at their fifth annual BSR conference in Boston that November. "Sure," he said without hesitation. At that point, he wasn't about to turn down an opportunity to share his message with a few other business people. Several days later a packet of background materials arrived in the mail. *Whoa!* David thought as he sifted through the brochures. BSR, it turned out, was a 1,200-member national association known for initiatives that improved the environment, the community, workplace policies, human rights, and business values. David scanned the rest of the pamphlet and noticed that the member companies included heavy hitters like AT&T, Ford Motor Co., and one of his own retail outlets, the Home Depot. There, at the top of the list of directors, was Ray Anderson, chairman of Atlanta-based Interface, Inc., one of the nation's top floor-covering manufacturers and a leader in the growing "green" movement. *Small world*, David thought. *Here's somebody else in the industry who's trying to make a difference in the world, and he's just down the road from us.*

But it wasn't until David arrived in Boston and glanced at the printed program that he realized just how important this conference might be. There, under the listing for his own breakout session, "Integrating Disabled Individuals into the Workplace," and other workshops led by executives from mega-bucks corporations like Coca-Cola and smaller humanitarian businesses like Yonkers-based Greyston Bakery, was the name of that night's guest speaker: former Israeli prime minister Shimon Peres. *I'm speaking the same day as a Nobel Peace Prize winner?* he thought. *Now that's pressure.* For the first time since he'd started lecturing, David was nervous. In fact, he was pretty darn overwhelmed.

David was scheduled to speak on Day Two of the conference, so he spent the first one floating from workshop to workshop and absorbing as much as he could from the other lectures. He took notes and tried to figure out what he'd say to reporters if they asked him a question. Then he did something completely out of character. He wrote a speech.

On the morning of David's session, he stepped to the podium, surveyed the crowd, and took a deep breath. Then he set down what he'd written. "I prepared a cheat sheet," he told the audience. "But I've changed my mind. I'm better at expressing what's in my heart.

"I've never been this nervous in my life," he continued. "It's a real honor for me to be in the presence of such highly respected, socially responsible business people. There's no way I can top what you all have said, so I won't even try. All I can do is tell you about my small manufacturing company in Rossville, Georgia. The reason we've been so successful is quite simple, really: I hire the people no one else wants to hire." For 90 minutes, David talked about his special workers, what they meant to him, and how they had made Habitat much more competitive than it otherwise would have been. He fielded tough queries from other entrepreneurs who wanted to know how they could make this happen at their own companies. "Doesn't this require a lot of extra work for an employer?" they asked. "Won't we lose money if we hire people with disabilities? Won't they hurt our business in the long run?" Each time, David assured them that nothing was farther from the truth. When the session was over, they gave him a standing ovation.

Afterward, journalists from high-profile newspapers and magazines crowded around him, firing more questions: "What statistics can you give to support what you do? Exactly how many American people with disabilities are out of work? In specific numbers, how do your revenues stack up against a company that doesn't hire the disabled?"

David grinned. "Like I said in my presentation, I speak from the heart, and from years of experience," he replied matter-of-factly. "I'm not a statistics person. It's your job to find the data, not mine."

Back at home, the once low-key rug plant was becoming more visible in its own back yard. For several years, Habitat had been hosting tour groups from the local community, but the demand had increased after David's Olympic torch run and the notoriety that came with it. The interest wasn't just coming from northwest Georgia, either. After the stories came out, manufacturing supervisors and plant managers from across the U.S. began calling David to set up private tours. So did representatives from non-profit employment agencies, who wanted to see how people with disabilities could be hired outright, without government grants or other corporate incentives. Schoolteachers brought in their curious colleagues and showed them around.

It was fun to watch the reactions of first-time visitors, who knew very little about Habitat beyond what they'd read in the articles. First came the dropped jaws and gaping mouths, particularly when guests saw the crazy artwork and the radio station and basketball court. Then came the disbelief. "But everyone's working so hard here, and they're smiling," they'd say as if they had just seen the real Santa Claus. "And where are the managers? Don't these people need constant supervision?" And always, always, there were sighs. "The people in my plant don't smile like this. And they never walk up and shake my hand or ask me how I'm doing. What's your secret?"

"You're lookin' at 'em," David would say. "They know what needs to be done, and they do it."

Each year since 1994, Melinda Wallins Lemmon, executive director of

the Catoosa County (Georgia) Development Authority, had been bringing leadership groups to Habitat, but the company's media exposure
had made it even more desirable as a role model for other businesses.
Here was living proof that hiring people with disabilities could, and did,
work. For Melinda, demonstrating this concept to others was a personal
goal. Her mother, who had been born with a hearing impairment, had
earned a graduate degree and become one of the most respected trail-
blazers in her community.

Glenn Vaughn also had an ulterior motive for signing up for a leadership tour. The retired air traffic controller was an active Chamber of
Commerce board member, and his wife, Kaye, was president. They were
both politically ambitious and ran for public offices at different times.
Glenn also knew there was a shortage of workers in Catoosa County,
and this was one way to put an underutilized segment of the population
to work. But it wasn't the business tie that intrigued him. The connection was much more human than that.

The Vaughns' 7-year-old granddaughter, Jessica, had been born with a
severe visual impairment, autism, and other developmental challenges.
For years, Glenn, Kaye, and Jessica's mother had dealt with state and
federal programs supposedly designed to help people like Jessica. But
so far they had found all the paperwork and bureaucracy and misguided
intentions more frustrating than useful. Even worse, when the resources
actually trickled down to the people they were meant to help, it seemed
as if they had all but dried up. Glenn was amazed at how Habitat had
managed to bypass all the bureaucratic nonsense, resist the temptation
to accept government subsidies, and hire people with all types of challenges. Here was a productive, profitable company owned by good people
who gave others a chance simply because they wanted to, not for glory
or greed. And it had paid off for them in more ways than one. Throughout the tour, David stopped to introduce various members of his staff
and share their personal success stories—how long they had worked at
Habitat, what tasks they were best at, the difficulties they had overcome,
how they had struggled to become independent and won. Here was the
owner of a multi-million-dollar corporation, mingling with his employees, remembering details about them, and actually caring. It was obvious
that they loved him too. Glenn could see it in their faces as soon as their
boss walked up and draped his arm across their shoulders.

He was so impressed with David that he nominated him for the
Olympic torch run.

At the end of each tour, David encouraged the local business executives—mostly bankers and insurance agents and small-business entrepreneurs—to hire people with disabilities. "These are good workers," he'd say. "You just saw them for a few minutes, but they're like this every day. I realize that some of you may have fears or reservations about hiring people with Down syndrome or autism or some type of mental illness. But believe me, even though you might have to make an accommodation here and there, your fears are mostly unfounded. Tell you what—if you want to employ some of my workers, that's fine with me. That'll give them an opportunity to move up in the world, and it'll give me a chance to take on some more severely challenged employees and work with them, get them trained and confident about their own job skills. Then after a while, they'll also be ready to work at your offices, factories, and stores."

Every now and then a visitor would express skepticism or discomfort with the unusual workforce at Habitat, but for the most part, the reactions, including the written evaluations from local leadership groups, were extremely positive. Some business guests even left the building super-charged about starting their own disability-hiring programs. Despite their good intentions, however, most never did. A few actually tried, but failed. Some couldn't move past the liability issues or the fear that the workers couldn't keep up, and in some cases the human resources or public relations departments nixed the idea. Even Beaulieu's attempt to hire people with disabilities didn't work out. But David reminded himself that if his message showed one employer how to be more open to workers with challenges, if it helped one person with disabilities be regarded with more respect or eventually get a job, the payoff would have been well worth the effort.

It had been several years since David and Connie bucked the system and hired the first disabled clients from the Walker County Training Center. New personnel were coming on board at the agency, and the goals of its managers seemed more closely aligned with Habitat's. The tension between Habitat and the state of Georgia was finally waning; David had even been asked to help government officials set up a disability employment committee. And thanks to the media coverage, the on-site tours, and the speeches, the company now held a more prominent place in the community. It had earned the respect of its business peers, many of whom had previously shunned the offbeat rug factory with the weird sculptures in the parking lot.

In 1996, Habitat began receiving awards for its dedication to hiring people with disabilities. First came the Catoosa County Chamber of Commerce's O. Wayne Rollins Entrepreneur Award, given to Habitat for its strong support of special-needs workers. The award was named for the Catoosa County native who rose from meager beginnings as a poor textile mill worker to found Orkin Exterminating Company, Inc. and ultimately become a wealthy philanthropist. In 1997, Habitat was named Employer of the Year by the Tri-State Council on Disabilities, a non-profit consortium of business people from Catoosa, Walker, and Dade counties in northwest Georgia. Again in 2000 and 2002, Habitat would earn the group's Employer of the Year distinction, and in 2000 the organization named Martin Arney, the hard-working young man with cerebral palsy, Employee of the Year.

In 1998, an article about Habitat in *Nation's Business* won a prestigious Easter Seals Equality, Dignity, Independence (EDI) award for "raising awareness of disability issues and encouraging realistic portrayals of people with disabilities." That fall, David accepted the glass obelisk trophy at a gala awards ceremony in New York alongside winners from *Dateline NBC*, *Newsweek*, and other top media outlets. The same article resulted in a Blue Chip Enterprise Award from MassMutual and the U.S. Chamber of Commerce. Each time Habitat won an award, David shared the good news with an "atta boy" memo to all his employees, thanking them for making the company such a success.

Despite the prestige of the national awards, and the glamorous ceremonies that came with them, the honor that meant the most to David came from the state of Georgia, where for years officials had warned him he could never run a competitive business with full-time, disabled workers. Melinda Wallins Lemmon, the economic developer who arranged the annual leadership tours at Habitat, was so touched by what she'd seen at the plant, year after year, that in 2001 she nominated the company for an Existing Industry Appreciation Award from the Georgia Economic Developers Association (GEDA). For Melinda, there was never a question of who the candidate should be. The 1,100-member organization apparently agreed. "Your investment of dollars and resources in physical and human capital show uncommon leadership in bettering the quality of life in your community, region, and state," wrote the GEDA president, David Luckie, in a letter of congratulations.

At the awards luncheon in April, David stepped up to the podium at the Georgia World Congress Center, surveyed the packed audience, and proudly received the top honor in the small-manufacturer category. Cullen Larson, GEDA's executive director, praised Habitat for consistently giving traditional jobs to non-traditional workers: "This is proof that, with the right commitment and people, no matter what their challenges, a company can be as productive as any other, and maybe even more so." *Finally*, David thought to himself as he held the plaque high in the air. *We are accepted in our own community. And it only took 20 years.*

Habitat's good karma didn't stop with the publicity or the awards or the company's status as a model for other businesses. Ironically, one of its greatest financial rewards came in May 2002, at a time when some of Habitat's over-extended competitors were still suffering from the aftermath of 9/11. Corporations across the U.S. were being forced to shut down, lay off workers or, at the very least, restructure the way they did business. But David and Saul, now semi-retired from the family enterprise and spending much of his time in Florida, had steadfastly stuck by their debt-free philosophy. That wise decision had cushioned them against financial loss, even when the company's growth stalled in the economic downturn in 2001. While other rug manufacturers were trimming their expenditures to the bare bones and letting good workers go, Habitat was still going strong.

And David and Jim hadn't let up on their aggressive marketing. In the spring of 2002, they and one of their sales representatives, Chuck Gearhart, prepared to bid on a major account for Lowe's, a national home-improvement chain with dense clusters of stores east of the Mississippi River. For several years, Habitat had been invited to make annual presentations to the Lowe's buyers, a requisite for landing some of the company's 850 retail outlets. So far they'd finagled about $1 million a year in spring and back-to-school promotions of boxed grass rugs, but a couple of large competitors still held a monopoly on the permanent 8-foot displays of ready-to-go carpet. In spite of their ambition and go-getter attitudes, and a track record of slaying giants, David and Jim went to each presentation knowing the odds were stacked against them. Habitat was miniscule compared to most of the other manufacturers vying for the account, and it didn't look like the big boys were going to be pushed aside anytime soon.

Still, when it was time for the annual bidding process to begin in 2002, David and Jim created a knockout display, complete with rugs, labels, and signs, exactly as it would appear in the store. They would, as usual, go to the meeting at Lowe's corporate headquarters in North Carolina with a healthy balance of optimism and realistic expectations.

Maybe the presentation would, at the very least, help solidify their seasonal promotions for another year. Who knows? They might even win a handful of Lowe's stores on a year-round basis.

On the day of the final presentation, David, Jim, and Chuck Gearhart, the sales rep, met with Chris Williams, the buyer for Lowe's, and several of Chris's colleagues. Habitat's proposal called for a single bay with three types of rugs—grass, needlepunch, and carpet remnants—so that a customer who wanted a low-priced item could choose from several types in a one-stop-shopping display. None of the other candidates had presented such an innovative concept, and the buyers seemed impressed, even remarking out loud on the attractive design and the smart approach of the packaging. When David and Jim had finished their pitch and the buyers had exhausted all of their questions, Chris asked David to spend a few minutes sharing the Habitat story with the other representatives from Lowe's. "I think they should know what your company does," Chris told him. "Not just what you produce, but who does it."

Not one to pass up an opportunity to brag on his employees, David gladly described his special workforce and their role in helping his company prosper. As they filed out of the meeting, David whispered to Jim and Chuck, "I thought it went well. Maybe we'll get a few of the stores after all."

On May 31, the Friday after Memorial Day, David's secretary patched in a call from Chuck. "Are you sitting down?" asked the sales rep when David picked up the phone. "David, you got the account."

"That's great, Chuck," David replied. "How many stores—50? 100? 200?"

"No, David, you don't understand. I mean all the stores," Chuck said, barely able to curb his excitement. "Habitat has won all 850 Lowe's stores.

"Of course that's the good news," he added. "The bad news is you're gonna have to work like banshees to fill all these orders." David almost fell out of his chair.

He would never admit it, of course, but David, Jim, and Chuck suspected the buyer had harbored a soft spot in his heart for Habitat and its innovative hiring practices. Out in the plant, David made the announcement to the employees. "We won this because of who you are," he told them. "It's because they appreciate what you're doing." To remind them of the windfall they had received in the middle of a national economic slump, David hung signs throughout the plant that read "The Year of the Lowe's." That Christmas, in addition to the heftiest bonuses they'd ever earned, the employees would also receive Lowe's gift cards. The new account was worth about $5 million in annual revenues, and the Habitat management did, after all, believe in giving back.

Chuck was right. The Habitat employees would have to hustle to meet the demands of stocking 850 Lowe's outlets. There was no time to ship the products to the retailer's distribution centers, as was customary; that process would have to come later. For now, the orders would go directly to each store—signs, display cartons, and all. The employees were so proud of the company's coup that they offered to work weekends to get the job done. With smiles on their faces, they quickly cranked out the first order of 80,000 rugs, as many as Habitat had produced in an entire year when the company started.

With this much new business, however, Habitat needed more people. In the late 1990s, Connie had started volunteering at the local Community Kitchen and its adjoining homeless shelter, and she'd shrewdly noted the Kitchen's convenient access to a nearby temporary labor agency. Many of the shelter's staff members already knew about Habitat's atypical hiring practices and had taken vanloads of homeless people to Habitat's summer picnics. So they quickly agreed that if any of their clients were employed at Habitat, they would provide transportation. "Hey, David," Connie asked when it was time to bring in more help to fill the Lowe's orders. "Why don't we funnel some of this work to the people down at the shelter?" Before long, homeless temps were running the entire shipping department at Habitat.

Like the employees with disabilities, the homeless workers were used to being stereotyped. And like their disabled counterparts, they promptly blew all those misconceptions out of the water. Each day, the hard-working temps reported to the staffing agency by 5 A.M., rode the van to the Rossville plant, and, once there, began loading a dozen tractor-trailer trucks by hand. If an order wasn't quite right, if a label had been inadvertently pasted upside down or a box top had been torn, they either corrected the mistake or brought it to the attention of Connie or Sandra.

David knew there was always a risk in hiring them, just as there had been with the disabled employees. Some were a bit rough around the edges, and a few were angry at the world. But when they realized they were being treated like real people, not like misfits or bums, most of them relaxed. Something else happened too. Without even trying, the employees with disabilities motivated the homeless temps to do their best. It was next to impossible, after all, to feel sorry for yourself while working next to someone who had sustained a brain injury or been born with mental retardation. Both segments of the population had often been stereotyped as apathetic or lazy, or worse. Here at Habitat, both had been given a break. And both were knocking the socks off the competition.

Thanks in large part to the new Lowe's account, Habitat enjoyed its largest growth spurt ever in 2002. By the end of 2003, sales had tripled. And the consistency of the orders had helped stabilize Habitat's revenue, even as other U.S. manufacturers struggled to make a profit and retain enough good, loyal workers to keep them afloat.

The company's good fortune also created a ripple effect for other regional businesses. New partnerships began to take shape, and existing ones were strengthened as Habitat won over new customers and suppliers with their pricing, quality, and commitment to the special workforce. The more open Habitat became about its unorthodox hiring practices, the more other companies wanted to do business with them. In an unusual partnership with another former competitor, Habitat began contracting the manufacture of remnant rugs to Chicago-based Jefferson Industries and the firm's 140-employee rug plant in Chatsworth, Georgia. Just as the labor-intensive cutting and packaging hadn't been a good fit for Beaulieu's operations, the sewing and binding of remnant rugs didn't work well at Habitat.

There was only one problem with all this success: Habitat had completely outgrown its space at the Rossville location. In October 2003, after 17 years at the revamped chicken hatchery, the company moved its operations to a much newer building in Chattanooga, placing it just a mile off busy Interstate 75, doubling the size of the plant and boosting production from 5,000 rugs a day to 12,000. Gone were the chopped-up rooms, awkward loading docks, and narrow driveway of the old place in Rossville. Here, in this roomier building, the workers and forklifts could move around much more easily, which streamlined production and shipping and boosted employee morale. The move not only enabled Habitat to keep up with the demands of Lowe's, the Home Depot, and other retailers, but it also prompted greater diversification. To complement its new line of steel yard art, the company introduced high-end Giclée printing for professional painters, photographers, and other artists. And Habitat forged a two-way agreement with Millennium Packaging Solutions, a Chattanooga-based division of Georgia Pacific. Habitat bought all its corrugated boxes from Millennium, and Millennium hired

Habitat workers to assemble large oven boxes called "buildups" that protect the appliances during shipment. Like Beaulieu, Millennium was highly automated and could greatly benefit from a hands-on partner like Habitat.

But the greatest advantage of the new, larger facility couldn't be measured in square footage or new innovations, or even the fact that by the end of 2004 annual production had risen to 1.5 million rugs. Here, at this spacious plant, Connie could hire even more people with mental and physical disabilities. David could give more homeless workers a chance. And employees like Terry, Lonnie, and Daniel could keep inspiring others with their persevering attitudes, strong work ethic, and courage. For Habitat, the process of hiring "the people no one else wants to hire," of allowing them to go farther than they ever dreamed, had just begun.

Thirteen

Sharon:
Cinderella

ONCE UPON A TIME there was a beautiful sister, the oldest of four. But there was something different about Sharon, something only the grandmother noticed at first.

If this were a fairytale about Sharon Adams, this is how it might begin. But Sharon's story doesn't necessarily fit the magic fable format. Happy endings, after all, take on different forms, and they don't always include pumpkin carriages and wish-granting godmothers who crystallize out of thin air.

Sharon's disability was so subtle at first that Helen Adams didn't know her child was developing more slowly than she should. Harvey, the girl's father, didn't see it either. One day when Harvey's mother came for a visit, she announced, "There's something wrong. Sharon's not holding her head right."

"I don't see anything," Helen replied. "And besides, I'm sure that all babies aren't exactly alike." It took Helen, a registered dietician, and Harvey, a homebuilder, almost a year to agree that Sharon was slow. It wasn't a physical thing; like many young children, she was so energetic her parents often had trouble chasing her down as she raced through their house in the hills of north Georgia. It was also apparent that Sharon was a perfectionist. After she played with her toys, she neatly stashed them away. Later on, when her sisters Vanessa, Valerie, and Rhonda were born, she put theirs away too. Her room was always the neatest one in the entire house.

But Sharon didn't communicate very well. She had a speech impediment and seemed uncoordinated and awkward when playing with other kids. She tried hard to learn, but for some reason she just couldn't grasp the nuances of the English language, and she showed poor eye-hand coordination. Vanessa was a year younger than Sharon but she seemed far more advanced. So when it was time for Sharon to start first grade, her parents enrolled her in a special school for children with developmental disabilities.

In spite of Helen's objections, school administrators placed her daughter in a class for kids deemed profoundly mentally retarded. Some couldn't talk at all. Others couldn't walk. Some threw temper tantrums. It was obvious that Sharon needed to be with kids who were functioning at a higher level. "You're not being objective," school personnel told Helen. "You're her mother. Of course you think she can do better."

But even the most adamant naysayers soon realized that Sharon had been wrongly pigeonholed. The teacher noticed that the other kids gravitated toward her, not because she shared their level of cognitive ability, but because she was good at mothering them. She wiped their runny noses. She urged them to pick up their toys. When they were unruly, she helped calm them down. Not only was Sharon able to take care of herself, she was capable of caring for others as well. And she did it with grace and ease. To Helen's relief, the administrators moved Sharon up to a more advanced class.

According to the Arc of the United States (originally called the National Association for Retarded Children and later the Association for Retarded Citizens), one in 10 American families is directly affected by mental retardation, and up to 7.5 million people have it. Just under 90 percent will be mildly affected, like Sharon, and slower than average in retaining new information.

Throughout her early childhood, Sharon went to academies for disabled students. But by junior high she was attending special-ed classes at a regular school and eventually graduated from the same high school as Vanessa. Sharon was still quite the perfectionist and she'd get extremely flustered if she couldn't master a word or concept or technique in the classroom. She'd push and push and push herself but sometimes, no matter how hard she tried, she couldn't quite reach her goals.

Despite her disability, Sharon was very, very smart. Her handwriting was impeccable, and she loved to sit and painstakingly form alphabet letters for hours on end, making sure she shaped each one just right.

She learned how to ride a bicycle and became accomplished at maneuvering it on the streets in her neighborhood. To her mother's advantage, she was good with directions and often helped Helen find her way back from a new place they had visited in the car. Sharon's reflexes were sharp as well. "Watch out!" she'd shout if Helen was too distracted to spot a car pulling in front of them. More than once, Helen felt her daughter's ability to pay attention had saved her life.

But the tall, slender girl with the porcelain, caramel skin was painfully shy around other people. This may have been one of the reasons she fit in so well at the Walker County Training Center in north Georgia, where in 1985 she joined the state-funded vocational program and began spending her days assembling ink pens. In those days, the Center's clients weren't allowed to talk to the person sitting at the next station and were expected to focus instead on the work, something Sharon knew how to do very well. What's more, she had inherited her parents' high morals and strong work ethic. When it came to putting together ink pens, she was fast, really fast, and she rarely made a mistake. When she did, she made up her mind that she wouldn't mess up again. Every other week, Sharon received a small check from the state for her work at the Center.

But there was one problem: Sharon could do a lot more.

In 1989, four years after she started working at the Walker County Training Center and two years after the center began transporting clients to area businesses to learn new job skills, Sharon began working at Habitat, not as an employee but as a recipient of state funding. Helen and Harvey were impressed with the company's willingness to host enclaves of people like Sharon and give them a chance. They weren't aware of many businesses that would do that.

Sharon had always been a quick study, so she fared well at Habitat. She went straight to work on the cutting table, fashioning golf putting greens, and as usual, moved as if she had wings on her feet. But she was still shy and reserved. She averted her eyes from people she didn't know and hardly spoke a word except to Becky and Wendy, her closest friends from the center. Particularly self-conscious around men, Sharon would look away or lower her head if David or Jim ventured out to the plant.

After Sharon was hired outright in 1993, along with the rest of her enclave, her Habitat co-workers began noticing changes in her personality. Wendy and Becky remarked on them too. So did Sharon's parents. She was still bashful, and more comfortable with one-on-one conversations than talking in front of a group, but if someone spoke to her, she nodded and smiled. She stood just a bit straighter, like a person who had achieved something important and was proud of it. She even spoke a little more clearly. And she no longer cringed if Jim yelled, "Good morning!" Now she yelled "Good morning!" back.

At the end of her first week on the Habitat payroll, Connie handed Sharon an envelope. It was Sharon's first paycheck. It was from a real company, and it was all hers. Positively giddy, she could hardly keep from jumping up and down. That weekend, she would go shopping with *her own money*.

Sharon was one of the most conscientious workers Habitat had ever hired. She caught on quickly. She was adept at training new hires. And she always tried hard to please. She was also one of the most rapid workers in the plant, often finishing first and out-producing her colleagues. Where Terry's sole speed was *slow*, Sharon could only work *fast*. Connie began testing the mettle of new employees, and those suspected of laziness, by pairing them up at a table with Sharon; if they could move swiftly enough for Sharon *and* live up to her high quality standards, they would do fine. Tammy, a woman with a hearing impairment and a sweet disposition, "apprenticed" under Sharon, and the two became best of friends.

But there was a down side. A stickler for perfection, she was quite the impatient taskmaster when it came to her training techniques. Not everyone could work at Sharon's speed, and that frustrated her. Aggravated, she would accelerate her pace even more, all the while churning out error-free products. Faster and faster she folded the rugs, until her poor co-worker was either exhausted or completely confused. If Connie caught Sharon pushing too hard she would take her aside. "Sharon, this is his first day. You have to be patient with people. Not everyone works as hard or as fast as you do." Sharon didn't deal well with criticism and at first she would cry when Connie corrected her. Later on, as she gained more confidence, the self-pity stopped. If Sharon's friends were standing nearby when she prodded somebody too hard, Connie simply gave Sharon a stern look to calm her down. Connie knew better than to embarrass Sharon in front of other people. One disapproving look was enough.

Sharon's perfectionism worked against her in other ways too, especially when it came to rolling the rugs. Where the other employees might do nothing more than glance at the length of carpet they were rolling, Sharon wasn't happy unless all the edges met with total precision. She was hyper-aware if the carpet didn't line up exactly, and that upset her. The task must be done right or not done at all.

The managers marveled at how Sharon could stay so neat and clean even while leaning against filthy machines that smeared the other workers in dirt and grease. And she never seemed to perspire. They decided to eavesdrop on Sharon and discovered that she had learned how to work so efficiently, and with such a healthy posture, that she didn't have to lean across the equipment to do her work.

Each morning when Sharon arrived she retrieved a broom and swept her work area. She wiped down the break table with a wet paper towel. At lunchtime she wiped it again. Like Sharon's bedroom at home, her space always stayed clean and orderly. Not surprisingly, David's innate sloppiness drove Sharon mad, and vice versa. After a while they began teasing each other, but eventually learned to accept their quirky differences and be friends.

Working in the Habitat factory was never easy, even for the strongest of bodies and minds. It required standing for long periods of time, and completing repetitive tasks in a hot, stuffy building. That kind of labor could take its toll on just about anyone. Not Sharon. She never complained; as a matter of fact, she would do just about anything to avoid missing even one day of work. David refused to lay off employees when Habitat lost a big account or orders were sparse, but a few times he was forced to temporarily cut hours to avoid letting anyone go. Sharon hated the weeks when she only worked part-time. She quickly gained weight out of boredom, and she was miserable.

Sharon also dreaded snow days. Like much of the South, the Chattanooga-north Georgia area never seemed quite prepared for even a sprinkling of the white stuff. Residents scanned the news for forecast updates and when snow was predicted, flocked to the supermarkets to stock up on bread, chips, and soup. Snowplows were scarce, and there weren't enough clean-up crews to go around. Sharon, on the other hand, didn't see what all the fuss was about. To her, it was just another workday.

"Sharon, the schools are all closed today and I don't think the Habitat bus can get up here to us either," Helen would say.

"I don't care if school's out," Sharon replied. "I can still go to work."

More often than not, Helen was right and the bus driver chose not to risk traveling on the roller-coaster of hills near Sharon's house. Bored and agitated, she couldn't wait to get back to work.

Even when business reached a near-feverish pitch and the employees needed to work weekends, Sharon still looked forward to being at Habitat. One day Connie was talking with Helen when she learned that one of Sharon's sisters, who lived in Atlanta, had recently had a baby. "Why didn't you let me know?" Connie asked. "Sharon could have taken some time off."

Helen was stunned. "Well, she told me you were real busy and that she couldn't take off."

"Mrs. Adams, Sharon can take a day off if she needs to. I don't have a problem with that," Connie responded. "She's got vacation days saved up, and besides, she's such a hard worker she ought to take a break every now and then."

The next time Connie saw Sharon, she brought up the subject. "Sharon, you need to go see that new baby," she teased.

"No, ma'am, I'm working," Sharon said, never taking her eyes off what she was doing.

After the plant moved from Georgia to Chattanooga, Sharon and several other employees who lived near the old location still rode the small, state-funded bus to work every day. Because of the longer distance and some dozen stops along the way to pick up other employees, the bus driver picked Sharon up at 5:45 A.M. and dropped her back off at home shortly before 6 P.M. The 12-hour days were grueling, but when Harvey and Helen suggested she look for an easier job, she wouldn't hear of it.

Like Terry, Martin, Daniel, and Lonnie, Sharon knew where she belonged.

Fourteen

Leading By Example

IN MOST COMPANIES, words like "love," "caring," and "compassion" are all but taboo. They're rarely used in the workplace and when they are—most often at team-building events and workshops—they tend to make corporate executives squirm in their seats.

At Habitat International, Inc. such language is not only allowed; it's encouraged. In fact, it's unavoidable. Employees with Down syndrome are just as apt to hug a stranger as someone they know. The sweet-natured workers with mental retardation don't seem to know how to be cruel to their colleagues. Those with mental illnesses are more concerned with helping newcomers than in jealously guarding their own positions. It's not uncommon for an employee with a brain injury to say, "I love you" to a co-worker, and mean it, as he leaves the plant for the weekend.

While some people are uncomfortable with such emotional intimacy at work, the managers and administrators at Habitat seem to take it in stride, even thriving on it. But they didn't always feel that way. Thanks to their disabled co-workers, they assert, they've become better people, more caring and compassionate, and more adept at handling life's punches. They are also quick to point out that the real disabilities aren't found in the imperfect bodies of the "distracted" workers, but in the hearts of the so-called "normal" employees, including themselves.

Here are their stories.

The Coal Miner's Daughter
CONNIE PRESNELL, TEAM PLANT COORDINATOR

I understand what it's like to be traumatized, to go through hard times.

I grew up in a family of 10 children, in the small mountain town of Whitwell, Tennessee. We were incredibly poor, but we were happy. Our chores were physically demanding, but when we were finished, we spent the rest of the day climbing trees and swimming in the creek, which flowed through our back yard. Our nearest neighbor lived a mile away, so we had plenty of room to spread our wings, and our imaginations. Sometimes we built playhouses from stones on the property. Other times we transformed the house into a "church," with my brother as the "preacher" and the rest of us as the "choir." It was truly the ideal place to be a kid.

Our perfect life was yanked away in the summer of 1963, when my father, a coal miner, was murdered on his way to work. There had been a strike going on in the mines for several months, but Daddy couldn't afford to join in. He had too many mouths to feed. He was riding to work one evening with another night watchman when five men in a car blocked the road and opened fire. The newspaper reports said my father died instantly.

I was 9 years old. My daddy and I had been very close, and I missed him terribly, so it was hard enough to deal with his death. But that wasn't the only thing we lost that summer. Without him, there was no way my mother could oversee the garden and chop trees for firewood and do all the other things it took to run a farm. Three of my siblings had already grown up and moved out of the house, so my mother packed up the seven of us who were left and we all went to live in a housing project in Chattanooga. Drug dealers and criminals hadn't overrun the neighborhood yet, so at least we didn't have to worry about that. For the first time in our lives we had electricity, running water, and a real bathroom—not an outhouse—simple, modern conveniences my mother had always wanted. I hated it. I ached for the wide-open spaces we'd left behind, and the freedom we'd enjoyed on the farm. In the projects, the only refuge we could call our own was a 3' x 3' porch, and if we stepped off it, we were on someone else's turf.

When we left Whitwell, we naïvely thought we could trust everyone, that most people were just naturally pleasant and nice. We soon found out that was not the case. The Chattanooga kids were street-smart, and they were mean. They poked fun at our clothes and our country accents, and they tried to beat us up. We defended ourselves with the slingshots Daddy had taught us how to make.

One of the things that puzzled me most was the way the city kids taunted my oldest sister, Ann. I had no idea what they were talking about when they called her a "retard," so I asked my mother to explain. My momma told me to ignore the kids, that they just didn't know Ann very well. It wasn't until about five years later, when the rest of my brothers and sisters married and left home and Ann stayed behind, that I finally understood what "mentally retarded" meant.

My mother died of cancer when I was 20. Losing both parents at an early age made me stronger, I think. So did the adjustments I was forced to make when we moved from the country to the harsh city. And growing up with a sister with a mental disability taught me compassion and tolerance, especially since my parents never treated her any differently from the rest of us.

After a succession of unfulfilling jobs as a dental assistant, I went to work for the state of Georgia, first as a house parent assistant at a group home for men with severe disabilities. The clients were barely functional. I shaved them. I bathed them. I fed them dinner. I drove them to Kmart so they could purchase their toiletries. After a while I became a job coach at the Walker County Training Center, and that's how I became acquainted with Habitat International, Inc. I'd never seen a place quite like this, where whole enclaves of clients with disabilities could work, be productive, and have fun at the same time. David tried to woo me away from my job at the state, but I didn't want to lose all the benefits I'd built up over the years, so I kept turning down his offers. Eventually, I gave in. Just like David, I was frustrated. I knew the disabled clients were capable of more, and I wanted to help make that happen. I wanted to be part of the change.

We've overcome a lot of challenges at Habitat since I came to work here, but they've all been worth it. The people with disabilities have, first and foremost, humbled me. Every time I think I've got them figured out, they surprise me by accomplishing much more than I'd assumed.

Don't get me wrong. I still have a reputation as the "hatchet woman," and I've earned it. We have certain work ethics at Habitat, and just because someone has a disability does not mean they don't have to follow the rules. I treat everyone equally here. If someone takes a few extra minutes at break time, I deduct it from their pay, whether they have a disability or not. Even if they've been babied all their lives, even if they come here thinking they can slack off just because they have a particular challenge, well, it doesn't take many paycheck deductions before they learn what they're supposed to do when the bell goes off in the plant. Just this morning, an employee named Ryan came to work with a streak of shaving cream on his face, and he was wearing a dirty shirt. I told him to go look in the mirror. He came back to me and said, "Connie, you were right. My mom says I need to look in the mirror before I come to work, and I didn't do it." I sent him home, and he came back cleaned up and ready to cut carpet.

When I hire someone, I look for enthusiasm, a good attitude, and a desire to work. Those characteristics make everything else fall into place, and with the right outlook, they'll end up achieving a great deal. I've found that if you pat them on the back, tell them how much you appreciate what they're doing, and give them a little encouragement every now and then, they'll work circles around people without disabilities. They even amaze themselves with how much they can do. All they want is to make a positive contribution to society, earn an honest living, and know in their hearts that they're valued and loved. Isn't that what we all want?

Where Have All the Problems Gone?
JIM THOMISON, PRESIDENT

In my previous job as vice president of a rope manufacturer, it wasn't uncommon for me to spend two or three days a month in labor court, trying to settle employee disputes. Sometimes a worker would intentionally try to get hurt so he could stay home and claim workman's compensation. Others would show up a few days a week—if it was convenient for them. Those employees showed a blatant disdain for the rules of the workplace and for us, their supervisors. Occasionally a worker's angry defiance would become so out of control that, if I fired him, he'd lunge across the desk or threaten to kill me. And accidents were much too frequent. Several times I was awakened by a call in the middle of the night only to pick up the phone and learn that another employee had lost a finger or broken an arm on the job.

Those issues are pretty much absent at Habitat. The attitude problems are minimal. You don't hear the negative, backbiting talk you normally hear in a workplace. You don't have to question whether the people have ulterior motives for being nice to you. They just *are*. Not one of our disabled employees has ever gotten hurt on the job. They show up when they're supposed to, they work hard, and we have very little turnover.

They even offer to come in on weekends when we have major orders to fill. To my knowledge, in the 13 years I've been working here, we've never back-ordered one item. That's how efficient our workers are. We also have built-in quality control. If the carpet isn't lined up straight or we're running low on supplies or someone's goofing off, Terry or Sharon or Daniel is going to let me know about it, and fast. This morning I was walking through the plant and one of them shouted out to me, "Hey, Jim, come here, look at this!" The employee was assembling boxes and discovered that the glue seam on three of them was busted. He had set the defective cartons aside to make sure we got our money back on them. Here at Habitat, the personnel problems you typically see in a manufacturing plant simply don't exist.

I first met David and Saul in the early 1980s, when they were ready to hire their first employees. I helped them find some great Cambodian workers who had escaped the terror of the Khmer Rouge, and had come to America under the sponsorship of a Chattanooga church. We had hired several Cambodian refugees at the rope company, and they turned out to be fabulous employees, very dedicated and hard working. In fact, our turnover rate dropped significantly after they came on board. David took my advice and employed a few members of the Teg family, and some of them still work at Habitat.

I remember telling my boss that David and Saul were way ahead of their time when it came to marketing and computerized inventory. When a product shipped from a Habitat warehouse on the west coast, the east coast computer automatically invoiced the customer. That was a pretty advanced concept for a small manufacturing company in the early 1980s.

Over the years I not only admired what they did, but who they were and what they stood for. So when David offered me a job in 1991, I jumped at the chance. Believe me, it took me a while to get used to our differences. I'm a neat freak; I keep all my papers lined up in uniform stacks on my desk and I can't stand to feel disorganized. David, on the other hand, is like Pigpen, leaving a messy trail wherever he goes. Somehow, we came to accept each other's quirks and put them in perspective. He and the other employees have even helped loosen me up over the years. I realize now that I don't have to be perfect at everything, all the time.

It also took me a while to get used to the enclaves of disabled people from the Walker County Training Center, in the days before we hired them outright. It wasn't that they were especially difficult or demanding;

I'd just never been around people with physical or mental challenges. I wasn't sure what to say around them, and I pitied them because they were different. But it didn't take long for them to burst my stereotypical bubble and show me how wrong I'd been. Now I feel sorry for others who view people with disabilities the way I did 20 years ago.

The reason this works for us is that we actually listen to our employees and treat them as individuals, whether or not they have a disability. We've learned how to push aside our pre-conceived notions of what people with Down syndrome or bipolar disorder or a hearing impairment should be like. Honestly, the best thing you can do is just let them be themselves. But that seems to be a difficult thing for business people to do. I have friends in management who sign up for expensive, time-consuming workshops to learn how to be tolerant or interact with other people, and that sort of thing just makes me jump up on my soapbox. Business is simple, really; you buy raw material, convert it into a product, sell it for a little more than it cost you, and make a profit. That's it. In the long run, it's the people part that makes it all happen. If you work together, everyone benefits. If you can't come together as a team, your production will suffer. It's that easy, really, but business executives often try to make it much, much harder than it is.

We're very picky about the way we do business, but we seldom go by the book. There are no daily production reports at Habitat, no formal quality-control program, no hidden agenda to lay off workers if our profits don't match last year's numbers. We don't hover around our employees like gadflies or breathe down their necks, counting the pieces of carpet they cut in a day. We respect them and they know it, and because of that, they don't let us down. Even the homeless people who work here are extremely conscientious and do their best to make us look good. I can't say enough complimentary things about them.

Our methods are out of the ordinary, our employees are not what you'd expect in a manufacturing plant, and the crazy artwork can be a shock to visitors who don't know us. I've never been a real touchy-feely type, and when I first came here I didn't know quite how to act, and I didn't talk much. In college, before I switched to a business degree, my intention was to major in geology so I could be outdoors and work in one of those field jobs where you don't have to interact much with people. I can still be hard to read when you first meet me, but I've learned to love people, all types of people. I've still got a laid-back temperament, and sometimes I'm even a pushover. But if I hear you making fun of the disabled employees or putting them down, I'll be the first to set you straight. They're the ones who've made Habitat such a success. They've shown us you don't have to be serious all the time to be productive. They're family, and for that reason we feel a strong sense of responsibility when it comes to their welfare, even when times are lean. We'll do whatever it takes to keep them working, and happy.

Finding Her Inspiration
SANDRA BALL, TEAM SHIPPING COORDINATOR

Ever since I can remember, my mother has had a mental illness, but back then it wasn't called bipolar disorder. About once a year, she'd have a "spell," and sometimes it would be several months before she'd come out of it. When she was in one of her manic phases, she was extremely violent and it took a lot to contain her when she got out of hand. If she wanted to do something dangerous and my brother and sisters and I tried to stop her, we might as well get ready for a physical struggle because she'd blow up and want to fight. I didn't understand her mood swings but I learned, over time, to deal with them. And as she got older the episodes seemed to lessen in severity.

I have no doubt that my mother's outbursts prepared me to work with people with mental disorders. That's one reason I could deal with people like Jason, the man with autism who sprained my hand when he grabbed it during one of his rages, and Daniel, whose brain injury caused him to lash out and call us names when he really didn't mean a word of what he said. Working with people like that really forces you to go the extra mile, to reach out to them with compassion, instead of losing your temper. And that really pays off. Once you give them the love and acceptance they crave, they'll return it to you tenfold.

I came to Habitat as a temporary worker in the summer of 1998. My life hadn't turned out the way I had planned, and I needed a chance almost as badly as the people with disabilities. I was barely 13 when I gave birth to my son—I was a baby, really, having a baby—and I wasn't prepared for the responsibility of being a parent. Years later, I was strung out on crack cocaine. I didn't think I could make it through the day without drinking a few beers and smoking a joint. Eventually I was fired from my longtime job at a fiberglass plant in a small town in east Tennessee. My bosses covered for me as long as they could in spite of my addiction, but after a while I was just too undependable. That's when I moved to Chattanooga and signed up with a temporary employment service. They sent me to Habitat, which I'd never heard of, and as soon as I walked in the door, I said to myself, "Lord, what have I gotten myself into?"

There was all this weird artwork hanging from the ceiling, and there was more out in the parking lot, but that wasn't what bothered me. What upset me was the sight of all these people working so hard. I had been out of work for about six months, and at the fiberglass plant I had driven a forklift, a job that seemed a lot less physical than standing on my feet and cutting carpet all day. I wasn't sure I could do it, or that I even wanted to try.

One day I was folding sheets of 9' x 12' carpet at a table in the middle of the plant when I found myself falling behind. It was sweltering hot that afternoon, and the sweat dripped off my forehead and onto my shirt. *I just can't do this*, I thought. *I just can't. It's too hard.* I had made up my mind that I wasn't coming back when I happened to look around at some of the disabled employees. There was Lonnie, who sometimes heard voices and saw images that weren't there. And Sharon, who was mentally retarded. And Jason, who was autistic. They were working as hard as they could, and smiling at me. How could they do this, day after day, without complaining? I looked down at the table, then back at them, and it suddenly hit me: if *they* could keep on, so could I.

Over the years, they've taught me to accept myself just the way I am, weaknesses and all. They inspire me with their innocence and joy. They're never catty; they don't talk about me behind my back or put up a fuss if I ask them to do something.

I've come a long way since the days when I didn't think I could get through the day without marijuana or a hit of cocaine. I married a wonderful man and kicked my drug habit. I am now an ordained minister, and I rely on God, not drugs, to see me through the rough spots. The disabled people I work with help lift me up too. Oh, they're not perfect, any more than I am. And some have tested me far more than I wanted to be. But every day, I come back. And every day I thank God for giving all of us a chance to reach our potential.

Mechanical Whiz
JERRY TREADWELL, PLANT ENGINEER

I've always had a knack for mechanical things. Gears, sprockets, motors, hydraulic equipment, you name it—somehow I just know how they work. Sometimes I wake up at night with an entire blueprint in my mind. I can see it. I never draw it on paper; I just build the machine from what's in my head. Maybe I was born with it. I don't really know. Then again, I probably picked the skill up as a 10-year-old, when I went with my dad on Saturdays to the plant where he designed sewing machines to make chenille bedspreads. He taught me how to sew and weld and build things. And I was a quick learner.

For years I worked as a machinist, starting part-time at a rug manufacturer at age 14. In the summertime, the staff electrician showed me how to bend conduit and run electrical circuits. He was a wonderful mentor. Throughout my career, I have held different mechanical and electrical engineering positions in Chattanooga, New Mexico, and Texas. I served in Vietnam in the '60s and at one time worked for Delta Airlines. In the mid-1980s, I returned to Chattanooga where, in addition to my full-time job at a foundry, I began taking on contract jobs with another electrician. That's how I met David and Saul. They had just moved their operation to Rossville, Georgia, and needed some electrical work done on the old, rundown building, formerly a chicken hatchery.

Habitat wasn't like any manufacturing plant I'd ever seen. The outlandish artwork wasn't up yet, but the enclave of disabled people from Orange Grove was there. I watched them fold carpet and assemble boxes and really admired them for what they were able to accomplish. I thought it was wonderful that David and Saul would take the time to give them a chance, to help them gain valuable job skills. All of them amazed me—the Morrises and their unusual workers—and I found myself hanging out at the plant more and more.

Once David realized I had a talent for modifying equipment and fabricating workstations from scratch, he started hiring me to do other things—odd jobs at first, then larger projects. I built racks for the press, and cutting tables, and a carpet cutter. I brought in my own tools and we set up a little workshop for me in the back. Each morning, after I'd worked all night at my full-time job, I'd head straight for Habitat. Over the years, when I spotted an ergonomic challenge, when I saw a way to make a job easier and safer for one of the employees, I talked to David about it, and more often than not, he gave me the green light to get started. I made a few special tables high enough to accommodate people in wheelchairs. Every now and then I'd adapt a piece of equipment so someone could reach it better without straining his back. In 2004, when Habitat and Millennium Packaging Solutions formed a partnership and some of our workers began putting together appliance boxes, I built the rack and some guides to make the process quicker and easier. The manager at the box company stopped by a couple days later and said, "I'm totally amazed. How did you do this so fast?" And I said, "Hey, all it takes is a little initiative. That's what Habitat is known for." He was blown away.

I've been blown away too, by the special employees and what they've taught me. They've shown me how to have fun and how to be proud of what I can do, and they take my mind off my troubles. I'm kind of an up-and-down guy, emotionally; I don't stay on an even keel all the time, and I let my personal problems bother me too much. When I went through a painful divorce a few years ago, the Habitat employees were there to cheer me up. You can't be too sad around people who are always telling jokes and trying their best to make you smile.

They also have a way of looking past the details to see the big picture of things. Many times, they've helped me come up with solutions that were so simple even I couldn't see them. They've taught me tolerance too. I grew up in northwest Georgia, where people with disabilities weren't seen very often, and they certainly weren't part of your circle of friends. There were even fewer of them in the military and in the industrial settings I worked in over the years. So I had no idea what someone with Down syndrome could do.

I was probably closest to Jeff Brown, one of the original workers hired from the Walker County Training Center. Jeff passed away in 1998, the same year as my divorce, and I still miss him. He was a tall, lanky guy with a protruding jaw and a form of mental retardation. When he first came to Habitat, he was painfully shy and hardly said a word. We started kidding around with him—he loved women and we'd say things like, "Hey, Jeff, what do you think about that gal over there?" or "Isn't she pretty?"—and after a while, he just opened up. He even started asking me to write love notes for him to Connie, and he'd tell me what to say. He could sign his name, but he printed his letters backwards. I'd take him and Ken Jones to baseball games, and we all went line dancing. Jeff wore his brand new snakeskin boots, and a gold necklace. Boy, did he love those boots. Most of all, though, he loved Habitat. Sometimes, if we were out on the town, we'd stop by Lowe's or one of the other retailers that carries our products. Jeff would just grin from ear to ear when he saw the Habitat rug display. He'd look around at the other customers and proudly ask, "Do you think they know who we are?" as if we were movie stars.

Calming Influence
PATTY KEITH, NATIONAL/INTERNATIONAL SALES COORDINATOR

When I first began working at Habitat in 1993, I was reminded of a girl I'd gone to school with named Pearl. She was mildly mentally retarded, and was always laughing and singing on the bus. Here at Habitat, the people with disabilities are always making me laugh. I'll never forget Ken Jones finagling his own business cards, writing down "orders" for rugs on his clipboard, and playing Santa Claus at our Christmas parties. And Jason, who never seemed to meet a stranger. He'd always walk up to you and say, "Hi. What's your name? How old are you? Are you married? Do you have kids?" There was no way to keep a low profile in the plant if Jason was around. Sharon used to be really shy, but now she loves to tease and have fun. Sometimes she'll say to me, "I get two checks today, right?" And I'll tease right back and say, "No, you don't get one this week. I'm going to take your check and go shopping with it." That always makes her laugh.

The employees with disabilities are great at handling unforeseen problems, and they stay much calmer than I do. I'm very high-strung and tend to get really stressed if there's a glitch in my day, even a small one. If I'm freaking out about something, they'll come up to me and say, "It's okay. You can do it." And it just stops me cold. Even when Ken's father passed away, he somehow accepted it and handled it far better than I would have. "He's in a good place," he told me. "His spirit is still with us. It's okay."

I just wish I could be more like them sometimes.

Accepting Each Other
DAMITA FAVORS, OFFICE AND ACCOUNTING COORDINATOR

I was one of Habitat's first employees, at the original plant on Jersey Pike in Chattanooga. The Cambodian people were already working there, but the enclaves of disabled clients hadn't started yet. Over the past 20 years I've watched the company evolve and hire more and more people with "distractions." And it's been a wonderful experience. They don't look at a stranger and say, "Oh well, they're beneath me" or "Maybe they're above me." They just look at you and see another person, period. And they're always so giving, no matter who you are.

For some reason, I've really never made a big deal over people who have disabilities, and I've always been drawn to the underdog. One of my earliest memories in school is of a girl with one leg. She walked with an artificial limb and she was extremely smart. She didn't act as if there were anything unique about her, and I didn't think of her as any different from myself. Years later, as a single mom, I taught my own kids to accept other people, regardless of what they looked like or what their abilities were. I was pleased when David hired a girl with a visual impairment to work in the office with me. It didn't work out, but not because she couldn't key in the data fast enough. She had been babied a great deal throughout her life and in my opinion her neediness was more of a challenge than her disability.

Most of our disabled employees aren't like that. Just like "normal" people, some don't make it here, for various reasons. But if you give them an opportunity to do a good job, then step back and let them do it, they usually will. The more you encourage them, the more you show your appreciation, the better they do. It makes me feel good when I see how happy one little compliment makes them.

I'm really a very shy person at heart. Twenty years ago, I would hardly speak unless spoken to and I shied away from conversations unless I knew someone extremely well. Working around these friendly employees with disabilities has pried me out of my shell; now I no longer have trouble talking to people I've never met. In public, I smile and say hello to everyone. Sometimes I even stop for a few minutes to chat. My philosophy now is: I accept you, you accept me, so let's go from there.

Fifteen

Carl:
The Company Grandpa

THE FIRST TIME HE SAW HER, in the summer of 1955, he thought she was the prettiest girl he had ever seen. Twenty-four-year-old Carl Wallace was taking a routine break from his job in the spinning department at DuPont, a major manufacturer of nylon yarns and one of Chattanooga's top employers, when he spotted the tall, slender woman laughing and talking to friends. He immediately made up his mind to find out more about her. And when Carl wanted something, he wouldn't stop until he got it.

Her name was Juanita, and she was 28. She worked in the draw twist division. She wasn't movie-star glamorous, but there was something about her that Carl couldn't resist. Maybe it was the way she carried herself. Or the way she smoothed back her hair. Or the intriguing self-assuredness of an "older woman." He couldn't stop thinking about her.

Carl found out that another DuPont worker, a friend of Juanita's named Greg, had been giving her a ride home from work every day. One day she exited the plant to find Carl waiting for her instead.

"Where's Greg?" she asked, suspicion rising in her voice.

"He went on vacation," Carl replied. "Come on, hop in."

Juanita raised a perfectly arched eyebrow. "But I don't know you."

Carl grinned. "You will."

Back then, people were more trusting, so Juanita finally relented and slid into the passenger seat. But she wasn't about to give in to Carl's unabashed flirting, and she grumbled all the way home.

"Greg won't be picking you up anymore," Carl said when he dropped her off. "So I guess you'll be riding with me from now on." Juanita responded by rolling her eyes.

True to his word, Carl became Juanita's new chauffeur, even as he concocted excuses to keep Greg away from her. Before long, instead of staring ahead in aggravation as they rode home from work, she found herself glancing at him out of the corner of her eye. He was nice-looking, she mused, with blue eyes and a mop of strawberry-blonde hair. He was stubborn, but so was she. When she finally let down her guard and began having real conversations with him, she discovered he wanted to wed and have children.

In September, three months after they met, they were married.

Over the years, Carl and Juanita raised two girls and a boy. Even while they were dating, Juanita knew Carl had a bad temper, especially when someone disagreed with him. After the wedding it worsened. If things didn't go his way, at work or at home, his face would turn red and he'd yell and blurt out mean things to his wife. When it came to disciplining the kids, Juanita believed in stern reprimands. Carl's response was to yank the young culprit up by the arm and spank him hard, right then and there.

Carl was just as restless in his professional life. Early on he left his job at DuPont and began selling life insurance, then dabbled in real estate, then again in insurance. He once helped in his brother's carpentry business. For a time he and Juanita and the kids lived on a dairy farm, overseeing its operations and raising calves. The children loved the freedom, and the Wallaces would always remember this as one of their happiest times. Juanita left her job at DuPont to care for the kids, selling Bibles and World Books and Avon cosmetics to help make ends meet. Later on both she and Carl were hired at a frame shop, where they learned how to mat and frame customer prints. Enthralled with the idea of going into business for themselves and pocketing all the profits from their hard work, in 1977 the Wallaces opened their own frame shop in Fort Oglethorpe, Georgia, on the outskirts of Chattanooga. As they had hoped, the money was good, at least at first, but like any other entrepreneurial venture, there were lean times. Nothing, however, could compare to their greatest challenge, which came 30 years after Carl began wooing Juanita in the DuPont parking lot.

One day in 1985, just before Thanksgiving, Carl complained of a terrible headache that wouldn't go away. The couple's 2-year-old granddaughter,

Cassie, was spending the night, and they had planned to eat dinner at Shoney's. Carl insisted on going despite the piercing sensation in his head.

"Are you sure you're up to it?" Juanita asked. "We can do this another time."

"No, maybe it'll make me feel better," Carl said. He didn't want to disappoint anyone, including himself. Cassie loved Shoney's, and Carl and Juanita loved dining out.

But the meal failed to ease the sharp pain. On the way home, Juanita noticed that Carl acted a bit strangely. For a brief moment, he swerved slightly, toward the shoulder of the road. Then he did it again. Cassie was being fussy, and Juanita was too busy tending to her granddaughter to dwell on Carl's goof. *Something must have caught his attention*, she thought. *He probably just looked away for a second.* Juanita couldn't remember the odd thing her husband said next; all she would ever recall was that he had mumbled a jangle of words that didn't make sense.

Carl went straight to bed that evening, but he couldn't sleep. "Juanita, this is the worst headache I've ever had in my life," he said, downing more aspirin. He walked out to the living room, sat down in his favorite chair, and muttered another nonsensical phrase. Before his wife could catch him, Carl had fallen out of the chair. She gently held him by the elbow and helped him to the sofa.

"Carl, what's wrong?" she asked, fear welling up inside her. "Talk to me." But all he could do was slur.

Juanita picked up the phone and called the kids and Carl's sister. "We'll be right there," they said.

The ambulance arrived six minutes later and transported Carl to the local county hospital. X-rays showed that a vessel had burst and blood had seeped into the left side of his brain. He had suffered a hemorrhagic stroke. The rupture, the doctors noted, was due to a malformation most likely present from birth. There had been a time bomb inside Carl's head for 54 years, and no one knew until it was too late. "We're sending him to Erlanger," the physician said, referring to the larger, trauma-care hospital in downtown Chattanooga. "He's got a 50/50 chance of living, and they're the only ones who can help."

At Erlanger, the neurologist gave only one option: emergency surgery. "If we don't operate, he could have more of these," the surgeon told Juanita. "One of them could kill him, and soon.

"There's one more thing," he added. "Surgery will save his life, but it will also probably change his personality. He won't be the same Carl."

To Juanita, *any* Carl was better than *no* Carl. They had been through a lot together, and this was the time in their lives when things were supposed to get easier. Three hours later, the surgeon had removed part of Carl's cranium, drained the pooled blood, and replaced the severed part of his skull.

Juanita brought Carl home the day before Christmas Eve. Then, and only then, did she begin to realize how much work her husband's recovery was going to be, and not just for him. Like half of the 700,000 Americans who have strokes every year, Carl was partially paralyzed on one side. The "cerebral accident" had occurred on the left half of his brain, affecting the right side of his body. This not only left him with speech problems and memory loss, but would also, from that point forward, cause him to move more slowly and with deliberate caution. (Strokes that hit the right side, on the other hand, are apt to trigger a quick, inquisitive behavioral style and vision loss.) He'd have to learn how to walk and talk and write his name all over again, and he had a long road ahead of him. So did Juanita.

Once home, Carl was an overgrown infant who needed constant care. A hospital bed was installed and Juanita had to turn her 200-pound husband every two hours, even throughout the night, to avoid bedsores. The nurses showed her how to manage his catheter and change his soiled clothes. Most days she ran on adrenaline, never stopping to ponder the fact that she'd just made the bed with fresh sheets and that they already needed changing again. When Carl was able to sit up, Juanita used a lift to deposit him in his wheelchair and move him to the living room. One time when she turned the lift the wrong way, Carl fell and his buttocks hit the floor with a thud. He chuckled, and Juanita couldn't help but laugh too. She needed the comic relief.

A home healthcare nurse couldn't help but notice how stressed and exhausted Juanita was. "You know, nearly every time somebody has a stroke, the spouse who is well ends up leaving the sick one," the nurse mused.

"Why would they do that?" Juanita asked. The thought of abandoning Carl had never even occurred to her. She had taken a vow three decades ago, and she and Carl were in this together, in sickness and in health.

A physical therapist, a friend of the family, came out to the house twice a day, morning and evening. He'd sit for hours, sweat beading up on his forehead as he moved Carl's legs back and forth, back and forth, in a bicycle motion, as Carl lay on a quilt on the floor. Eventually the therapist began using a sheet for a belt to hold his frustrated patient upright while urging him to take one more tiny, faltering step. Juanita was almost glad Carl hadn't learned to talk again yet; if he had, she knew, he would surely be cursing the therapist at the top of his lungs. It took about six months for Carl to walk on his own, and eventually those little steps turned into brisk walks in Carl's new neighborhood. Juanita had sold the old place, and the shop, to help pay the medical bills.

When it came to language, Carl had all but become a blank slate. The speech therapists brought little primer cards to teach Carl his ABC's. He learned how to write, but it wasn't the same as before. When he printed the word C-A-R-L, he did it all in one motion, without ever lifting the pen from the page. Each day Juanita, a shrewd mom who knew how to motivate without overpowering, coaxed Carl into practicing his newfound language. "Let's check your eyes today," she'd say, retrieving the newspaper. "Can you say those words right there?" It often took him a while but sooner or later Carl would read the sentence aloud.

The doctor had been right about Carl's personality change. Almost immediately Juanita noticed her husband was gentler, and easier to get along with. His hot temper seemed to be gone. And he laughed more. *Well,* she thought to herself, *at least something good came of this.*

The Veterans Administration had declared Carl totally and permanently disabled. But the doctor didn't think it was wise for Carl to sit at home every day and watch TV. "You need to get out in public again," the physician said. "It'll be good for you. Try to find something to do with your time."

In 1988, three years after the stroke, Carl began applying for jobs in Chickamauga, the small north Georgia town where he and Juanita now lived. Each time, he was met with a smile and a polite but firm "no." Juanita suspected it was because Carl's peers knew what had happened and were afraid to hire him. She decided to talk to the manager of a grocery store in a nearby town. "Well, sure," the manager told Juanita when she explained. "I'd be glad to give him a chance."

Carl went to work as a bag boy, starting a few hours a week and gradually adding more until he became a full-time employee. He had been there eight years when he and a co-worker, another elderly gentleman, got into a heated argument and the other fellow struck Carl. The manager fired both of them on the spot. Carl worked at another supermarket, then a drugstore, but both times the boss let him go for talking too much to customers and wandering away from the job. He was fired from a third grocery store, presumably because he couldn't handle the heavy trains of carts.

In 1999, friends told Juanita and Carl about Lookout Mountain Community Services, the mother agency for the Walker County Training Center, where Habitat International, Inc. had found its first employees with disabilities. Juanita signed Carl up. An acquaintance recommended him for employment at Habitat, and Juanita wasted no time making an appointment with Connie. But there were no job openings. Connie, who remembered meeting Carl years before when he framed some of her needlepunch, also had her misgivings about hiring a 68-year-old man when a younger one might need the job. Still, Juanita persisted. She called Connie frequently, sometimes every day, and often dropped by the Habitat plant, with Carl trailing on her heels. Eventually her efforts paid off thanks, in part, to Sandra.

"Connie, please give him a job," Sandra begged. "We'll be old someday and I'd like to think somebody will give us a chance when we are."

Connie sensed that Carl was going to be a troublemaker, but she gave in to Sandra's pleas and hired him anyway. As usual, her intuition was right on target. Some of Carl's old orneriness had returned, and he didn't like being told what to do. When Connie tried to correct him about a task he was doing the wrong way, he would curse, raise his fist, and threaten to hit her. Later he would apologize. In the beginning, she would punish him for the offense by making him stay at home the next day without pay. But Juanita, who was depending on Carl's check to help supplement their social security income, would have none of that.

"Connie, let's punish him some other way," she would say with all the persuasive tact she could muster. "He loves to go out to eat, especially on Saturday mornings when we go to Cracker Barrel. What if I just refuse to take him when he acts up?"

Connie agreed, and the strategy worked.

Carl's memory, or lack of it, posed another set of problems. Because of his stroke and subsequent brain disease, he was extremely forgetful. Sometimes he'd return from break time and not be able to recall what he'd been working on. More than once, the managers found him wandering in Jerry's workshop or outside in the parking lot. Carl loved to talk, and he would approach anyone who came into the plant—truck drivers, new employees, visitors—and try to engage them in conversation. More often than not, Y, Cheng, or Terry would act as informants. "Connie, there goes Carl again," one of them would say. And off Connie would go to nab Carl and steer him back to his post.

As always, she maintained a healthy sense of humor. The first time she heard Carl sing, she thought someone had been hurt on the job and it nearly scared her to death. Then she laughed at her own jumpiness. "Oh, Lord!" he cried out, loudly enough for the whole plant to hear, before launching into a rousing church hymn. Other times he would sing a few lines from a favorite folk tune. "All day I face the barren waste," he crooned. "Without the taste of water, cool water...."

All those years of daily walks on the Georgia back roads had paid off for Carl, especially when it came to the cutting table, where employees were required to move back and forth for hours at a time. After the stroke, he couldn't raise his right arm very high, but if he and one other person shared the cutting table, that never got in the way. When deadlines were tight and Connie was forced to speed up the process by adding more workers—the more people on the table, the faster the assembly line—she let Carl move to a workstation that wasn't quite as demanding. No matter what he was doing, though, he stayed with it, and he was productive.

It took some time, but Carl came to love Habitat, and the other employees came to love *him*. Jason Cook, one of the first Habitat workers with autism, started calling him Grandpops, and other employees did the same thing. Carl simply nodded in reply. After a while, he didn't even notice the other "distractions" around him; he particularly liked Lonnie, whose laid-back demeanor set him at ease. Carl appreciated the bonuses and the fact that if he wanted to, he could work straight through vacation time and make extra money. (He stopped drawing V.A. disability supplements when his salary reached a certain level.) He was especially impressed when he saw David and Jim and the other Habitat managers working alongside their employees—helping out in a pinch, cutting carpet, carrying out garbage, or anything else that needed to be done. Despite his occasional outbursts and nomadic behavior, Carl was happier than he'd been since the stroke. He even greeted Connie with a handshake every morning.

But Carl's strong point was loyalty. Like Sharon and Martin and some of the others, he didn't want to miss a single day at Habitat, not for any reason. In fact, he worked several years without missing work due to illness, but was so sick one time that Connie insisted he stay at home. Day after day, he gladly got up at 5:20 A.M., boarded the Walker County Training Center bus at 6 A.M. and worked until 4 P.M. before returning home. Sometimes on weekends he forgot he could sleep in and rose early to get dressed for work. Juanita would have to remind him to come back to bed.

Sandra's hunch had been right, and as the years passed, Connie was glad she'd hired Carl. What family, after all, would be complete without a "Grandpops"?

Sixteen

Love Is Contagious

T HE HABITAT PHILOSOPHY of acceptance and love has not only impacted the people inside its walls; it has created a ripple effect in the local community and beyond. A bank president borrowed the Habitat "positive distractions" slogan to motivate his employees at Christmas. The director of a non-profit organization that helps ex-prisoners make the transition back into the work world has used Habitat as a model. Specialists from a major rehabilitation hospital routinely bring patients to Habitat to show them that, yes, there is life after a debilitating injury or stroke. Even the most stalwart business executives have been touched by what they've seen in the plant, and have become more tolerant of people different from themselves.

Here, various members of the extended "Habitat family" share what they've learned from this unusual workplace, and explain why they hope other employers will take a chance and hire people with disabilities:

THE TEACHERS

Robin Leventhal,
special-education teacher, vision services
WALKER COUNTY (GEORGIA) SCHOOL SYSTEM

For seven years Robin Leventhal worked with severe and profoundly disabled students in her job as a special-ed teacher at Ridgeland High

163

School in Rossville, Georgia. "The people at Habitat showed me that my students could do so much more than I ever thought they could. I was shocked at what my kids could do because I didn't have any way to give them that experience in a classroom. It showed me that I might have been selling my own students short."

One of the reasons special-ed kids tend to do so well at Habitat, Robin asserts, is that they are given the space and the opportunity to learn socialization skills, to see for themselves what will and will not be tolerated in a real workplace. As problems arise, the kids can be gently steered in the right direction by their teachers and supervisors.

After she'd been taking her students to Habitat for several years in a row, her school's principal and an assistant administrator accompanied her to the plant to see what all the fuss was about. "They were shocked. I mean, they were totally amazed at how our kids worked. They said things like, 'These are the same kids?' It was a good experience for these administrators to come out and see that our kids can do much more than they've seen them do at school."

It will be hard to emulate the Habitat environment now that the company has moved across the state line, from Georgia to Tennessee, Robin says. "I think it just does a service that nobody else is willing to do or has thought about doing or *can* do. Not everybody makes it at Habitat, and that's okay too. It can't be everything to everybody. But the people there are so accepting of the differences in other people that it gives [the special students] the confidence to go out in the world and say, 'Oh, man, maybe I can do it. Maybe I can go somewhere.' I think the acceptance factor at Habitat is like none other.

"For my kids it was an awesome experience," she adds. "I don't know that there'll be another one like it, but I sure can hope there will be."

Wadene Livingston Bartoo, special-education teacher
RIDGELAND HIGH SCHOOL, ROSSVILLE, GEORGIA

Like her former colleague Robin Leventhal, Wadene Livingston Bartoo has been teaching special-ed classes for more than two decades. She began taking her students to Habitat in 1996 and soon fell in love with the place. Over the years, Wadene and her colleagues recruited other host companies, but none, she says, even came close to Habitat. "It offers more for the kids with more [severe] problems," she says. "In a lot of the businesses we go to, the kids have to deal with the public. And some of our guys are not good with that, particularly those with autism and the kids in wheelchairs that can't get around too well. It really limits their choice of places to work. Habitat's a place that is willing to work with anyone, even those with the worst disabilities. Even the kids with the most limiting disabilities—we could find something for them to do at Habitat."

One of the reasons more students aren't effectively making the school-to-work transition is that the parents are not supportive enough of their kids. Some are overly protective and want to shield their children from prejudice or the mistakes they might make on the job. Other parents lack a strong work ethic themselves or would rather rely on welfare or government-funded disability income. "They won't go that extra mile to see that their kids get to work and are on time, so a lot of the kids just end up sitting at home."

Even though a few other job sites in the vocational program did pan out, Habitat was by far Wadene's favorite. "Some of the kids liked it, and some of them didn't, because it can be pretty labor-intensive. But I think that overall the kids experienced a great deal of success there. If they mastered this level of making boxes, there was always another level they could go to, where they had more responsibility. And I think *that* was the great thing that I loved about Habitat—just watching the kids move step-by-step up the ladder to more difficult jobs."

Mike Carter, teacher
Catoosa Crossroads Academy, Fort Oglethorpe, Georgia

Mike Carter met David and Saul when they bought the former chicken hatchery in Rossville, Georgia, from his father-in-law. Mike's relationship with Habitat was further cemented by the fact that he lived right next door to the factory. One day he was talking to David and casually mentioned his vocational program for at-risk youth in Fort Oglethorpe, Georgia. Mike was a teacher at Catoosa Crossroads Academy, a public alternative school for middle- and high-school kids with behavior problems, truancy violations, and poor academic achievement. The program focused on positive reinforcement, character education, and small classes designed to keep students in school until they graduated.

David took Mike up on his offer to visit the Academy, and Mike introduced David to Jack Towns, the school's vocational director and the instructor of a metalwork class. Before long David had helped Jack acquire scrap metal to use in the workshop, and had agreed to a formal request for grant money to purchase a welding machine. After that, the students were invited to Habitat's annual picnics and Christmas parties, where they immediately connected with the disabled employees. "My students are very, very sensitive to people with special needs," Mike says. "We have a severely emotionally disturbed program at Catoosa Crossroads Academy. Not all of these kids, but some of them are really on the level of a kid that might go to Orange Grove (a Chattanooga-based center for the developmentally disabled) or something like that. You see TV programs and stuff where people bully and make fun, but I've never seen that with my students. That's something we reinforce also. We tell them, 'There are people that don't have the abilities that you have, but they're worthy people and they're valuable people and they're a part of our society.'"

Mike continues to be impressed with the way David Morris "puts his money where his mouth is" and follows through on philanthropic ideas. "Even though he's very independent, he's willing to listen to what you've got to say," Mike points out. "He's a very successful businessman and he doesn't have to serve his fellow man, but he does."

Deanna Baker, special-education teacher
BOYNTON ELEMENTARY SCHOOL, RINGGOLD, GEORGIA

Deanna Baker first became aware of Habitat International, Inc. when she toured the plant with one of the leadership classes from Catoosa County, Georgia. At the time, she was coordinating the local Partnership 2000 program, a statewide business-education partnership that helps provide financial and volunteer resources to local schools. Arriving at Habitat, she was impressed with the serenity of the water fountain in the lobby and with David's cultured but down-to-earth style. But what really captured her attention was what she saw in the plant: an employee with Down syndrome working next to people with schizophrenia, autism, and the aftermath of a stroke.

Later, a few of her leadership classmates told her they felt uncomfortable seeing "those people on display." "I didn't feel that way at all, and I don't think David presented it that way at all," Deanna says. "I think he's very proud of the people who work for him. They are his family. They are his friends. He treats them no differently than he would treat you or me. He has expectations of them to do a good job and they do it, and he values them. So I think the issues that some people had were their own."

Now a special-ed teacher at Boynton Elementary School, Deanna admits that until she saw the workers at Habitat, she had no idea people with physical and mental disabilities could accomplish so much. "I was guilty just as everybody else of thinking that they could do something menial and would probably have to have a lot of assistance and could never really be self-supportive. But David doesn't see an individual with a disability. He sees inside their heart and he sees that they're capable and he makes it so that they can be successful.

"I just think all of us too often make the mistake of stereotyping and putting people in boxes sometimes just so they can fit in our comfort zone, so we can keep them at a distance," Deanna adds. "They belong *here*, and I belong *here*, and that's the way we want to keep it. David is not that way. He's about uniting people and bringing out the best in people and finding value in every individual. It's not the people with disabilities that have a problem, because they are capable and can do it if someone will give them a chance. I think it's the rest of us who have these hang-ups, and that's what we've got to get past."

THE BUSINESS ASSOCIATES

Carl Bouchaert, chairman and CEO
Ben Hahn, national marketing director
Hans Bakker, director of product management
Kim Brown, customer relations manager
David Bagby, bypass distribution manager
BEAULIEU OF AMERICA, DALTON, GEORGIA

At one time they were staunch opponents, warily keeping an eye on each other's standing in the packaged-rug industry. Today, Habitat International, Inc. and carpet giant Beaulieu of America work in tandem to supply the Home Depot with grass and needlepunch rugs. The relationship between David Morris and the Beaulieu executives, including Carl Bouckaert, the company's founder and CEO, is now built on mutual admiration and shared business goals. The trust factor is extremely high.

By the time the two companies began doing business together in 1997, Carl had already known David's father, Saul, for many years. "He was the ultimate salesman," Carl recalls. "Customers loved him. He had a real good vision on products, and how his home center customers could make money with the products that he would develop. And he had a way about himself. Customers just couldn't say no to him. He was just an incredible, incredible guy—very charming, very persuasive, very genuine, just a good man."

Still, Carl wasn't prepared for what he saw when he visited the Habitat plant for the first time. He was so touched by the sight of the workers with Down syndrome and brain injuries and obvious mental disorders, and so amazed by their high productivity level, that he closed Beaulieu's rug-cutting division and partnered with Habitat to produce the same items for the Home Depot, all under the Beaulieu label. "It's just beautiful to see that people like that get a chance in life and actually can do a lot of the work that you would not necessarily expect them to be able to do," Carl points out. "And they really, really rise to the occasion and you see so much happiness. To me it's just a very satisfying feeling, a rewarding feeling, to see that that can be the case."

Carl's longtime managers weren't so sure about Habitat, at least not until they visited the Rossville plant with the wacky artwork plastering the walls. "The building was smaller and there were just stacks and stacks of things everywhere and we're just like, 'How is this really going to work?'" says Kim Brown, Beaulieu's customer relations manager. "But then over time, and dealing with the individuals and the management there, you see that their people have more pride in what they're doing than some of the people we work closely with today. I mean, they worked seven days a week for us, even lately, and they handle it, where the 'normal' person would be growling. It's good to see that there's somebody not disposing of people because they don't exactly fit the mold. I even took my kids to the Habitat picnic and explained to them that there's a difference in the people, but there isn't a difference in their spirit."

Like Kim, her colleagues, Ben Hahn, national marketing director, and David Bagby, bypass distribution manager, grew up in small Southern towns where people with disabilities were often sheltered or hidden from public view.

"At Habitat," Ben says, "you have people who have been neglected and you have people who have not been given an opportunity and you go there and it's kind of like a fresh look at your own self. It's like you know these people aren't different than us. They've got different challenges than we do. And I think I took a lot out of it. I don't look at things the same way I used to."

David Bagby occasionally drives up to Habitat and slips in the back door, unannounced, so he can observe the workers without being noticed. "They take pride in what they do, and they work hard," he says. "They're not asking, 'When's my next break time?' like us so-called normal people do. They just continue to work and don't really think about it. You have to say, 'Okay, guys, we need to take a break and let's eat lunch now.' They're involved with the job and they enjoy it. And for us so-called normal people, rolling that grass all day long for eight hours, we wouldn't last long at all. I wouldn't. I'd be going nuts."

Because sudden disruptions in the daily routine can be troublesome for some people with mental disabilities, Habitat's special workforce does require strong organization and a commitment to staying on schedule, says Hans Bakker, Beaulieu's director of product management. That means that if a load of Beaulieu carpet is slated to arrive at Habitat at a certain time, it better be there. "With [David's] workforce, it needs to be planned," Hans says. "He cannot go from blue to red [carpet] within a minute. That is even difficult for our folks that are so-called normal. So I think it is very important to him to have a good flow and to have changes come in a gradual way."

David Bagby's impromptu visits prove that the Habitat employees work hard all the time, and aren't simply showing off when someone tours the plant. He and the other Beaulieu executives have been impressed with something else too: the cheery, disabled workers act the same around everyone friend, stranger, buyer, truck driver, CEO. "The thing that hits you the most is when you walk in, whether it's a dinner or anything, lunch, Christmas, they're all smiles," says Kim. "It doesn't matter who you are. It doesn't matter if you're Carl Bouckaert or if you're David Bagby. You're all on an even playing field. There are no status quos. There's none of this, 'This is my business card. This is who I am.' They are who they are, every day. They are the very same—natural, down-to-earth. And it doesn't change no matter how many suits walk in the building or whatever. They'll come up to you and say, 'How are you? I'm so-and-so.' If everybody 'normal' had that same feeling then I guess it would be a better world."

Chuck Gearhart, partner
GEARHART & SUTTON, ROANOKE, VIRGINIA

Chuck Gearhart was part of the Habitat family long before the colossal do-it-yourself retailers like Lowe's and the Home Depot had eclipsed the small, regional home center suppliers. In the mid-1980s, Chuck began purchasing Habitat rugs in his job as a floor-covering buyer for Moore's Lumber & Building Supplies, a DIY company based in Roanoke, Virginia. Saul's down-to-earth credibility and unrivaled knowledge of the industry played a role in Chuck's decision to switch all of the company's business to Habitat instead of splitting it between two suppliers, as they had in the past. So did the fact that Habitat was outperforming its competitors with aggressive pricing, quality products, and reliable shipping. And then there was the matter of David and Saul's humanitarian hiring practices.

"It seemed like a pretty ordinary workplace and then Saul took me out in the plant," Chuck recalls. "What struck me up front is that Saul and David have never been shy about who they hire, and they seem to take a real pride in letting you meet these people. I was a buyer, and I was giving them my business, and David was very, very open and introduced me to the people one by one and let me get to know them a little bit. When you toured the plant, you just got a real feel of the enthusiasm of the people and how seriously they took their work, and how happy they were to be functioning in a society where most people would probably discard them. You felt like you were giving your business to a company that was doing good in the world, and it made you feel good."

Even after Chuck left Moore's, he remained friends with David and Saul, and they kept in touch throughout the years. For the past decade he has worked as an independent manufacturing representative, selling Habitat products to major retailers, particularly Lowe's. Chuck was just as shocked as David when Lowe's awarded the entire boxed-rug account to Habitat in 2002.

"I don't ever want to say that somebody gave Habitat business just because of [its disabled workforce] but when you show the Habitat video at a sales meeting, they very, very quickly learn how Habitat does business. You know, David is not the most polished guy in the world. He doesn't wear a three-piece suit, but when you go into a meeting, he's believable. And when David says something, he does it. He's just like his dad. And I think the people at Lowe's learned that very quickly and they respect that about him.

"To be completely honest, a piece of carpet is a piece of carpet is a piece of carpet. Yes, it's got to be to a quality standard, but after you do that, what do you have to sell somebody? Hopefully you sell them yourself and your company and what you can do and what you're all about, and I think that's exactly what David's done. Almost every meeting we would go in, he would have a new write-up on Habitat and he would share that with the buyers, and I think that impressed them. I think it helped business-wise. It didn't get the business, but I think they enjoy doing business with the company, no different than when I was a buyer."

As someone who's worked for years on both sides of the floor-covering fence—sales and purchasing—Chuck believes Habitat is a beacon of light in the sometimes-unscrupulous corporate realm. "I think what other business people could learn from Habitat is that you can do business the right way and still be very successful. You can treat your people the right way and still get a lot of productivity out of them. You can take a special group of people that most companies wouldn't even consider hiring, and get more productivity and more pride out of that group of people than you would a 'normal' workforce. They've invested in their people and their company and they've done business the right way."

Dan Cellura, director of purchasing and procurement
Mike Renahan, director of product development
Izzo Golf Inc., Macedon, New York

Thanks to the marketing fluke that turned a putting-green sample into a hot seller, one of Habitat's strongest customer segments over the years has been retail sporting goods. Izzo Golf Inc., which also sells golf accessories under the Top Flite and Gold Eagle brands, contracts with Habitat to make a dozen different driving and putting mats. Mike Renahan, director of product development, became aware of Habitat through a referral from a salesman and visited the plant for the first time just after 9/11. He was stunned. "The thing that stuck with me the most was the family atmosphere there," Mike says. "There was no corporate, industrial hierarchy. It was a whole bunch of people in there working together making it happen."

Dan Cellura, director of purchasing and procurement, flew down to the Georgia facility soon after that. "When I was there, one of the employees came up and actually shook my hand and introduced himself," Dan says. "That's not common in plant tours—somebody working on the line coming right up to you and saying, 'My name is so-and-so. What's yours?'"

It didn't take long for the Izzo executives to commission its golf accessory products to Habitat, and they've been consistently pleased with the quality of workmanship, competitive pricing, and accessibility of the Habitat managers. Still, says Dan, who has participated in state-funded programs in which disabled workers have packaged products for Izzo, the greatest appeal may lie in being involved with a company that's doing the right thing by its workers. "We're all in business, so if somebody is 10 percent cheaper, you have to put your business there," Dan admits. "But if everything is apples to apples, of course you feel like you want to help."

Fred Schnair, chairman, Des Plains, Illinois
James Gibson, vice president and general manager
of Georgia operations, Chatsworth, Georgia
JEFFERSON INDUSTRIES INC.

When Habitat landed the big Lowe's account in the spring of 2002, the Rossville, Georgia, rug company teamed up with one of its former competitors, Jefferson Industries Inc., to supply the remnant rug portion of the orders. Jefferson chairman, Fred Schnair, whose 140-employee company is based near Chicago, had known Saul for 35 years and the two men would chat at trade shows, passing the time and "solving the world's problems." He also knew of Habitat's reputation as a merchandising dynamo. So he was delighted to learn that Saul's son, David, was looking for good suppliers to help him keep up with the demand from the 850-store Lowe's chain. The next step, of course, was a visit to Habitat.

"My first impression was total infatuation, really," says James Gibson, vice president and general manager of Georgia operations. As he and Fred trekked through the plant with David, he couldn't take his eyes off the assembly line of employees who were cutting carpet, folding it, and placing it in boxes, all in one synchronized motion. "The people were so fast. You would never believe that David was working anyone with any handicaps whatsoever. They were very productive. I told Fred I was simply amazed. [David] doesn't sacrifice anything in quality and packaging because of the employees that he has. As a matter of fact, I think it's the opposite. I believe David's employees produce more per man by far than our employees."

Fred believes that the specificity of the job functions at Habitat, plus the company's concentration on two basic materials—grass and needle-punch—allow the disabled workers to become experts at what they do. But he doesn't think it would work without the patience and caring of supervisors like David and Connie and Jim. He should know. At one point Jefferson Industries Inc. contracted with what was then known as the CARC (Chicago Association of Retarded Children) to sew small pillows for the airlines industry. "It takes very special people to work with the disabled. Not everybody can do it," Fred says. "I hate to admit it, but we found it extremely difficult. It's very difficult to accommodate. You've got so many other factors in business that you have to deal with."

When they hear that David routinely hires people with disabilities, some industry executives assume he does it in exchange for government incentives, such as supplemented wages or tax breaks, says Fred. "And at Habitat this is not the case. They pay the people normal salaries. They turn down benefits and help from various state agencies and so forth. And this is something that is really not too well known amongst the trade. Not only do they deal with the issues, many of which would be insurmountable to most people, but they seem to be able to overcome them and deal with them and successfully put it together. And it's a remarkable thing. The thing that Habitat is to be most commended for is the fact that they do this because they want to and not for the monetary benefits that can be derived from doing it. That overshadows everything as far as I'm concerned. That, to me, says something."

Rick Parris, general manager
MILLENNIUM PACKAGING SOLUTIONS, CHATTANOOGA, TENNESSEE

One of the core goals at Georgia-Pacific, a leading manufacturer of tissue, pulp, paper, packaging materials, building products, and related chemicals, is to encourage minority, women, and disabled-owned businesses to compete for its business. So when Rick Parris, general manager of Millennium Packaging Solutions, a division of Georgia Pacific, saw an opportunity to hire Habitat workers to help out with one of its labor-intensive tasks, he jumped at the chance.

For the past year, Millennium, which makes corrugated boxes at its Chattanooga-based factory, had been supplying all of Habitat's packaging. One day Rick was talking to David Morris, who happened to mention his desire to diversify the company's services, so he could hire more people with disabilities and provide even greater job security for the ones he already had. "Well, why don't you give me a price on what it would cost for your team to assemble my oven boxes?" he asked David before leaving the plant that day. The figure turned out to be more cost-effective than making the boxes on-site, using Millennium employees.

Soon after, Habitat workers began making the "build-ups" that fit on the bottom of stoves during shipment.

"The quality that they put out is amazing," Rick says. "They've done an outstanding job for us. They're doing them better than we could do them. There's no limit to their work ethic, or in the quality of what these special folks can do."

The fact that the two companies are now each other's customers has shown just how much a business-to-business relationship can pay off. "Hand work, where a box requires something else glued to it or requires us to break items apart, is really not what we should be doing," Rick points out. "We should be making boxes and shipping them out the door and not touching them again, but we do them because there's other business at stake. David's helping us take the cost out of our plant. And because of the work that they're doing over there for us and the quality of what they're sending back to us, there's gonna be a heck of a lot more opportunities for them."

THE PARENTS

Phyllis Schwarz, Lonnie Jacobs's mother

Lonnie Jacobs was just 16 when his mental illness surfaced for the first time and he emerged a different person from the one his family had known. His mother, Phyllis, hates the word "schizophrenia" because of the stigma associated with it. To her, Lonnie is simply Lonnie. "He is very compassionate. He always has been," she says. "There are some traits that he has not lost. He is very loving and considerate. He's always been a joy that way."

Lonnie began working at Habitat in 1995 and, thanks to the right medication, is quite productive in spite of the fact that, according to Phyllis, "he still hears voices and probably always will. There's no cure. He has a low tolerance for stress. Right now he's at the age where it's almost like he's getting a little bit forgetful and stuff like that. This is to be expected. He's got his ups and downs, just like you and me."

Lonnie now lives in his own duplex and pays his own bills. "But without Habitat, where Lonnie can go every day and leave with a sense of accomplishment," says Phyllis, "I hate to think where he would be."

Lisa Blair, Martin Arney's mother

Martin Arney absolutely refuses to give in to his cerebral palsy. Thanks in part to a strong mom with a stubborn streak of her own, he's always been that way.

Since 1996, Martin has been one of Habitat's most loyal employees, often coming to work when he's sick and working extra hours whenever he can, despite the fact that a *regular* day leaves him completely exhausted. When asked what Habitat has meant to him, he cracks a few jokes with his trademark wit, but his mother, Lisa, is quick to point out that he loves working there.

"It gives him something to do every day," she says. "He's on a schedule. It's interesting, especially when they get different temporary people in there. He gets to meet all kinds of people. It's his social outlet, actually, because he doesn't go out a whole lot. And they're good to him. They're really good to all their employees—they show their appreciation at Christmas time, the dinners, and the company picnics where everybody gets together. We always go."

Betty Davis* and Tony Davis, Terry Davis's mother and brother

Betty Davis was ecstatic when Connie Presnell called to offer her son, Terry, a job at Habitat. The first thing Betty did, as usual, was to sit down with the entire family, including Terry, to get everyone's input. The discussion didn't last long; they quickly agreed it was a great idea.

"I was gonna take him out and hunt him a job," Betty remembers. "[My husband] James and I wanted him to work. But we were just debating on where to take him because we didn't really know who might work with him 'cause he's slow."

Terry, who has Down syndrome, had just graduated from his special-ed class at Ridgeland High School in Rossville, Georgia, and he'd been part of the vocational program at Habitat for several years. He was just as thrilled as his mom that Connie was going to hire him. "He was so excited about Habitat and them wanting him to come and work for them," says his brother, Tony. "He was real positive about it and it seemed to lift his spirits."

* Betty Davis passed away in late 2004, after being interviewed for this book.

Each day he would go home and tell his parents how many boxes he'd assembled or how well he'd rolled carpet, and give them a detailed description of how he and David had arm-wrestled during the break. "He was very anxious to go to work every day," Betty says. "He was tired when he came home, but he was really anxious to go to work every morning, and he still is. He's so excited about what he's done to help the company, and I wish that people would stop holding a birth defect against a person, instead of giving them a chance to prove themselves."

The Davises feel a sense of belonging at Habitat too. "This is home," Betty says. "We all feel welcome here. It doesn't matter whether we come up by surprise or whether we're invited for a dinner or whatever, they treat us like we're family."

Yes, they admit, Terry still works at one speed—slow—and he's not perfect. But he fits in perfectly at Habitat. Tony recalls a day not long ago when David challenged Terry to a rug-rolling contest. "And I hate to say this," says Tony, "but Terry's roll looked better than David's."

Helen and Harvey Adams, Sharon Adams's parents

Sharon Adams is one of the first clients David and Saul hired from the Walker County Training Center in 1993. Never mind that she was born with mild mental retardation. She's always been a perfectionist, and a hard worker, and she's never been able to use those skills more than at Habitat. Still, although she "worked" at Habitat through the state program for several years, it wasn't until she became a real, full-time employee that her parents noticed a vast difference. "Her self-esteem improved," says her mother, Helen. "I think she speaks a lot better. She's not as shy as she was. She never looks for the opportunity to be off of the job. She loves working and she loves that paycheck."

Sharon's dad, Harvey, notes that the job has provided his daughter with the self-support she's always craved. "I think if she didn't go to work at Habitat, she'd probably sit down and cry. She loves it there."

Like many parents whose grown children are employed at Habitat, the Adamses wish more families would help their disabled sons and daughters find meaningful work. "It really motivates them when they go out and work and earn money," Helen says. "It means a lot more to them than getting government funds. That's always there, I feel like, if you need it. You could still get it if it ever came to that. That's where some more education needs to be done, making people aware this is there for you when you need it. And it just means so much more to them as a person when they're actually earning. I know *I* feel different when I go to work."

THE GOVERNMENT WORKERS

Jim Moon, director
LOOKOUT MOUNTAIN COMMUNITY SERVICES, LAFAYETTE, GEORGIA

By the time Jim Moon became director of Lookout Mountain Community Services, the mother agency that oversees the Walker County Training Center and its counterparts in three other north Georgia counties, the connection between Habitat and the state program had all but been severed. David and Connie just hadn't gotten along with the previous state personnel, and they felt hampered by what they perceived as insistence on labeling clients and keeping them from achieving their true potential. One of the first things Jim did when he took over the reins of the program in 1998 was to re-establish the link with Habitat, but with a twist. These days the Center actually serves as a placement service by sending job candidates with disabilities to the plant when there are openings. And since transportation is a major issue for many people with physical and mental challenges, the Center provides van service for several Habitat employees who live in north Georgia. (The enclaves, incidentally, now serve as short-term investments in on-the-job training, rather than as permanent work groups for people with disabilities.)

Habitat has turned out to be a wonderful source of jobs for his agency's clients, says Jim. "It didn't make sense for us *not* to utilize them as a resource. They actually view a person with disabilities as a person that has *capabilities*. So they look beyond the disability into what that person can actually do. They don't treat them any differently than anybody else that works there. They're all one group of employees. It's not *them* and *us*.

"In reality, a person with a disability just wants a chance to prove that they can work and wants to be paid a respectable, decent wage for that work, and Habitat does that," Jim adds. "They pay people for the work that they do. They don't fall back on a sub-minimum wage for the people who are working there with disabilities, which is what happens with programs like we have here, where we do contracted piecework. Centers like that tend to rely on a sub-minimum wage certificate that's authorized by the Department of Labor to pay people at less than minimum wage per hour, but the person with the disability may not be able to work fast enough to make that minimum wage. Habitat has been able to take a person and have them perform the job they need performed and then pay him or her at least that minimum wage and typically more, which is very unusual."

Another rarity, Jim says, is that Habitat is not only *open* to hiring people with disabilities, but actively *seeks* them. That's because the company's managers defied convention, gave employees with challenges a chance to prove themselves, and quickly learned what he's known for some time. "A person with a disability is typically gonna be more stable than someone who has *no* disability," he says. "They're gonna be more motivated to work and to keep their job, and generally they're gonna be better trained because they do want to do a good job and they do want to have that job on a long-term basis. That's one of the things we try to sell to the employers when we go out: that our people will be well-trained, that they will be dependable because they'll be at work every day, and if they can't be at work then we've got a backup. So you don't have to worry about coming into work one day and the parking lot being empty because everybody decided to take a holiday or whatever. It's a dependable workforce."

Jim has seen a definite shift in public perception since he began his career in the early 1970s. He recalls the days when most people with disabilities didn't work at all, when doctors were advising parents to place their developmentally delayed children in institutions, rather than bring them home from the hospital, when insensitive passengers would stare at the "retards" on a bus. But a lot of work still needs to be done to educate the general community, he notes.

"The attitudes have changed a great deal, but not enough, not enough," he says. "I had a rather heated conversation with an area physician about whether or not a person with mental retardation should be on the list as a heart recipient. You're talking about a person with as much education as anybody would ever have in our society, and the attitude was, 'Well, that person is not worth anything. Why would we want to give them a perfectly good heart?' So the negative attitudes—they're still out there. And I don't know how you overcome that except through some sort of an education process and showing people that we're all alike. The doctor that I talked to, I got his attention when I said, 'Your son or daughter is only a heartbeat away from being a person with a traumatic brain injury. All it takes is making the wrong turn at a stop sign and getting broad-sided.'

"So when you're talking about changing attitudes toward people with disabilities, it's one step at a time, and Habitat is a good step. The more people we can place in jobs and prove that people with disabilities have capabilities, the better. That employer will tell other employers who will tell other people. Disabilities can usually be overcome, minimized in a lot of different ways. It's a whole lot easier to build on people's capabilities, and that's what people need to learn. Open your eyes, open your mind, and see what value and worth that person has to you as an employer and then capitalize on that."

Tom Henderson, vocational rehabilitation counselor
GEORGIA DEPARTMENT OF LABOR, LaFAYETTE, GEORGIA

Tom Henderson knows how hard it is to convince some business owners to hire people with disabilities. "I'm in this every day and most employers, the first thing they're gonna say is, 'Well, my insurance is going up because people with disabilities are more likely to have accidents.' And they feel like they're gonna be absent more and all this stuff, and none of it's true. I'd say the majority are really leery about hiring anybody with a disability," says Tom, who frequently tries to place workers in his role as a vocational rehabilitation counselor with the Georgia Department of Labor. His agency serves about 500 people with disabilities, although only about 20 percent successfully find paying work.

Habitat was, of course, an exception. Tom had just started working as an employment coordinator at the Walker County Training Center in 1987 when he talked David Morris into hosting the first enclave of eight disabled clients. They would later be hired as full-time employees.

"David was always real supportive of them," Tom recalls. "At breaks and lunch and so forth, he was out playing with them. He had basketball courts set up for them and he was always interacting with them. They thought the world of David. There wasn't anybody any better to them than David, and he was very patient with them and he'd hang in there with them until they got their speed built up to where they could handle the job. And David would do stuff like picnics and take them to ballgames and just all kinds of things like that. And really, they worked hard for him 'cause they liked him so much."

The tension that once existed between the state and the crusading managers at Habitat is gone and "they've gained an immense amount of respect" in the community, Tom points out. "David is really admired.

And the clients, after they're there a few days, they just fall right in and they want to do their best and be productive. I think the people in the community that know David and know about Habitat are really positive about him and what he's done."

The reason Habitat has flourished, Tom says, is really quite simple. But its winning approach is not that easy to find in the corporate environment. "Before I was in this field, I was a plant manager for a company that at the time had 80,000 employees," Tom says. "There was always so much pressure. You didn't mess up or you were terminated. The emphasis was on the dollar. Make a dollar, make a dollar. At Habitat, people work there because they're loyal to David. And they do a good job. They're not under all that pressure. It just shows me the way David has operated—he's been patient, compassionate, caring—if you do that, if an employer cares about their people and tries to meet *their* needs, they're going to perform. I think if more companies would operate their business like David they'd be a whole lot more successful. It's just a matter of treating others like you want them to treat you."

Melinda Wallins Lemmon, executive director
Bartow County (Georgia) Department of Economic Development, Cartersville, Georgia

Growing up as the daughter of the "4-H Lady," Melinda Wallins Lemmon listened as her hearing-impaired mother told stories about fighting the stereotypes other people tried to thrust on her. It was hard for Melinda to believe that her mom, a county extension agent widely respected in the community, could have ever been belittled by her classmates. "She was treated as inferior and even stupid and teachers would put her in the back of the classroom, which is the last place she needed to be," Melinda says. "She read lips but she needed to be in the front of the room to do that, and it wasn't until third grade when she had a male teacher and the lower tones of his voice helped her hear better [that everyone realized what was happening]. He put her in the front of the classroom and it made all the difference in the world. And she wound up overcoming her challenges once she realized what it was and once they realized, 'Hey, this is a straight A student. Why are we putting her in the back of the room and treating her as inferior?' She wound up in the top 10 percent of her class, beating all the boys in math and science and going on to college and earning her masters degree."

Melinda was a young intern at the Catoosa County (Georgia) Chamber of Commerce when she first met the people at Habitat in the summer of 1987. Later, as executive director of the Catoosa County Development Authority, she coordinated leadership tours of area businesses, including Habitat. She was delighted to find a local company where employees with disabilities could thrive, but she soon discovered that Habitat was an oasis in a sea of dubious manufacturers, many of whom feared that people with disabilities would create a liability for the company or inhibit production. What she saw at Habitat, on the other hand, were employers who, instead of trying to make their workers conform to a traditional manufacturing line, found ways to help each one be successful, even if it took a little extra training or a minor tweak of a machine.

"To me, the whole reason behind economic development, working with new and existing industries, is to provide jobs for people who work in that community," says Melinda, who nominated Habitat for the Georgia Economic Development Association (GEDA) Existing Industry Appreciation Award in 2001. "Everyone has a need to work, to feel self-fulfilled. There are so many good things that can go along with just having a job and feeling independent. However, it's difficult for someone with special challenges to find a job, either to be able to prove themselves as a worthy employee to those who may not give them a chance, or to overcome some other stigmas and stereotypes that our society has of them.

"My whole desire in doing economic development, which I learned I wanted to do at a pretty early age, was to serve the people of the community and help them find good jobs. And that meant *everyone*. David demonstrated to the other manufacturers that you *can* take a chance on these folks. They'll be some of your hardest and best workers. I would match his productivity and results to just about any manufacturer."

THE COMMUNITY LEADERS

Alan Smith, president
FIRST CITIZENS BANK, CLEVELAND, TENNESSEE

For Alan Smith, writing a motivational letter to his employees has become a Christmastime ritual. Each year, the president of First Citizens Bank, a 10-branch holding company based in Cleveland, Tennessee, sends his entire staff a memo that is part business wrap-up, part human-interest story. After attending a holiday open house at Habitat's new plant in 2003, a year that had been particularly difficult for several bank employees and family members who had been diagnosed with cancer, Alan had no doubt what he would write. He began by describing the curious Habitat motto, *A Company of Positive Distractions*.

"If anyone should be bitter, it would be the 'company' (people) of Habitat," he penned. "Ironically, their conditions have allowed them to discover a very simple and profound truth that takes some people a lifetime to understand and yet [is] artfully conveyed in their five-word motto. Their message is clear: we all have "distractions," or if you prefer, "challenges," "setbacks" or "misfortunes"; however we choose how we view and react to them…As we begin a new year, keep their example and motto in mind as they may afford you the strength to persevere through your own certain future 'distractions.'"

Alan had been itching for a good excuse to tell his employees about Habitat ever since David and Saul began doing business with his bank nearly three years earlier. On his second visit to the Rossville location, David showed Alan around. "I've been on a lot of plant tours," Alan says. "And normally what you see is nobody talking to each other, a 'these are our jobs, we're getting them done' kind of sterile environment. And when you walked around Habitat, everybody stopped and talked. As a business person, I am used to shaking hands with the president and not really creating a dialogue with the people that work in the plant. And you can't go through a plant tour there and not do that, because people just came up and they were very curious about who we were, what we were doing, and they were more physical."

In fact, it took Alan a while to get comfortable with the touchy-feely atmosphere at Habitat. It's not every day, after all, that a banker is hugged by a bunch of complete strangers, who seem genuinely happy to see him. As the months passed, he came to expect such friendly behavior at Habitat. He found himself looking forward to his visits there, and not just for business reasons. "We feel like it makes us better by being associated with them," Alan admits. He began sharing their story as an example of perseverance in his Sunday School class for teenagers, many of whom expressed the usual complaints about adolescence. When he tells a new group of edgy teens about Habitat, Alan says, "It will stop them dead in their tracks."

That's one reason he decided to write an employee memo about Habitat's unusual workforce. Maybe, just maybe, it would help his own staff feel better about their problems too. "You think of how life has thrown you this curve ball and how you're gonna get through it," he says. "And you stop and you think about the people who work there, and you ask yourself, *Who's been dealt a rougher card? Who has a harder hand to deal with?* If *they* can find a way to get up every day and come to work, be productive, be responsible toward one another with the circumstances that they bring to the table, what does that tell you and me?"

Darlene Jenkins, vocational consultant
SISKIN HOSPITAL FOR PHYSICAL REHABILITATION, CHATTANOOGA, TENNESSEE

Darlene Jenkins was "shocked" when she walked in the door of the Habitat plant in the fall of 1997. She had just gone to work as a vocational consultant at Siskin Hospital for Physical Rehabilitation in Chattanooga, Tennessee, and was acquainting herself with local companies willing to employ people who had sustained brain and spinal cord injuries.

"The thing I remember most was watching the school kids come in," she says. "They were so excited and they were so alive and they were smiling. And they knew where to go. They hit that door running. They could not wait to get to their workstations. And I stood there in awe thinking, *Wow, if the rest of the world did this, what a great place we'd live in.* I mean, I was just totally taken aback by how they were so passionate about what they did. It was one of those life-defining moments when you stood there and you were the observer and you watched what was happening and it just took your breath away."

After that, Darlene called Connie Presnell whenever she had a severely disabled client who couldn't work elsewhere. They would arrange for a half-day "test run" to make sure the person could handle the job. Once, when Darlene brought a client to Habitat, the man began having seizures. They soon realized that any type of change, including a switch in environment, would trigger the episodes. Despite their patient approach and experience in handling crises, that was too risky for even the Habitat managers to deal with on a daily basis. Clients who simply needed a repetitive, manual job, on the other hand, generally fared well at Habitat. The company turned out to be a good fit for most people with brain injuries, because it allowed them to bypass their problems with short-term memory, problem solving, and multi-tasking.

About four times a year, Darlene and her colleagues request tours of Habitat for clients in the hospital's community re-entry program to show them that yes, there *is* life after a car accident or stroke. And she sometimes visits alone to recharge her emotional batteries and help regain her perspective. "There would be times that I'd just go out there simply because I needed a refresher, because clients can be draining, especially when you're working with them over and over. I would go there to get nourishment and remind myself that what we were doing [in the rehabilitation program] was right."

Tim Dempsey, executive director
CHATTANOOGA ENDEAVORS, CHATTANOOGA, TENNESSEE

Tim Dempsey's first thought when he was introduced to Habitat's special workforce was, *This looks like one of the special-ed classes my sister used to be in.* The next thing he noticed was that the factory provided much more than jobs. "It's hard to tell if it's a culture or if it's a business," he says. "It's got a life of its own. And the thing that struck me when we went out there was that the people that were coming to work there were really coming to live. I mean, you walk into a plant very often and people are punching in and as soon as they punch the clock they've got a frown on their face. And then they keep it up for eight hours and then they punch out and they go home and then they do it again the next day and the next day and the next day, and it's drudgery. But here you've got people that punch the clock and as soon as they do there's a shine on their face, and that's very, very different."

As executive director of Chattanooga Endeavors, a transitional program that helps ex-prisoners find and prepare for employment, Tim could identify. Many of Habitat's disabled workers have had to deal with "the same kind of stereotypes we get hit with, that 'an ex-offender is always gonna be an ex-offender, that eventually they're gonna recommit a crime and they're gonna do it on my shift.' And so they hesitate to hire them."

Habitat's practice of employing "the people no one else wants to hire" has shown Tim that despite the hesitations and fears of many employers, there are some willing to take that risk. David Morris now serves on the organization's New Ventures committee, and is working with Tim to help start a group of self-sustaining, for-profit companies operated by ex-prisoners.

"The thing that David really demonstrates well is that it's not only possible but it is *inevitable* that a group of people will profit by doing the right thing," Tim says. "And he shows that in every corner of his organization. Every time you turn the page, David's doing the right thing, and the right thing results. And I think that really speaks against the kind of deception that you see in common business practices and common social-service organizations. It's not that he's got a *unit* in his business that acts that way, he's got an *entire company* that acts that way, which is very unusual."

Glenn and Kaye Vaughn
RETIRED CIVIC LEADERS, RINGGOLD, GEORGIA

Glenn Vaughn had a personal reason for wanting to tour Habitat with one of the county leadership groups in 1995. It wasn't because he was politically active in the community and wanted to drum up support, or because he'd retired from his job as an air traffic controller and had too much time on his hands. It wasn't even because his wife, Kaye, was president of the Catoosa County (Georgia) Chamber of Commerce.

The Vaughns' granddaughter, Jessica, had been born blind, autistic, and with severe learning disabilities. They knew they could help care for her while she was young, and that she might even grow up to be healthy and happy. But what would her adult future be like? The job prospects for Jessica, or lack of them, worried Glenn and Kaye more than anything else. During the Habitat tour, Glenn recalls, "It was like seeing that there is hope, that at some point in our granddaughter's life she will either be lucky enough to be employed at a place similar to this, or she will have someone that will be an advocate for her in her adult-hood as much as David is for the folks that work for him."

The Vaughns knew firsthand how critical advocacy could be to the well-being of a disabled child. For years they and Jessica's mother had struggled with government agencies, and they had grown weary of all the paper shuffling and bureaucracy and general pessimism about Jessica's chances for employment when she got older.

"People like Jessica," Kaye says, "have the same desire for social relationships that we all have, and they're pretty much isolated when they're going through school, even though a lot of them are mainstreamed. And when they go to Habitat, they're not different anymore. It's just so encouraging to know that there are places where people like that can reach their potential."

Glenn admired David Morris so much for routinely hiring people with disabilities that he nominated him to carry the Olympic torch in 1996. And the two men became good friends. Jessica is now enrolled in a college for the visually impaired, studying to become a caregiver, and has become far more independent than the social-service workers ever thought she would be. "It's always going to be a challenge," says Glenn. "But we're so excited that there are [companies] out there like Habitat."

Greg Sundell, executive director
ARKAY PERSONNEL INC., TAYLOR, MICHIGAN

Greg Sundell read about Habitat in a magazine article and was so intrigued by the notion that a business owner could "run a for-profit, manufacturing company with the ideals of an entrepreneur who also cared about and loved his employees" that he flew down from Michigan and spent a couple of days with David and his special workforce. By the time he left, Greg, the executive director of a non-profit agency that finds jobs for adults with disabilities, was so fired up about what he'd seen that he vowed to start a similar, for-profit venture in his own town. Greg even wrote a letter to his congressman, describing his visit to Habitat and asking the lawmaker for advice on how to run a factory with disabled workers, just like Saul and David had done.

Unfortunately, Greg's idea never quite got off the ground. It wasn't that he didn't try. But he didn't know much about manufacturing and he couldn't seem to find the support he needed to turn his dream into reality. In his role as a job placement specialist for people with cognitive disabilities, he encounters the same kind of resistance. "I haven't come across another manufacturing company that's willing to do the same thing that David has," says Greg, who also teaches as an adjunct professor of special-education at Wayne State University in Detroit. "People think there's a magic pill for working with people with disabilities. There isn't. People think they come with acting-out behaviors. Well, so do people without disabilities, you know?"

Another problem, Greg notes, is that even if an employer *does* hire someone with special challenges, when corporate belt-tightening is necessary, the disabled person is often the first to go if he can't work faster or double his production. "When we think of a great employee, we think in terms of speed and accuracy of their work. But we also look to see if they're trustworthy, if they're loyal, if they're enthusiastic and willing to learn. And many of the folks with disabilities have those qualities, but may take a little bit longer to learn the components of a job and the individual steps. But it's well worth it, because what makes a company grow is in fact not just speed and accuracy but also those other qualities. You have to *care* about the speed. You have to *care* about the accuracy of the work. Look at David's model. It works."

Seventeen

The Habitat Advantage:
Why the Company's Unconventional
Workers Outproduce the Competition

DESPITE ALL THE KUDOS from visitors, customers, and industry associates, it's difficult for some hard-nosed business managers to believe that a company like Habitat can truly be more efficient than its conventional competitors. Yet the data shows that it can, and does. In this chapter, we'll give the no-frills facts about Habitat's high productivity rate and the reasons behind it.

Today, Habitat employs about 80 people, most of whom have a physical or mental disability, or both. Contrary to public perception, because of their strong work ethic, company loyalty, and ability to focus on tasks for a long period of time, the disabled workers are generally *more* productive than their able-bodied counterparts at other companies. This distinction can even be seen in one of the company's sideline services, in which Habitat employees assemble large oven boxes for Millennium Packaging Solutions, a Chattanooga-based division of Georgia Pacific. Before the box company contracted with Habitat to handle this labor-intensive task, it took three or four of Millennium's own employees an entire week to produce 1,200 pieces. At Habitat, it only takes two people *a day and a half* to do the same thing.

Habitat visitors can't help but notice the difference. When James Gibson, vice president of Chicago-based Jefferson Industries, walked through the Habitat plant for the first time, he was shocked at the speed and accuracy of the disabled employees who were cutting, folding, and boxing grass rugs. "I kept looking around and thinking, *These people are so efficient at what they're doing*," says James, whose 140-employee corporation used to compete with Habitat, but now supplies them with remnant rugs for a major account. "I believe [their] employees produce more per man *by far* than our employees."

Despite the hands-on nature of the business, Habitat's labor costs total only about 5 percent of gross sales, a fraction of the 25 to 30 percent of most comparable cut-and-sew carpet operations. And it's not because the employees are underpaid. Very few, in fact, make only minimum wage; most earn the industry average of $7 to $12 per hour, with some making as much as $18 per hour and managers earning much more. All receive hefty year-end bonuses and other perks.

They've certainly earned them. Here's why:

1. **Zero back orders in 24 years**. The overall fill rate is 99.9 percent. The 0.01 percent of unfilled orders stems from outside factors, such as shipping mistakes caused by freight lines.
2. **Product defect rate: Less than one-half of 1 percent** . Fewer than 10 rugs have been incorrectly cut in the company's history, and the return rate is so negligible it is not even recorded.
3. **Zero accidents among the workers with disabilities**. Since Habitat opened for business in 1981, there have only been three on-site accidents. All three involved "able-bodied" supervisors, not disabled employees.
4. **Practically no absenteeism**. Sickness, inclement weather, and other challenges seldom keep loyal Habitat employees from coming to work. Many times, their supervisors have had to insist that they see a doctor or stay home when they have the flu.
5. **Very little turnover due to job dissatisfaction or firings**. When employees do leave the company, the single biggest reason is lack of transportation. Tammy, a hearing-impaired woman and one of Habitat's best workers, was forced to quit her job when the plant moved from north Georgia to Tennessee (farther away from her home) because she didn't feel comfortable driving in interstate traffic to get there. Even when someone quits or takes a sabbatical because of a physical or mental disability, the person often returns to Habitat months later.
6. **Cross-training for all employees**, thereby ensuring job flexibil-

ity and reducing the need to call in extra workers to fill in for someone who's out. The entire staff, even the most severely disabled, can perform at least three out of four job tasks, and most are trained on every single function in the plant.

7. **Fewer supervisors, not more.** In many factories, productivity slides when supervisors are away. At Habitat, however, there is no need to micro-manage employees. They do their jobs, and do them well, whether or not the boss is around. Two managers oversee the entire plant, even on high-volume days.

8. **Less time and money spent tracking comparative data.** Because some events, such as accidents and firings, are extremely rare, there is no need to keep detailed quality-control records, thereby saving additional administrative costs.

Entrepreneurs from Maine to Washington have heard about Habitat's unusual success story, and contacted the company's executives for advice on how to set up their own disability-hiring programs. They are often surprised at the minimal investment required to get started. Initially, the Habitat managers were prepared to make concessions on a regular basis, but they soon realized that the special treatment was neither necessary nor particularly welcomed and that, for the most part, the employees with challenges didn't want to be treated differently from anyone else. It might take an extra week or two, at most, for someone with a severe developmental disability to master a new job. And occasionally plant engineer Jerry Treadwell spends a couple of hours adapting a jig, at no additional cost to the company.

The payoff for a few extra hours of training time is well worth the effort, asserts Habitat CEO, David Morris. Without the company's dedicated employees, Habitat's high profit margin and resilience in the face of a shifting marketplace would be much more difficult to maintain. Because employees are family members, not faceless numbers with quotas to meet, they feel better about themselves and therefore produce more.

That's one reason Habitat doesn't keep records that show how the company's disabled workers stack up against their able-bodied counterparts. To do so, say the Habitat managers, would be highly prejudicial, even unethical—similar to comparing the productivity of Caucasian workers to that of minorities, based on the assumption that one group can outpace the other. Here, as in any workplace, an employee's productivity ultimately depends on his or her individual abilities and attitude. Although the number of rugs a worker can cut, roll, or package varies from person to person, at Habitat it all evens out in the end, with some workers taking longer to complete their job tasks, and others able to work three times as fast as the "normal" employees.

Quite by accident, what began as a humanitarian effort to give "the people no one else wants to hire" a chance to prove themselves has given the company a concrete advantage in an increasingly competitive marketplace. Despite the fickle nature of the $12 billion carpet industry, Habitat's rug orders are on the rise and daily production is higher than ever. By July of 2004 the company had already met its gross revenues for all of 2003.

Eighteen

You Can Do This Too

AFTER HIS SPEECH at the national Business for Social Responsibility conference in 1998, the audience bombarded David Morris with questions:

"Won't it cost my company a lot of money to start a disability-hiring program?"

"How can I possibly take time to do this when my day is already stretched thin?"

"What will our customers think?"

"But don't they have more accidents on the job than 'normal' people?"

"Won't this negatively impact my bottom line?"

Not one to mince words, David explained the advantages *and* challenges of hiring people with disabilities, but his response to each question circled back to one core philosophy: If you do this, you *will* have a better company, financially and otherwise. "The best advice I can give is to open your heart a little and trust in people," David says. "They do make mistakes, but so do I. All it takes is changing your paradigms and your mindset and realizing that disabled people aren't dumb."

Over the years, David and the other Habitat managers have heard just about every excuse in the book for not hiring people with disabilities. Yes, they admit, it requires patience, creativity, and a willingness to be flexible. And it may not be suitable for every company and every disabled person. Just like their non-disabled peers, some physically and mentally challenged employees just don't have the work ethic or the stamina or the desire to do a good job. At Habitat, those workers are either fired or will quit on their own.

The main reason more employers don't hire the disabled, say David and his managers, is the same one that holds people back from pursuing their dreams: *fear*. They're afraid they'll lose money. They're afraid it will slow down production. They're afraid it will hinder the performance of the other workers. Most of all, they're afraid to take a risk.

That explains why companies like Habitat International, Inc. are still in the minority, and why *two-thirds* of working-age people with disabilities are unemployed. In a 2003 *Work Trends* study conducted by the John J. Heldrich Center for Workforce Development at Rutgers University, only 25 percent of the 501 employers interviewed said their company has at least one worker with a physical or mental disability. Less than half provide training to educate other employees about working with people with disabilities. And many are even more hesitant to hire special-needs employees during tough economic times. The report notes that "people with physical and mental disabilities continue to be vastly underrepresented in the American workplace" and that this group represents "an untapped pool of labor."

When asked to name the greatest barrier to hiring disabled workers, one-third of the survey respondents said that people with disabilities couldn't effectively perform the required job tasks. But national job studies show that people with disabilities have *equal or higher* performance ratings, better retention rates, and less absenteeism.

The second most common reason for not hiring people with disabilities, according to the *Work Trends* survey, is the fear of having to make costly accommodations. Yet among the respondents who said they have actually hired disabled workers, three of four said no workplace changes at all were needed. When accommodations *were* necessary, the average cost was under $500, less than many had anticipated. The reality, says David, is that the most important modification employers must make is not in a piece of equipment or in the ergonomics of a workstation but in their own perceptions. They must learn to see past the disability and view the person as simply that: a person.

If you're a business owner or a human resources manager or a supervisor in a manufacturing plant, office, or store, read on for suggestions on how to implement a disability-hiring program. If you work for a social-service agency, rehabilitation center, or other organization that serves people with disabilities, these suggestions may help you become a better advocate for your clients. And if you're the parent, caregiver, or teacher of a disabled child who's old enough to work, this advice applies to you too. Even if you're not currently in any of these roles, the following tips may help cast a fresh perspective on someone you work with or live near or sit next to in church:

- *Open your mind.* Look past your own prejudices and fears and make a commitment to giving it a try. Remember that physical appearance, even in someone with Down syndrome or a facial deformity, can be misleading. Understand, too, that hiring someone with disabilities isn't simply about adhering to state mandates or the requirements of the Americans with Disabilities Act (ADA). This is about treating others as you would want to be treated. It's about taking a chance and giving someone else a chance to excel. Go into this with a positive attitude and a willingness to see it through. Stretch your paradigms and watch what happens.
- *Find a role model*, preferably in your own community, and take a tour of the business. Interview the owner or managers about their hiring practices, special challenges, and the benefits of hiring people with disabilities. Ask if they'll serve as a mentor for you as you learn the ropes.
- *Contact your state or local mental health association and disability organizations*, especially those that help special-needs workers find jobs in the community. See if the Chamber of Commerce or manufacturers association in your area has a supported-employment program. Ask these groups for employee referrals and advice on how to get started. Establish a good rapport with someone you can call when you have questions or concerns.
- *Cultivate relationships with special-education teachers* and invite them to bring their disabled students to learn on-the-job skills at your company. In many cases, these educators are just as concerned as parents about what will happen to their students after graduation, and they actively look for ways to help them make the transition into the real world. Through on-site vocational programs, students learn valuable job skills and supervisors can "apprentice" future employees, with no liability. (The school system is responsible for the individual as long as he's going to school, so you do not need to provide workers' compensation.) By the time the students graduate from high school, they should be comfortable with the job requirements and ready to work for real wages.

And you'll be aware of their special talents and needs. Start by calling the director of special-education for your county's school system and ask about hosting a couple of students from the high school nearest your place of business.

- Another low-risk way to employ people with disabilities is to *team up with a temporary placement agency* where disabled workers go to find jobs. Be sure representatives from "regular" temp agencies are aware that you welcome physically and mentally challenged employees. Ask them to let you know when an appropriate candidate applies for a position.

- *Do not rely solely on formal evaluations* of the disabled. Get to know each person as an individual. Do you automatically assume that tall people can do only one thing, or that redheads aren't capable of performing certain tasks? Of course not. People with special challenges are no different; they're merely human beings with unique personalities, needs, and abilities. If possible, when hiring people with disabilities, bypass the intermediaries and work directly with the individuals and their families. Accepting referrals from state agencies does not mean you are obligated to follow their guidelines.

- *Start small* by introducing a few workers into a single department or unit. Don't try to bring in a dozen mentally challenged employees at once if no one in your organization has ever worked around people with disabilities. It doesn't matter whether you manage a 5,000-employee corporation or a mom-and-pop restaurant or a tiny floral shop; there is most likely a place in your organization for at least one disabled person.

- *Educate management first.* Help them understand what you're doing, and why. Your managers *must* be sold on the idea before they can help other employees accept it. Communicate openly with everyone on your staff and be prepared to address fears and answer tough questions. Realize, too, that you can't wipe out prejudice in the workplace, at least not overnight. Give your "regular" workers a chance to accept the newcomers. Chances are they'll see for themselves just what a valuable contribution disabled workers can make to the workplace.

- *Be patient—or hire a supervisor who is.* Consider bringing on board a manager already familiar with the nuances of working with people with disabilities—a former teacher, perhaps, or a job coach used to overseeing clients with special challenges. You may feel more at ease with an experienced staff member who understands the frustrations of people with disabilities and can handle problems as they arise.

- *Steer parents and caregivers to the right resources* so they can better understand how full-time employment will affect their children's supplemental income. Bringing home a paycheck does not mean a disabled person will automatically lose her Medicare, Medicaid, or other medical coverage. She may have to give up a portion of her SSI benefits, but if she ever stops working, she can reapply for SSI, and the checks will start arriving again in a few weeks. During the job interview, offer to put the parents or the disabled person in contact with the local Social Security office, so they'll have all the information they need to feel financially comfortable.

- *Understand the possible medical implications* of hiring the disabled and make sure other employees and managers are trained to handle emergencies. People with disabilities are just as conscientious about taking prescribed medications as the rest of the population, so that shouldn't be a major concern. On the other hand, if the person you hire is prone to seizures or other life-threatening problems, be sure your staff is aware of procedures and knows what they're expected to do during an episode.

- *Integrate people with disabilities into the general workplace.* Don't try to segregate them from the rest of your staff, or relegate them to a corner of the factory or office. Otherwise, you're just perpetuating an "us vs. them" mentality. And that's exactly what you *don't* want to do.

- *Let the disabled employees mentor each other.* You'd be surprised how much a person with Down syndrome can teach someone just like him, and without feeling threatened that the rookie is after his job. More often than not, people with disabilities want to help others succeed. And everyone benefits in the process.

- *Keep a sense of humor.* People with disabilities don't always take themselves seriously. Why should you? Find ways to turn mistakes and foibles into reasons to laugh.

- *Follow your own style.* David Morris is quick to point out that the Habitat model isn't for everyone. You don't have to go to extremes with wacky artwork, a basketball court, or an in-house radio station. You don't have to be physically affectionate with your employees. All you need is an open heart and a willingness to accept, and honor, their differences.

- *If greed is your motivation, forget it.* You'll defeat the whole purpose if you hire people with disabilities just so you can take advantage of tax breaks or save money by paying cheap wages. Like foster parents who house more kids just so they can pocket the government subsidy—not because they care about the children and want to give them a better life—you can't accept government incentives and expect to cultivate a "family" of healthy workers. They'll know, somehow, what you're up to. Likewise, you can't look at this as a charity or use it as a public relations tool to boost your own philanthropic image or your company's standing in the community. There are plenty of other ways to do that. If, however, you do the right thing, for the right reason, if you hire people with disabilities because you're convinced they'll be valuable members of your organization, then they'll work hard for you and you'll watch your revenues grow.
- *Consider the ripple effect.* Remember that hiring people with disabilities:
  - Reduces their dependency on government subsidies, shifts responsibility for their income to the private sector, and lifts the financial burden from taxpayers. When disabled citizens work, they stop relying on federally funded Supplemental Security Income (SSI) or the sub-minimum wages they might otherwise earn in state-funded programs. They become fully participating members of the community who pay taxes, no longer depend on government aid, and contribute to or take care of their own living expenses.
  - Builds on the investment of special-education programs in which high-school-age students learn valuable vocational skills. These skills are of no use to them if they don't find jobs after graduation.
  - Offers an alternative for American business owners who feel that the only way to stay competitive is to outsource and hire low-paid workers in other countries. The Habitat approach, on the other hand, helps keep jobs at home by building a team of loyal, productive, quality-driven employees who look out for your company's interests.
  - Gives you, as a business person, the chance to reach a whole new segment of the population. Disabled employees relate better to customers with disabilities, who represent $1 trillion in annual consumer spending.

Epilogue

An Open Letter from David Morris
CEO, HABITAT INTERNATIONAL, INC.

"No poor, rural, weak, or black person should ever again have to bear the additional burden of being deprived of the opportunity for an education, a job, or simple justice."
—JIMMY CARTER, in his inaugural address as governor, Atlanta, January 12, 1971

Through his unfaltering human-rights activism, former President Jimmy Carter continues to show that every person, regardless of color or economic status or physical ability, is entitled to a "normal," fulfilling life. Maybe that's why, nearly 35 years after he spoke these words at his first gubernatorial address, he is still one of my most inspiring role models.

So are the "distracted" people who work with me at Habitat. They have taught me so much about life, love, and doing business the right way. Time and again, they have demonstrated what it means to keep carrying on despite ugly prejudice and misconceptions and muscles that don't always want to cooperate. They have broken down my own barriers with their kindness and loyalty, and have shown me the power of the human spirit, no matter what body it's housed in. They have made me a better person than I ever could have been without them.

Over the years, I've also witnessed a gradual, positive shift in public attitudes and in the way government-funded agencies run their disability-hiring programs. I've seen the old-school bias against people who are "different" start to lessen a bit. Educational mainstreaming has helped make people with disabilities more visible and less segregated from the rest of society. So has the activism of well-known celebrities like the late Christopher Reeve. But we still have a long way to go. Many business people still cling to old myths—"Disabled employees don't perform as well on the job," "It will cost me too much to hire them," "They will disrupt my other workers"—that keep them from hiring people with disabilities.

Hopefully this mindset will change even more within the next decade, and employees with Down syndrome, brain injury, and other physical and mental distractions will become more commonplace in the business world. This will, however, call for compassion, something most MBAs aren't taught in business school. You'll have to learn that on your own. But if you hire people with so-called disabilities, I can guarantee this: it won't take long for them to teach you about genuine love and caring just by being themselves. When you see a person who's been told "no" every day of his life and is now saying, "Yes, I can do it," it's hard not to get inspired. And you'll be the one who grows.

If you're an employer, I urge you to let go of your fear and your preconceived notions and hire individuals, not labels or categories. Substitute the word "able" for "disabled" in your own mind and see what happens.

If you're a parent or caregiver of a person with a disability, I urge you to take a leap of faith and allow your loved one to spread her wings in the workplace. There are ways to help keep her government-funded medical benefits intact if necessary.

If you're a working-age person with a disability, I urge you to seek employment with a socially responsible business. They are out there. Even if the company has never employed a person with special challenges, go into the interview with a "yes, yes, I can" attitude. Let the person who's hiring see your confidence in your own abilities, and explain how you can help him build a better workplace. Regardless of whether you get the job, you'll undoubtedly make an impact and help pave the way for future employees with "distractions."

My father, Saul, who passed away in 2004, took a giant risk when he asked me to start a small indoor-outdoor rug business with him back in 1981. He didn't always agree with my crazy ideas, but he still let me pursue them, even in the early days when we weren't making much money. He did it because he believed in his son, because he was a wise parent who knew how to step back and let me become the person I was meant to be. Even when he wasn't so sure of the outcome, he knew my intentions were worthwhile, so he kept giving me chances, over and over again. All I ask is that you do the same thing. Give someone a chance and watch him exceed your highest expectations. Hire someone you might otherwise have passed up and watch her blossom right before your eyes. Do the right thing, and I promise the right thing will come back to you.

Bibliography

Most of the information for this book was culled from personal interviews. Additional facts and figures were provided and/or substantiated by the following sources:

PREFACE

What is Stroke? About Stroke, Impact of Stroke, American Stroke Association Web site, www.strokeassociation.org.

Bipolar Disorder, National Institute of Mental Health Web site, www.nimh.nih.gov/publicat/bipolar.cfm.

Overview of Schizophrenia, An Introduction to Schizophrenia, www.schizophrenia.com.

Introduction to Mental Retardation, Introduction to the Arc, the Arc of the United States Web site, www.thearc.org.

Down Syndrome Facts, National Association for Down Syndrome Web site, www.nads.org.

Cerebral Palsy—Facts & Figures, United Cerebral Palsy Web site, www.ucp.org.

Who Are We?, What is Brain Injury?, Brain Injury Association of America Web site, www.biausa.org.

What is Autism?, Autism Society of America Web site, www.autism-society.org.

Supplemental Security Income (SSI), Social Security Online home page, www.ssa.gov/notices/supplemental-security-income.

The Americans with Disabilities Act of 1990, Titles I and V, the U.S. Equal Employment Opportunity Commission Web site, www.eeoc.gov/policy/ada.html.

The Top 10 Reasons to Hire People with Disabilities, Economic Participation: Finding Good Jobs, National Organization on Disability (NOD) Web site, www.nod.org.

"Universal Design Good for Business," *Aging Today*, bi-monthly newspaper of the American Society on Aging, May-June 2004, pages 9 and 11.

"Restricted Access: A Survey of Employers About People with Disabilities and Lowering Barriers to Work," *Work Trends* survey, John J. Heldrich Center for Workforce Development, Rutgers University, March 2003.

Myths and Facts About People with Disabilities, Easter Seals Web site, www.easterseals.com.

CHAPTER 2: THE TEST

Carpet Industry: Overview, The New Georgia Encyclopedia Web site, www.georgiaencyclopedia.org.

Carpet Capital of the World, Dalton-Whitfield County (Georgia) Chamber of Commerce Web site, www.daltonchamber.org.

From Sideshow to Genocide: The Khmer Rouge Years, www.edwebproject.org.

Khmer Rouge, www.encylopedia.com.

Welcome to Orange Grove Center, Orange Grove Center Web site, www.orangegrovecenter.com.

"Hubert Shuptrine: Chronicler of the South," *Watercolor* magazine, Spring 2002, pages 121–127.

CHAPTER 4: BUCKING THE SYSTEM

Supplemental Security Income (SSI), Social Security Online home page, www.ssa.gov/notices/supplemental-security-income.

"Night Watchman at Grundy Mines Shot and Killed," *Chattanooga Daily*, June 22, 1963.

"Trio Charged in Mine Death," *Chattanooga News-Free Press*, June 22, 1963.

"3 Men in Grundy Free Under Bond," *Chattanooga Daily Times*, June 26, 1963.

"Chattanooga Man Dead in Gunfight With UMW Leader," *Chattanooga Daily Times*, July 5, 1963.

"UMW Man Slain; Grundy Foreman Will Be Charged," *Chattanooga Daily Times*, July 16, 1963.

"Foreman Sought in Layne Killing," "Deputy's Store Hit By Dynamite Stick," "Firm Closes Grundy Mines," "Grundy Grand Jury Clears All 5 Charged in Mine Guard's Death," *Chattanooga Daily Times*, dates unknown.

"Murder Charged to 3 Palmer Men In Slaying of Coal Company Guard," "Mine Killing Trial Reset," "3 Men Seized in Mine Death," "2 More Charged in Mine Slaying," "More Palmer Men Charged," "Slaying Goes to Jury July 8," *Chattanooga News-Free Press*, dates unknown.

CHAPTER 5: TERRY: THE LOVE BUILDER

Down Syndrome Facts, National Association for Down Syndrome Web site, www.nads.org.

CHAPTER 6: WHAT WERE WE THINKING?

Bipolar Disorder, National Institute of Mental Health Web site, www.nimh.nih.gov/publicat/bipolar.cfm.
What is Autism?, *Common Characteristics of Autism*, *What Causes Autism?*, Autism Society of America Web site, www.autism-society.org.

CHAPTER 7: MARTIN: MR. DETERMINED

Cerebral Palsy—Facts & Figures, United Cerebral Palsy Web site, www.ucp.org.
Supported Employment, Signal Centers Web site, www.signalcenters.org.

CHAPTER 8: WE ARE FAMILY

Congratulatory letter to David Morris from the Atlanta Committee for the Olympic Games, dated January 30, 1996.
Congratulatory letter to David Morris from Vice President Al Gore, dated February 29, 1996.

CHAPTER 9: LONNIE: THE ENCOURAGER

Overview of Schizophrenia, *An Introduction to Schizophrenia*, www.schizophrenia.com.
About Our Clubhouse, AIM Center Web site, www.aimcenterinc.org.

CHAPTER 10: DAVID AND THE GOLIATHS

Beaulieu of America, LLC, Hoover's Books Web site, www.hoovers.com/beaulieu-of-america,-llc/--ID_43067--/free-co-factsheet.xhtml.

Leading International Riders Top the Bill at the North American Beaulieu Classic Horse Trials, March 10, 2004, National Equestrian Communications Web site, www.necomms.com/News/Mar10.asp.

Darlington School 3-Day Eventing coed, college preparatory, boarding (9-12) and day (PK-12) school in Rome, Ga., July 27, 2003, Horses in the South Web site, www.horsesinthesouth.com/Articles/darlington_school.htm.

About Us, *FAQ*, *Brands*, Beaulieu of America Web site, www.beaulieu-usa.com.

Carpet Industry: Overview, The New Georgia Encyclopedia Web site, www.georgiaencyclopedia.org.

General Felt Industries, Div.: Profile, General Felt Industries Web site, www.designbiz.com/web/CompanyWebsite.asp?CompanyID=57449.

CHAPTER 11: DANIEL: MAN OF COURAGE

Who Are We?, *What is Brain Injury?*, Brain Injury Association of America Web site, www.biausa.org.

About Erlanger, Erlanger Medical Center Web site, www.erlanger.org.

CHAPTER 12: DOING WELL BY DOING GOOD

"People Are Its Most Important Products," *Chattanooga Free Press*, May 12, 1996.

Letters to David Morris in response to various magazine articles and the Habitat story on product packaging.

Published letter to the editor, *Southwest Airlines Spirit* magazine, July 2003.

Business for Social Responsibility (BSR) brochure, 1998.

Program from BSR conference, Learning from the Global Village: Corporate Responsibility Around the World, November 18-20, 1998.

"More Than a Workplace," *Southern Living*, April 1998.

"An Enabling Work Force," *Nation's Business*, June 1998.

Easter Seals EDI Awards program, October 5, 1998.

Insights and Inspirations: How Businesses Succeed, 1999 edition, MassMutual—The Blue Chip Company, pages 163–165.

Letter from David Luckie, president, GEDA, to David Morris, dated March 20, 2001.

"Habitat Award Sweet for Owner," *Chattanooga Times-Free Press*, May 29, 2001.

CHAPTER 13: SHARON: CINDERELLA

Introduction to Mental Retardation, the Arc of the United States Web site, www.thearc.org.

CHAPTER 15: CARL: THE COMPANY GRANDPA

What is Stroke?, *Impact of Stroke*, *What Are the Effects of Stroke?*, American Stroke Association Web site, www.strokeassociation.org.

CHAPTER 16: LOVE IS CONTAGIOUS

Letter from Carl Bouckaert to Saul Morris, dated December 11, 1998. Memo from Alan Smith to his employees, December 2003.

CHAPTER 17: THE HABITAT ADVANTAGE: WHY THE COMPANY'S UNCONVENTIONAL WORKERS OUTPRODUCE THE COMPETITION

Carpets & Rugs to 2005 (Study #1396), Hoover's Online, www.hoovers. com.

2001 National Industry-Specific Occupational Employment and Wage Estimates, SIC 227—Carpets and Rugs, U.S. Department of Labor, Bureau of Labor Statistics Web site, www.bls.gov.

About The Author

N ANCY HENDERSON WURST is an award-winning writer who enjoys pursuing stories that break societal stereotypes and challenge readers to look at human issues in a new light. She has published hundreds of articles in major periodicals ranging from *Parade* and the *New York Times* to *Family Circle*, *Woman's Day*, and *Southwest Airlines Spirit*. In recent years, two of her primary areas of expertise—human-interest and business—have "accidentally" meshed into a specialty that focuses on people who are making a difference through their work.

Nancy is a member of the American Society of Journalists and Authors and the Authors Guild. She has won two Print Journalism EDI (Equality, Dignity and Independence) awards from Easter Seals for "raising awareness of disability issues and encouraging realistic portrayals of people with disabilities." One of the honors was for "An Enabling Workforce," a story she wrote about Habitat International, Inc. for *Nation's Business* in 1998.

Nancy's magazine articles about Habitat have also prompted numerous calls and letters from socially conscious entrepreneurs, disability groups, and parents with disabled children, as well as many unsolicited invitations for Habitat owner, David Morris, to share his message at workshops for business, education, healthcare, and disability groups throughout the U.S.

Nancy and her husband, Mark, a photographer, live in Chattanooga, Tennessee, with the lovely Grizabella, a half-Siamese, half-tabby who rules the household. They enjoy being outdoors whenever possible and working together on travel assignments, from the upscale to the offbeat. Griz, however, prefers not to go kayaking with them.